Stonehouse Inn
624-4569
@ 8th ⓛ montverde
on Left.

MONTEREY BAY TRAILS

OUTDOOR ADVENTURES IN MONTEREY, SANTA CRUZ & SAN BENITO COUNTIES

David Weintraub

WILDERNESS PRESS
BERKELEY

Copyright © 2001 by David Weintraub
FIRST EDITION December 2001
Second printing January 2003

All photos © 2001 by David Weintraub,
  except author photo (p. 227) © 2001 by Steve Gregory
Book design by Margaret Copeland—Terragraphics
All maps © 2001 by National Geographic Maps, with trails added by the author
Cover photos © 2001 by David Weintraub
Cover design by Larry B. Van Dyke

Library of Congress Card Number 2001043785
ISBN 0-89997-248-9

Manufactured in the United States of America
Published by: **Wilderness Press**
            1200 5th Street
            Berkeley, CA 94710
            (800) 443-7227; FAX (510) 558-1696
            mail@wildernesspress.com
            www.wildernesspress.com

            Contact us for a free catalog

Cover photos: Grand Loop, Point Lobos State Reserve—Trip 24;
            (inset) Pogonip Creek Nature Trail—Trip 41
Frontispiece: Monterey Cypress

♻ Printed on recycled paper, 20% post-consumer waste

Library Of Congress Cataloging-in-Publication Data

Weintraub, David, 1949–
    Monterey Bay trails : outdoor adventures in Monterey, Santa Cruz & San Benito
counties / David Weintraub.-- 1st ed.
        p. cm.
    Includes bibliographical references (p.) and index.
    ISBN 0-89997-248-9
    1. Hiking--California--Monterey Bay Region--Guidebooks. 2.
Trails--California--Monterey Bay Region--Guidebooks. 3. Monterey Bay Region
(Calif.)--Guidebooks. I. Title.

GV199.42.C22 M659 2001
917.94'70454--dc21
                                                                    2001043785

Table of Contents

Acknowledgments

Preparing this book involved many miles of solo hiking and many hours of solitary writing. But during both activities, I was accompanied by wisdom and advice offered freely by park rangers, naturalists, docents, and others who help make our parklands the wonderful places we cherish and enjoy. These folks advised me on routes and trail conditions, and took time out of their busy schedules to read my manuscript and offer valuable comments, suggestions, and corrections.

Among those I wish to thank are Dave Dixon, Tom Moss, Glen McGowan, and Patricia Clark-Gray from California State Parks, Monterey District; Ralph Fairfield from California State Parks, Santa Cruz District; Bob Culbertson and Elizabeth Burko from Big Basin Redwoods State Park; the staff at Asilomar State Beach; Kenton Parker from Elkhorn Slough National Estuarine Research Reserve; Bruce Delgado, Roberto Maceira, and Eric Morgan from the Bureau of Land Management, Fort Ord Public Lands; Mike Branson from Carmel-by-the-Sea; Tim Jensen, Chris Reed, and Robert Chapin from the Monterey Peninsula Regional Park District; Rhonda Stevens and Al Miyamoto from the Monterey County Department of Parks and Recreation; Doug Stafford from the City of Monterey, Parks Division; Julie Armstrong from the Monterey Peninsula Visitors and Convention Bureau; Richard Bañuelos from Pinnacles National Monument; Chuck Bancroft from Point Lobos State Reserve; and Susan Harris and Mary Schweitzer from Santa Cruz City Department of Parks and Recreation.

A special thanks goes to Mary Ann Matthews, author of *An Illustrated Field Key to the Flowering Plants of Monterey County*, for her help with plant identification and naming. Thanks also to the folks at the San Carlos Inn in Monterey and the National 9 Motel in Santa Cruz for their hospitality.

My friends John Macchia, Angela Macchia, Steve Gregory, and Vickie Vann joined me on a few hikes and served ably as photographic subjects—thanks! The people at Wilderness Press know how to take an author's vision and turn it into reality, so I thank them too. Finally, I am grateful to my wife, Maggi, for her love and support.

Heads Up

Hiking in the backcountry entails unavoidable risk that every hiker assumes and must be aware of and respect. The fact that a trail is described in this book is not a representation that it will be safe for you. Trails vary greatly in difficulty and in the degree of conditioning and agility one needs to enjoy them safely. On some hikes routes may have changed or conditions may have deteriorated since the descriptions were written. Also trail conditions can change even from day to day, owing to weather and other factors. A trail that is safe on a dry day or for a highly conditioned, agile, properly equipped hiker may be completely unsafe for someone else or unsafe under adverse weather conditions.

You can minimize your risks on the trail by being knowledgeable, prepared and alert. There is not space in this book for a general treatise on safety in the mountains, but there are a number of good books and public courses on the subject and you should take advantage of them to increase your knowledge. Just as important, you should always be aware of your own limitations and of conditions existing when and where you are hiking. If conditions are dangerous, or if you're not prepared to deal with them safely, choose a different hike! It's better to have wasted a drive than to be the subject of a mountain rescue.

These warnings are not intended to scare you off the trails. Millions of people have safe and enjoyable hikes every year. However, one element of the beauty, freedom and excitement of the wilderness is the presence of risks that do not confront us at home. When you hike you assume those risks. They can be met safely, but only if you exercise your own independent judgment and common sense.

Western gull stands sentinel over a rocky Monterey coast.

✦ Introduction ✦

THE MONTEREY BAY AREA

The sweeping curve of the Monterey Bay coast gives shape to this hiking guide, which covers parklands in Monterey and parts of Santa Cruz and San Benito counties. Bounded on the north by Big Basin Redwoods State Park, and on the south by Garrapata State Park, most of the routes I describe are close to the Bay and its influence on weather, terrain, plants, and animals. But for the sake of variety, and also because they contain some wonderful trails, I have included a selection of inland parks stretching eastward to Pinnacles National Monument.

Beautiful Monterey Peninsula, at the south end of Monterey Bay, is where you find the towns of Monterey, Pacific Grove, and Carmel, each different and each with its own wonderful attractions. Monterey has a lively waterfront centered around Fisherman's Wharf and Cannery Row, a world-class aquarium, and an historic downtown with buildings that date from the Spanish and Mexican eras, when the town was the capital of Alta California.

Pacific Grove is a lovely town known for its Victorian homes, its lighthouse at Point Pinos, which has been shining brightly since 1855, and its monarch butterflies, thousands of which return each fall to seek shelter in pine and eucalyptus groves. Carmel, founded in 1904 as an artists colony, retains much of its small-town charm but offers visitors dozens of shops, art galleries, and restaurants, along with several gorgeous beaches, to enjoy.

Highway 1, California's premier scenic route, follows the shore of Monterey Bay on its way from San Francisco to San Luis Obispo. Between Pacific Grove and Carmel runs world-famous 17-Mile Drive, a toll road that winds along the rocky coast past such well-photographed attractions as Seal Rock, Cypress Point, and the Lone Cypress, and also past six championship golf courses. Heading east from Carmel is Carmel Valley Rd., a lovely highway that parallels the Carmel River. Inland from Monterey curves Hwy. 68, connecting the coast with the agriculturally-rich Salinas Valley.

On the north side of Monterey Bay is Santa Cruz, a laid-back surfing town known for its beachside boardwalk and Giant Dipper roller coaster, its recently renovated downtown, which had been destroyed in the 1989 Loma Prieta earthquake, and its campus of the University of California. Santa Cruz lies at the foot of the Santa Cruz Mountains, which contain some of the finest remaining stands of old-growth coast redwoods on earth. Heading northward from Santa Cruz are Hwy. 17, which connects the coast with the San Francisco Bay Area, and Hwy. 9, a superb scenic route that winds into the heart of redwood country.

Inland from the coast is the rich agricultural land of the Salinas Valley, made famous by author John Steinbeck in his books *The Grapes of Wrath* and *East of Eden*, and the farming communities of Salinas, Watsonville, and Castroville. Farther east, across the Gabilan Range, are the towns of San Juan Bautista, site of a historic mission and gateway to Fremont Peak State Park, and Hollister, gateway to Pinnacles National Monument.

The parklands of the Monterey Bay area are administered by a variety of federal, state, and local agencies. These include the National Park Service (NPS), the Bureau of Land Management (BLM), the U.S. Fish and Wildlife Service (USFWS), the California State Parks (CSP), the California Department of Fish and Game, the Monterey Peninsula Regional Park District (MPRPD), the Monterey County Department of Parks and Recreation, the City of Monterey Department of Parks and Recreation, the Carmel Department of Forestry, and the City of Santa Cruz Department of Parks and Recreation. Phone numbers for these agencies can be found in Appendix B. Lands along 17-Mile Drive are administered by the Pebble Beach Company, listed in Appendix B.

Climate and Weather

Weather is our day-to-day experience of the elements, whereas climate refers to seasonal conditions and trends over time. Although the Monterey Bay area has one of the world's most favorable climates, the weather here can still keep us guessing. The Bay itself and the Pacific beyond have a moderating influence on our weather. Along the shore, it isn't usually too hot or too cold—average daily temperatures stay within a fairly narrow range—and the air is moist. As you go eastward, each successive range of coastal hills diminishes this moderating effect by blocking ocean breezes and squeezing moisture out of passing clouds.

In general, we enjoy approximately six rain-free months, from May through October. During this time, two main factors determine whether you roast on the trail or need to don an extra layer: first, how close you are to Monterey Bay, and second, whether or not there is a fog bank pushing inland from the Bay. When fog blankets the coast, which it does more than 100 days each year, conditions there are cool and moist. The farther inland from the Bay you go, the hotter and drier it will be. This fact often determines where specific plants and animals can thrive. For example, coast redwood, a tree that depends on fog to obtain moisture, only grows within a narrow belt near the coast.

During the rainy season, which usually lasts from November through April, Pacific storms bring rain and wind that batter the coast. Snow is rare, except on the highest peaks. In the lull between winter storms, we often have our clearest, coldest days, when visibility is superb. The refreshed hillsides, sere in summer, turn green and lush. Creeks and rivers fill and flow, sometimes flooding their banks. All this water sets the stage for wonderful wildflower displays that begin in our area in late winter, peak in spring, and, with some species, continue through summer.

An otherwise perfect hike can easily be ruined by high winds or a sudden rainstorm. You can obtain the latest weather information and current forecasts from the National Weather Service, either on a weather radio (available at Radio Shack, outdoor stores, and other outlets) or on the National Weather Service Web site, *www.nws.mbay.net*.

Geology

The Monterey Bay area lies within the southern Coast Ranges, the name given by geologists to the complex system of ridges and valleys that extend south from San Francisco Bay to the Santa Ynez Mountains near Santa Barbara, and inland to the edge of the Central Valley. These ridges and valleys trend northwest to southeast, paralleling the San Andreas and other faults. Dominating the southern Coast Ranges is the

Rock pinnacles in Pinnacles National Monument are the eroded remnants of half an ancient volcano that was split by the San Andreas fault and moved northward by plate tectonics.

Santa Lucia Range, topped by Junipero Serra Peak (5862'). The major watercourse in the Monterey Bay area is the Salinas River, which gets its start in the Los Padres National Forest near San Luis Obispo, and empties into Monterey Bay south of Moss Landing.

The earth's continents and oceans are not fixed in place but rather travel on ever-shifting "plates," whose motions are controlled by forces deep within the earth. Geologists say that California's Coast Ranges were formed when the heavier Pacific plate was subducted beneath the North American plate, scraping off material and building it up on the continent's western edge. Forces then cracked and folded this material, forming the ridges and valleys we see today.

Much of the Monterey Bay area contains granitic rocks that originated eons ago in southern California. How did they get here? The rocks arrived during the last 25 million years thanks to sideways motion along the San Andreas fault, which runs through our area from Pinnacles National Monument, near Hollister, northwest to The Forest of Nisene Marks State Park, near Santa Cruz. Everything west of the San Andreas fault, a formation called the Salinian block, is moving northwest at the rate of about 1 inch per year. The Pinnacles themselves were part of a volcano created more than 20 million years ago. When the San Andreas fault formed, it bisected the volcano and carried half of it northwest 195 miles to its present location. The remaining half is in southern California near the town of Lancaster.

Also underlying the Monterey Bay area are sedimentary rocks formed in layers underwater when the sea covered the southern Coast Ranges. Uplifting within the past 10 million years brought these layers above sea level, and many have since been tilted and twisted by geologic forces. These unstable layers are easily eroded and prone to sliding during periods of heavy rains, sometimes causing millions of dollars in property damage. Prominent along Hwy. 1 in our area are coastal terraces, a series of plateaus rising step-like away from Monterey Bay. Each terrace represents a former shoreline with a steep, wave-eroded face. Uplift has reclaimed these ancient beachfront acres from the waves, at least for now.

Plant Communities

California has more than 5,000 native plant species and an estimated 1,000 introduced species. Of the native plants, about 30 percent occur nowhere else—these are called endemics. Among the most common endemics are many types of manzanita (*Arctostaphylos*) and monkeyflower (*Mimulus*). The state has some of the oldest species, in terms of evolution, and also some of the youngest. For example, coast redwoods date back to the dinosaurs, whereas certain species of tarweed (*Madia*) have evolved within the past several thousand years. Botanists divide the plant kingdom into several major groups: flowering plants, conifers, ferns and their allies, mosses, and algae. The members of these groups that grow together in a distinct habitat are a plant community. For this book, I relied heavily on *Plants of the San Francisco Bay Region: Mendocino to Monterey*, by Eugene N. Kozloff and Linda H. Beidleman. They classify the principal plant communities commonly found in our region as follows:

Valley and Foothill Woodland

The dry hills of Pinnacles National Monument are characteristic of this community, which is found at elevations between 300 and 3500 feet. Common trees and shrubs found in this generally open woodland, sometimes called a savanna, include various oaks, California buckeye, gray pine, Coulter pine, California bay, buckbrush, toyon, coffeeberry, snowberry, and poison oak. Especially with oaks, slope aspect and elevation determine which species occur where. Among the oaks in our area are coast live oak, valley oak, blue oak, canyon oak, and interior live oak.

Riparian Woodland

Members of this moisture-loving community are usually found beside rivers and creeks. Among the most common are bigleaf maple, white alder, red alder, California bay, various willows, wild rose, poison oak, elk clover, and giant chain fern. Trails that run along Garzas Creek in Garland Ranch Regional Park, and along many of the creeks in the Santa Cruz Mountains, give you opportunities to study this community.

Redwood Forest

Coast redwoods are the world's tallest trees and are among the fastest growing. Redwood groves once formed an extensive coastal forest that stretched from central California to southern Oregon. Commercially valuable, they were heavily logged. The remaining old-growth coast redwoods in the Monterey Bay area are confined to a few areas, most notably Big Basin Redwoods State Park, Henry Cowell Redwoods State Park, and Fall Creek State Park. Associated with redwoods are a number of other plants,

Light filtering through towering coast redwoods lends a cathedral-like feeling to the forest.

including tanbark oak, California bay, hazelnut, evergreen huckleberry, wood rose, redwood sorrel, and sword fern.

Closed-cone Pine Forest

Unlike other pines, whose cones open when their seeds are mature, closed-cone pines retain their seeds until heat, usually from fire, opens the pitch-glued cones and releases the seeds. There are two closed-cone species in the Monterey Bay area: Monterey pine and knobcone pine. Monterey pine, seen on many trails, has been planted extensively in our area but is native to only a few places on the central California coast. Knobcone pine can be seen along Ridge Fire Road in Henry Cowell Redwood State Park.

Douglas-fir Forest

Douglas-fir, not a true fir, is easily told by its distinctive cones, which have protruding, three-pointed bracts, sometimes called rat's tails. Douglas-fir and coast redwood are California's two most important commercial trees. Some of the common plants associated with Douglas-fir are the same as those associated with coast redwood, namely California bay, tanbark oak, and sword fern. Others include blue blossom, coffeeberry, and poison oak.

Chaparral

This fascinating community is made up of plants that thrive in poor soils under hot, dry conditions. Chaparral is very susceptible to fire, and some of its members, such as various species of manzanita, survive devastating blazes by sprouting new growth from ground-level burls. Despite the harsh environment, chaparral can be beautiful year-round, with certain manzanitas blooming as early as December, and other plants continuing into spring and summer. The upper slopes of many inland peaks in the Monterey Bay area are cloaked in chaparral. The word itself comes from a Spanish term for dwarf or scrub oak, but in the Monterey Bay area chamise, various manzanitas, and species of Ceanothus dominate the community. Other chaparral plants include mountain mahogany, yerba santa, toyon, and chaparral pea.

Hill and Valley Grassland

Few if any grasslands in the Monterey Bay area retain their native character. Human intervention, in the form of farming and livestock grazing, along with the mostly inadvertent importation of non-native grasses like wild oat, have significantly altered the landscape. Gone from most areas are native bunchgrasses, the perennial species that once dominated our area. Remaining, thankfully, are native wildflowers, which decorate grasslands in spring and summer. Among the most common are bluedicks, California poppy, checkerbloom, lupine, and blue-eyed grass.

Coastal Prairie

Lacking protection from trees and shrubs, these windswept grasslands extend inland from coastal cliffs, offering a toehold for hearty perennial grasses and wildflowers. Generally flat and smooth, coastal prairies are marine terraces that have been lifted above sea level by geological forces. Perfect for farming and grazing livestock, many of these terraces were cleared of trees and shrubs, creating human-made prairies. The Old Cove Landing Trail in Wilder Ranch State Park traverses a coastal prairie.

Coastal Scrub

Also called soft chaparral, this community consists mostly of shrubs and grasses growing near the coast. Among its most common members are California sagebrush, coyote brush, bush monkeyflower, berry vines, and poison oak. Coastal scrub is widespread in the Monterey Bay area.

Boardwalks such as this one at Elkhorn Slough allow hikers to explore fascinating ecosystems without harming salt marshes and other delicate terrain.

Backshores of Sandy Beaches

This shoreline community begins just back from the high-tide line. It consists mostly of wind-resistant and salt-tolerant plants. Among these are various beach grasses, including European beach grass, which was introduced to stabilize dunes, and low-growing succulents such as sand-verbena, searocket, and iceplant, another non-native dune stabilizer. The most common shrubs here are lizard tail, mock heather, beach sagewort, yellow bush lupine, and coyote brush.

Coastal Salt Marsh

Found at the edges of bays and estuaries, this community is made up of plants that can tolerate salt in varying degrees. At the lowest level of the marsh, which is flooded twice daily by the tide, are various cord grasses (*Spartina*). Higher in the

The Monterey Bay area affords a unique opportunity to enjoy and study a wide variety of plant communities.

marsh are pickleweed and salt-marsh dodder, a parasitic plant that sends out orange threads to encircle its host. At a level reached only by the highest tides grow salt grass, alkali heath, and sea lavender, also called marsh rosemary. Decorating the marsh nearly year-round may be the yellow flowers of brass buttons and Pacific gumplant. Coastal salt marshes are in decline, and each one lost deprives us of a highly productive ecosystem.

Plant Names

Naming plants puts writers in a quandary, because plants have no standard common names. The same plant may have two or more names, and the same name may apply to different plants. For example, a violet of the coast redwood forest, *Viola ocellata*, appears in one plant guide as "two-eyed violet" and in another as "western heart's-ease." My solution is to pick a plant guide for the region I am writing about and follow its choice of names. For the Monterey Bay area, I settled on *Plants of the San Francisco Bay Region: Mendocino to Monterey*, with a few modifications. Where it would not cause confusion to do so, I removed some hyphens, dropped some modifiers, such as "California" and "western," and renamed a few plants. Thus western poison-oak becomes poison oak, and common Indian-paintbrush becomes paintbrush. Hottentot fig and seafig, common coastal ground covers, I call iceplant.

Animals
Mammals

Besides deer, rabbits, and squirrels, you probably won't see many other land mammals on your hikes in the Monterey Bay area, unless you visit the parks near dawn or dusk. These are times when most other mammals are active, and you may be rewarded with a fleeting glimpse of a coyote or a bobcat. Large mammals, such as black bears and mountain lions, are rare and seldom seen. Other more common mammals in our area include gray fox, raccoon, skunk, opossum, and chipmunk.

Marine mammals—whales, sea lions, seals, and sea otters—can sometimes be seen from vantage points on the Monterey Bay coast, especially from Soberanes Point at Garrapata State Park, and from Point Lobos State Reserve. The best time of year to view migrating gray whales, which often travel close to shore, is from January to April. Sea lions, distinguished from true seals by the presence of external ears, congregate on offshore rocks and sometimes on harbor docks. Harbor seals are commonly glimpsed as they float in quiet bays and harbors, their heads just poking up out of the water. Otters are fond of kelp beds, where they feed and rest.

Birds

The Monterey Bay area is a wonderful place to see birds. Its location on the western edge of the Pacific Flyway, combined with the presence of so many different habitats, from rocky offshore islands to inland peaks and valleys, guarantees both a high species count and a large number of individual birds either resident, wintering, or passing through on migration. Elkhorn Slough, near Moss Landing, holds the North American record for most bird species, 116, seen from one spot in a single day.

Monterey Bay, rich in marine life, attracts a wide variety of sea birds, including petrels, shearwaters, and albatrosses, all of which can sometimes be seen from shore. The Bay's sandy shores and salt marshes are frequented by migrating and wintering shorebirds and wading birds. The area's pine, oak, and redwood forests host a wonderful array of songbirds, including such colorful denizens as acorn woodpeckers and Steller's jays. Circling high above open fields and meadows are common birds of prey such as red-tailed hawks, American kestrels, and turkey vultures.

Season, location, weather, and even time of day—these together help determine which birds you are likely to see. The timing of the tides is especially important for viewing shorebirds. If you learn "birding by ear," the technique of identifying species by their distinctive notes, calls, and songs, you will quickly expand your list, because many birds are frustratingly hard to spot, especially in dense foliage. Birding with a group also improves your odds of seeing and identifying a large number of species, including rarities. For the common names of birds, I rely on the American Ornithologists' Union (AOU) checklist for birds of the continental United States and Canada. In this checklist, old friends such as rufous-sided towhee and scrub jay have new names—spotted towhee and western scrub-jay.

Human History

Rich in history, the Monterey Bay area has often played center stage to a rich mix of people, cultures, ideas, and events. Many of the people who were involved with California's evolution from colony to statehood lived or passed through here. The first American flag to be raised over California, by John C. Frémont in defiance of the Mexican authorities, flew from a hilltop not far from the Bay's shimmering waters. Writer John Steinbeck memorialized the area in his novels. California's constitution was written here. During the Spanish and Mexican eras, Monterey was the capital of Alta California, the name used to distinguish the vast land north of Mexico from the slender peninsula of Baja California. Prior to the coming of Europeans, the Monterey Bay area was inhabited by the Ohlone Indians, who used the rich resources of land and sea to survive.

Europeans began arriving in 1542 when Portuguese navigator Juan Rodríguez Cabrillo, in the service of Spain, explored the West Coast looking for gold, jewels, and a rumored water route across the top of North America. Cabrillo's ships sailed past Monterey Bay, which the navigator named *Bahía de los Pinos*, or Bay of Pines. In 1602, Sebastían Vizcaíno anchored near the shore and renamed the bay *Puerto de Monterrey* after his employer, the fifth Count de Monterrey, viceroy of New Spain. The first land expedition to reach Monterey Bay, led by Gaspar de Portolá, arrived in 1769, and in 1770 a mission and a presidio, or fort, were established in Monterey. A year later, the mission was moved to Carmel, where it became the headquarters and residence of Junípero Serra, a Franciscan monk who came north with Portolá to establish Catholic outposts in the wilderness. A fine account of the Spanish exploration of Alta California is given by Barbara and Rudy Marinacci in *California's Spanish Place-Names*.

For many years, Alta California remained a far-flung colony of Spain, isolated from the rest of the world by its geography—high mountains, harsh desert, and treacherous coast. During this time, Native Americans were herded onto mission lands, where they were converted to Christianity and died by the tens of thousands from diseases to which they had no resistance. Many Indians resisted missionization, whereas others accommodated themselves to mission life. In 1821, Mexico freed itself from Spanish rule, and in 1834 the mission lands were secularized and divided into large ranchos. Any native-born or naturalized Mexican Catholic without a criminal record was eligible to receive grants to these ranchos. The ranching era in California had begun.

Joining the land-owning Californios, as they called themselves, were immigrants from the U.S. who began arriving mostly from the East through the Sierra Nevada passes. Monterey soon developed into an important Pacific trading port, made all the more so important by the friction developing between Mexico and the U.S., which had its sights set westward. Conflict also developed between the Californios and the new immigrants: should Alta California remain a province of Mexico, or should it become part of the United States? The answer came in May of 1846, with the beginning of the Mexican War which would reshape the American West.

The intrigue and skullduggery that preceded the war rivals any modern spy thriller, and the story is best told by David Lavender in his book *California: Land of New Beginnings.* Involved in the process that eventually wrested the province free from Mexico and led to statehood were heroes and blowhards, instigators and peacemakers, many of whose names are familiar today. They included John C. Frémont, captain with

When fully restored, the Wilder Ranch Cultural Preserve will feature a Native American village, a Mexican-era adobe, and 19th- and 20th-century ranch buildings.

the U.S. Corps of Topographical Engineers; Thomas O. Larkin, U.S. consul in Monterey; Juan Bautista Alvarado, governor of Alta California; José Castro, the governor's cousin and military comandante; Commodores John D. Sloat and Robert F. Stockton of the Pacific squadron; and General Stephen W. Kearny, leader of the Army of the West. On July 7th, a warship commanded by Commodore Sloat entered Monterey harbor and raised the American flag, effectively seizing northern California for the U.S. Two years later, the war ended with a treaty that took California from Mexico.

Almost as soon as the dust of war had settled, a new dust—this one gold—again transformed California. In the year of the Gold Rush, 1849, Monterey hosted California's constitutional convention, and statehood followed in 1850. Monterey County became one of California's original 27 counties. During the second half of the 19th Century, the Monterey area saw the development of logging, limestone mining, and commercial fishing, the latter largely pioneered by Chinese immigrants. Monterey's famous waterfront canneries, vividly described by Steinbeck, bustled with activity from around 1900 until 1950, when the Pacific sardine fishery mysteriously collapsed. In the 1880s, a tourism industry developed, thanks mainly to the Southern Pacific Railroad and the construction of Monterey's luxurious Del Monte Hotel by railroad magnate Charles Crocker. More than a century later, tourists continue to flock to the Monterey peninsula, many of them on Hwy. 1, California's first Scenic Highway.

The railroad brought tourism to Monterey and also to Santa Cruz, on the north side of Monterey Bay. Formerly the site of a Spanish mission, Santa Cruz became an important port and helped supply the new state of California with lumber, lime, leather goods, and agricultural products. The extension of a railway line from San Jose across the Santa Cruz Mountains to the coast in the late 1800s, and the construction of the Santa Cruz boardwalk and casino insured the town's future as a tourist destination. Better roads and more automobiles brought a steady stream of visitors to the area's scenic beaches and magnificent redwood forests, which today are still the region's main attractions.

Using This Book

A good hiking guidebook should do more than just get you from one place to another. It should stimulate your interest in a particular area and provide enough accurate information to get you safely there and back. While you are en route, the book should be a knowledgeable but not overbearing companion, pointing out features of interest and tidbits of natural and human history that pertain to your chosen hike. The route descriptions should capture the enthusiasm and spirit of adventure the author felt when hiking the trails for the first time.

Every guidebook author decides which areas and trips to include and which to leave out, which features to emphasize and which to diminish. Additionally, an author's interests and preferences almost always come into play. Here, in the interest of full disclosure, are some of mine. In general, I prefer loops to out-and-back routes. As a photographer, I love to climb high for great views, but as an aging hiker, I look for the easiest way down. Birds, wildflowers, and water of all sorts—the ocean, lakes, rivers, creeks, marshes—turn enjoyable hikes into memorable ones.

During the 18 months it took to prepare this book, I hiked each of the 48 routes, some more than once. Every day in nature is different, so your experience of a particular park or trail will probably differ from mine, depending on season, weather, time of day, and the acts of God and various federal, state, and local governments. I have tried to indicate this variability in two ways. First, by liberally using the word *may* in the text, as in, "Overhead you may be lucky enough to see swifts cavorting on the ocean breezes." Second, by being as specific as possible about when seasonal events occur, such as the blooming of wildflowers or the migration of birds.

Comments, corrections, and suggestions are certainly appreciated. Please send them to: Wilderness Press, 1200 Fifth Street, Berkeley, CA 94710. If your comments concern trail conditions, signage, or other park-related issues, please also send a copy of your letter to the appropriate government agency. A list of these is in Appendix B.

Favorite Hikes

Here are some of my favorite hikes in the Monterey Bay area, places I'd return to and share with my friends. A few parks—Garland Ranch Regional Park, Point Lobos State Reserve, Big Basin Redwoods State Park, Pinnacles National Monument—are so wonderful that I could not limit my choices, so I simply picked "All."

Park	Route	Highlights
Asilomar State Beach	Spanish Bay	Flora, Views
Big Basin Redwoods State Park	All	Flora, Redwoods
Fall Creek State Park	Lime Kilns	History, Redwoods
The Forest of Nisene Marks State Park	West Ridge	History, Redwoods
Garland Ranch Regional Park	All	Flora, Views
Garrapata State Park	Soberanes Canyon	Flora, Redwoods
Henry Cowell Redwoods State Park	Redwood Grove	Flora, Redwoods
Natural Bridges State Beach	Nature Trail	Monarch Butterflies
Pinnacles National Monument	All	Flora, Geology, Views
Pogonip	Lookout Loop	Flora, Views
Point Lobos State Reserve	All	Fauna, Flora, Views
Toro County Park	Ollason Peak	Flora, Views

Selecting a Route

The variety of terrain covered by this book is stunning, and the routes described will delight hikers of all ages and abilities. Many people come to the Monterey Bay area for the joy of being near the ocean, but those who desire the solitude of a redwood forest or the wide-open vistas surrounding a chaparral-clad peak will not be disappointed. Simply put, there are so many choices. Whatever you want—exercise, scenery, nature study, or just a walk in the woods—you can probably find it in the pages of this book.

When selecting a route, here are some questions to consider: First, when is the best time of year to hike? Although many of the parks can be enjoyed year-round, most are at their best during spring and fall. Winter brings rain, which can make trails muddy and streams swollen. Summer is the season when fog often shrouds the coast and inland temperatures soar. Second, how much time do you want to spend on the trail, and what kind of terrain do you want to cover? Third, what will make this a special experience: seeing wildflowers in bloom, watching sea birds on the wing, or learning about natural and human history?

Each route description is preceded by a snapshot of what the hike entails. **Length** measures round-trip distance from what I designate as the **Trailhead**, which is almost always adjacent to the parking area. **Time** is the estimated duration of the hike, including a few stops, based on my average hiking pace of 1.5 to 2 miles per hour. **Rating** indicates whether the route is Easy, Moderate, or Difficult. For this book, Easy means the route is mostly flat and can usually be completed in one hour or less. Moderate indicates a more challenging, hilly hike that will probably take two to four hours. Difficult means a hike is more than 6 miles in length, or involves an elevation gain of more than 1,000 feet.

The **Regulations** head tells you which agency has jurisdiction over the route (see Appendix B for any abbreviations used). I also indicate if a fee is required, and whether or not dogs, bikes, and horses are allowed on the route as described. In **Highlights**, you can find out the type of route—loop, semi-loop, out-and-back—along with the names of the trails you'll use. You can also see at a glance the main attractions of the route, such as wildflowers or great views. **Directions** gets you to the parking area from the nearest major roadway. **Facilities** lists things like water, toilets, or phones that may be near the trailhead. Finally, **Trailhead** tells you where to start your hike. For almost all the routes in this book, I designate the point at which you leave the parking area as the trailhead, and I measure the round-trip mileage from that point.

Most of the hiking routes in the Monterey Bay area follow dirt roads and single-track trails. Within the route descriptions themselves, the subjective terms *Gentle*, *Moderate*, and *Steep* indicate the grade of ascent and descent. A gentle grade, if you are reasonably fit, is almost imperceptible and requires no change of pace. A moderate uphill grade requires you to "shift down" a bit, but should not interfere with regular breathing or conversation. Climbing steeply uphill forces you to concentrate your efforts, and is best done by maintaining a slow but measured pace coordinated with deep breathing. Moderate and steep downhill grades, especially over loose, rocky ground, require caution—a walking stick or a trekking pole is invaluable here.

Distances given in the route descriptions are approximations, and they always refer to the start of the hike. Thus "At about the 2-mile point, you reach a four-way junction" means the junction is about 2 miles from the trailhead. Any map mentioned in a route description is the one produced by the agency having jurisdiction over that particular trail.

What To Wear

Boots

Lightweight, flexible, supportive, comfortable, durable—in the past you had to settle for only a few of these qualities when buying boots. Not any longer. Today's light hiking boots combine the weight, flexibility, and comfort of running shoes with the support and durability of heavier backpacking boots. Many come with Gore-Tex liners to make them waterproof yet breathable. A good pair of hiking boots will protect your feet and ankles, and provide essential traction on steep slopes. They will also help keep your feet dry in the event of a rain shower or a misstep while crossing a creek.

When buying boots, go to a reputable outdoor store with a variety of styles and sizes in stock. Wear the socks you plan to wear hiking when you try on boots (see below). A boot that fits properly will have plenty of toe room but will hold your foot snugly in place. Boots that are uncomfortable in the store, even slightly, will only get worse after hours on the trail. Above all, make sure the store will allow you to return the boots, provided you do not wear them outdoors. Wear them around the house for several days to make sure they fit.

Socks

Good socks can make the difference between happy feet and unhappy, blistered feet. Socks help cushion your feet and keep them dry by wicking moisture away from your skin. Most hikers wear two pairs of socks—a thin liner sock and a thicker outer sock. Look for liners made from synthetic materials, and outer socks made from wool or a blend of wool and synthetics. Avoid hiking socks that contain cotton—these will retain moisture and may cause blisters.

Other Clothing

Hiking clothes should provide you with comfortable protection from sun, wind, poison oak, and ticks. Adjusting to changing conditions is the biggest challenge, and most people find a layering system works best, allowing you to doff and don as needed. For warm weather, I prefer light-weight, synthetic pants that convert to shorts by means of zip-off legs, and a long-sleeved, sun-proof shirt. Light colors make it easier to see ticks on your clothing. If it is cool, I add a lightweight synthetic vest and a nylon windbreaker. A hat is an essential part of my wardrobe. I also carry a light pair of gloves and an insulating headband; these are very effective if it gets cold. If you are hiking during the rainy season, avoid cotton clothing. Instead, rely on synthetics like Gore-Tex and Polartec to keep you warm and dry.

What To Take Along

Some hikers like to travel light, and for them, many of the trails in this book require nothing more than a water bottle. Others look forward to a sumptuous picnic with all the trimmings. Here are some of the things I don't leave home without: plenty of water, snacks, extra clothes, trekking pole, sunglasses, sunscreen, insect repellent, flashlight, knife, and basic first-aid supplies. Also handy are a map and compass, binoculars, a hand-lens for plant study, and a pad and pencil. Try leaving your heavy field guides at home and instead make notes and sketches of birds or flowers you wish to identify. Please do not collect plant or flower speci-mens.

Trail Etiquette

Sharing the Trail

Many of the trails in the Monterey Bay area are multi-use paths shared by hikers, equestrians, bicyclists, and trail runners. A few trails are open to dogs. Each park has its own regulations, and it is your responsibility to

By obeying trail regulations, equestrians, cyclists, and hikers can peacefully share and enjoy multi-use trails like this one in Manzanita County Park.

Exploring on two wheels allows you to cover a lot of territory on trails where the rules permit bicycles, like this one in the Fort Ord Public Lands.

know, understand, and obey them. Before selecting a particular route in this book, check the **Regulations** section just above the route description. There you will find the agency having jurisdiction over the trails, along with specific restrictions concerning dogs, bikes, and horses on the described route. If you see or hear horseback riders approaching, step off the trail to give them the right-of-way and remain motionless until they pass. Bicyclists should slow down and call out when approaching hikers, and dismount when near horses.

Protecting the Environment

Public lands are just that: they belong to everybody. Treating them as a precious resource will ensure that they remain unspoiled for all of us to enjoy. Small, thoughtless acts can have unintended consequences, because everything in nature is interconnected. Effects of carelessness may be sudden and dramatic, or they may not show up for years. The rules of outdoor etiquette are simple and based on common sense. Obey all posted restrictions. Stay on marked trails and do not cut switchbacks. Pack out all trash, and do not disturb the park's plants and animals. In short, tread lightly on the land.

Preventing Fires

Although lightning-caused wildfires play an important role in maintaining the health of certain ecosystems, fires caused by human carelessness often result in damage to parklands and property, and even loss of life. Smoking is generally not allowed on park trails. Each jurisdiction has its own regulations about campfires, barbecues, and smoking; please obey them.

Controlling Dogs

Most parklands covered in this book do not allow dogs on their trails because of potential conflicts with other park users and with wildlife. Where dogs are permitted, they generally must be leashed. On those trails where dogs are allowed off-leash, they must be under *immediate* voice control. Dog owners must clean up after their pets. Hikers wishing to bring their dogs with them into a park should check the **Regulations** section just above the route description to see if dogs are allowed and what rules apply.

Safety on the Trail

Injury, Illness

It's been said that the most dangerous part of any outdoor activity is driving to the trailhead. In general, hiking is a relatively safe sport, provided you use common sense. Match the route to your ability and don't overdo it—fatigue, hunger, thirst, and environmental factors such as heat and cold can all contribute to accidents. Protect your knees and ankles with sturdy boots that have good traction, and consider using a walking stick or trekking pole for extra stability. Watch the ground in front of you when you're walking over difficult terrain, and stop walking to admire the scenery. Don't get so carried away by a beautiful vista that you literally go "over the edge."

Knowing CPR and first aid may help you feel more secure in the outdoors and may also enable you to help someone in distress. One illness you may encounter on the trail is heat exhaustion, also called heat prostration. Its causes are dehydration and physical exertion under hot, humid conditions. The victim may feel weak, have a rapid pulse, and experience headache, dizziness, and brief loss of consciousness. Get the victim out of the heat and provide fluids, especially those with salt. Untreated, heat exhaustion can turn into heat stroke, a severe medical emergency.

Getting Lost

Most of the trails covered by this book are well-signed and easy to follow. Still, it is possible to get lost by taking a wrong turn at a junction, venturing off the trail in search of a great view, or becoming disoriented. If you do lose your way, don't panic. Try to retrace your steps to a known point. Use landmarks to get oriented and refer to your map and compass if you have them. Altimeters are very useful if you have a map with elevation lines. Much has been said about Global Positioning System (GPS) devices, but unless a GPS unit has an unobstructed exposure to the sky, it won't record an accurate position. GPS devices are incredibly useful for activities that take place in the open, such as boating, but less so for hiking.

Poison Oak

This common shrub, a member of the sumac family, produces an itchy rash in people allergic to its oil. Learn to identify poison oak's shiny green foliage—"leaves of three, let it be"—and avoid it. In fall the shrub's leaves turn yellow and red, adding a wonderful touch of color to the woods. In winter, you can identify the plant by its upward-reaching clusters of bare branches. Staying on the trail is the best way to avoid contact with poison oak, and wearing long pants and a long-sleeved shirt helps too. Anything that touches poison oak—clothing, pets—should be washed in soap and water.

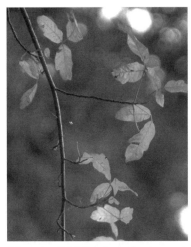

The splendid fall colors of poison oak are for the eyes only! Skin contact with the plant's oils can cause a severe, itchy rash.

Ticks

Ticks cause a variety of illnesses, but in recent years most attention has been focused on Lyme disease, which is produced by bacteria carried in our area by western black-legged ticks. These tiny insects are almost invisible, and often the victim doesn't know he or she has been bitten. Sometimes a "bull's-eye" rash appears, and the victim has flu-like symptoms. Lyme disease in the West is not as widespread as it is in the Northeast because the ticks here feed on western fence lizards, and the lizard's blood contains something that kills the disease-causing bacteria.

If the victim is not treated quickly with antibiotics, the disease can cause severe cardiac and neurological disorders. The best protection against Lyme disease is to wear long pants tucked into your socks and a long-sleeved shirt, use an insect repellent containing DEET on your clothes, stay on the trail, and shower and launder your clothes after your hike. If you find a tick attached, grasp it as close to your skin as possible and gently pull it straight out. Squeezing on an attached tick may cause it to inject the bacteria. Wash the bite area, apply antiseptic, and call your doctor.

Rattlesnakes

Although present in the Monterey Bay area, western rattlesnakes are shy and seldom seen. Most snake bites are the result of a defensive reaction: a foot or hand has suddenly landed in the snake's immediate vicinity. A rattlesnake often, but not always, gives a warning when it feels threatened. The sound, even if you have never before heard it, is instantly recognizable. Stand still until you have located the snake, and then back slowly away. Even if the snake strikes, it may fail to bite and inject venom. Clothing and boot material may absorb venom if the snake succeeds in biting—another reason to wear long pants and high-topped boots. Staying on the trail and not putting your hands or feet beyond your range of vision are other preventive measures. If you are bitten, seek medical attention as quickly and effortlessly as possible to avoid spreading the venom.

Coyotes, Mountain Lions, Wild Pigs

Coyotes are common residents of the Monterey Bay area, feeding on small mammals, birds, and, occasionally, deer. Coyotes generally avoid contact with humans and are not often seen. Mountain lions, also called cougars or pumas, are rarely seen in our area. They hunt at night and feed mostly on deer. If you do encounter a mountain lion, experts advise standing your ground, making loud noises, waving your arms to appear larger, and fighting back if attacked. Above all, never run, as running may trigger the animal's predator instincts. Report all mountain lion sightings to park personnel. Wild pigs are dangerous and should never be approached.

Maps

It would be nice if high-quality maps existed for each park covered by this guide, but that is not the case. The maps I used to find my way around the trails varied from professionally drawn topographic ones to sketch maps lacking contour lines and other features. In a few cases, no maps were available. When you visit a park that has a staffed entrance kiosk or visitor center, check there for a map. Sometimes maps and trail guides will be found in dispensers near the trailhead. Not surprisingly, bigger, more well-known parks have the best maps.

Point Lobos State Reserve is served by a good map published by the Point Lobos National History Association in collaboration with California State Parks. For Pinnacles National Monument, there are both the standard National Park map and a topographic map published in 1993 by Chad Moore, which is for sale at the Bear Gulch Visitor Center. For Big Basin Redwoods State Park, there is good map from the Mountain Parks Foundation in association with California State Parks, plus two from the Sempervirens Fund that cover the entire Skyline-to-the-Sea Trail (available from Wilderness Press). Appendix B has phone numbers of the agencies responsible for all the Monterey Bay area parks covered in this book.

The maps for this book were made using TOPO!, a computer program from National Geographic Maps (formerly Wildflower Productions). TOPO! uses USGS maps on CD-ROM combined with software that allows you to draw routes, insert text, measure distance, plot elevation gain and loss, and locate landmarks. You can even print your own custom maps right from your PC or Macintosh. An interface allows a GPS unit to transfer data to and from a PC. This lets you load waypoints from a map into your GPS so you can find them in the field, and the interface also allows you to take waypoints stored in your GPS during a hike and plot them on a map.

The California State Automobile Association (CSAA) gives its members free maps. Most useful for the routes in this book is *Monterey Bay Region*, taking in an area from Big Basin Redwoods State Park to the Ventana Wilderness and east to the Diablo Range. The CSAA also has maps for various towns and surrounding communities in the area, including Monterey and Santa Cruz.

Where To Get More Information

The best general-interest guidebook for the Monterey Bay area is *The Monterey Bay Shoreline Guide* by Jerry Emory, with stunning photographs by Frank Balthis. A list of other useful books about the Monterey Bay area and its natural and human history is provided in Appendix A. More information about the area's parklands and other resources may be found by contacting the agencies and organizations listed in Appendix B.

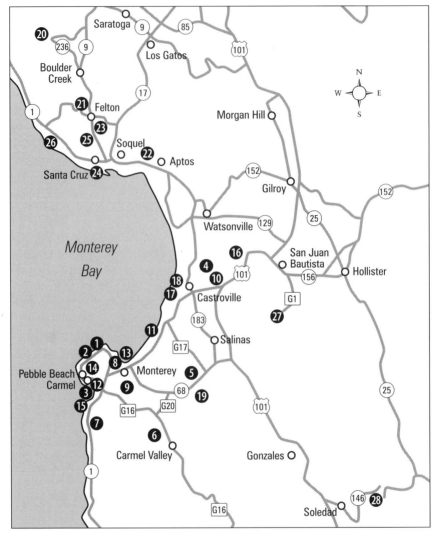

Hiking Area Locator Map

1. Asilomar Conference Grounds
2. Asilomar State Beach
3. Carmel River State Beach
4. Elkhorn Slough National Estuarine Research Reserve
5. Fort Ord Public Lands
6. Garland Ranch Regional Park
7. Garrapata State Park
8. Huckleberry Hill Nature Preserve
9. Jacks Peak County Park
10. Manzanita County Park
11. Marina State Beach
12. Mission Trail Park
13. Monterey State Beach
14. Pebble Beach
15. Point Lobos State Reserve
16. Royal Oaks County Park
17. Salinas River National Wildlife Refuge
18. Salinas River State Beach
19. Toro County Park
20. Big Basin Redwoods State Park
21. Fall Creek State Park
22. The Forest of Nisene Marks State Park
23. Henry Cowell Redwoods State Park
24. Natural Bridges State Beach
25. Pogonip
26. Wilder Ranch State Park
27. Fremont Peak State Park
28. Pinnacles National Monument

◆ Monterey County ◆

Asilomar Conference Grounds
DUNE BOARDWALK

Length: 0.8 mile

Time: Less than 1 hour

Rating: Easy

Regulations: CSP; no bikes; dogs on 6-foot or shorter leash.

Phone: Asilomar State Beach office, (831) 372-4076; concessionaire for conferences and lodging, (831) 372-8016.

Web site: *http://parks.ca.gov* or *www.visitasilomar.com*

Highlights: This easy loop on a boardwalk through the dunes in the historic Asilomar Conference Grounds introduces you to many of the plants successfully adapted to this harsh yet beautiful environment. (A brochure called "Living Dunes," describing some of the features seen from the boardwalk, is available from the park store in the Asilomar Conference Grounds social hall or from the park office, 804 Crocker Ave., on the east edge of the conference grounds.)

Directions: From the junction of Hwy. 1 and Hwy. 68 just south of Monterey, take 68 west toward Pacific Grove. At 3.3 miles, turn left onto Sunset Dr., here signed as Hwy. 68, and go another 1 mile to Asilomar State Beach. Parking is on the road shoulder on the ocean side; be sure your car is facing the correct way or it may be ticketed.

Facilities: Phone at the trailhead; nearby Asilomar Conference Grounds has water, rest rooms, store, dining hall, and lodging.

Trailhead: North side of Sunset Dr., opposite the entrance to Asilomar State Beach.

This easy stroll, which uses a boardwalk through the dunes, gives you a fine opportunity to learn about California's coastal dunes. The dune ecosystem is characterized by rolling hills of ever-shifting sand, and hearty, low-growing plants such as coastal sagewort and sand-verbena. Both may be seen here, along with a coastal variety of California poppy known as beach poppy, lupines, and paintbrush, also called seaside

(previous page) On the trail to Spanish Bay, Asilomar State Beach (Trip 2).

painted-cup. The thriving dunes here are the result of a massive dune-restoration project begun in 1984.

A pitched roof held aloft by two supports, called a "stile," welcomes you to the Asilomar Conference Grounds, originally created in 1913 as a conference center for the YWCA, to serve religious groups, college conferences, and women's training courses. Famed architect Julia Morgan designed many of the buildings here, and these are now a National Historic Landmark. California State Parks acquired the property in 1956, adding new buildings over the next two decades. A concessionaire runs the lodging and conference business for the state. The name Asilomar, created by the YWCA, is from the Spanish *asilo* (refuge) and *mar* (sea).

About 150 feet from the trailhead, you reach a junction where you turn left on a boardwalk heading north through the dunes. With the ocean briefly hidden from view by a dune, you pass a grassy area studded with clumps of coyote brush, poison oak, and mock heather. Two species of sand-verbena, pink and yellow, are at home in the dunes. Both have

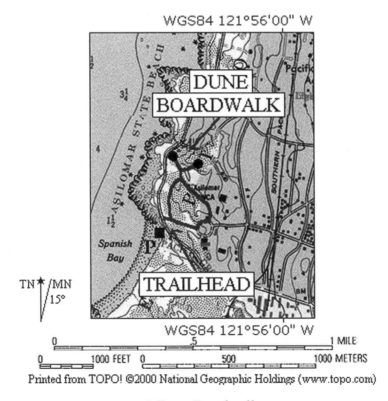

Printed from TOPO! ©2000 National Geographic Holdings (www.topo.com)

1. Dune Boardwalk

sticky leaves that trap particles of sand, creating an armor-like coating that helps protect the plant.

Now cresting a rise, you enjoy a stunning view south across Asilomar State Beach all the way to Spanish Bay and Point Joe. As the boardwalk curves right, you pass a rest bench on the right. Dense brush nearby provides shelter for black-tailed deer, which often come here to give birth in the spring. Reaching a **T**-junction, you turn left and in about 25 feet reach a fork. A stand of Monterey pines here is slowly succumbing to pine pitch canker, a fungal disease. According to scientists, perhaps 80 percent of California's Monterey pines will die within the next 30 years.

The fork's right-hand branch soon reaches a paved parking area near the Asilomar greenhouse. More than 450,000 plants representing 25 California native species have been propagated here, and then planted in the forest, in the dunes, and along the shoreline. The fork's left-hand branch heads north and quickly brings you to an overlook above a secluded pine hollow and the end of this part of the boardwalk. From here you retrace your steps to the **T**-junction mentioned above.

Continuing straight, you have the buildings of the Asilomar Conference Grounds on your left, marked by a line of Monterey pines, and a swale in the dunes to your right. If you pass through the dunes in spring and summer, the silver-green leaves and yellow-to-lavender flowers of bush lupine make a gorgeous display. Yellow sand-verbena offers its complement of color, and a nearby rest bench invites you to pause and take in the lovely scene. At about the 0.5-mile point, the boardwalk swings left and ends at a **T**-junction with a paved path. Turning right, you come in about 25 feet to a four-way junction with a paved road, where you turn right and head downhill for about a hundred feet.

At the next four-way junction, with the conference grounds' social hall and park store ahead and left, you turn right and follow a paved road that skirts a grassy field. The road soon curves left, bringing you to an entrance to the dune boardwalk, which is on your right. Once on the boardwalk, continue straight, returning to the trailhead just off Sunset Drive.

2 Asilomar State Beach
SPANISH BAY

Length:	3.8 miles
Time:	2 to 3 hours
Rating:	Easy
Regulations:	Pebble Beach Company; no bikes.
Phone:	Asilomar State Beach, (831) 372-4076; Pebble Beach Company, (800) 654-9300.
Web site:	*http://parks.ca.gov*
Highlights:	This out-and-back route, not to be missed, follows the Bay Trail through restored dunes from Asilomar State Beach to South Moss Beach at Spanish Bay, and then uses a trail beside 17-Mile Drive to bring you to a parking area south of China Rock. Coastal plants, migrating birds and whales, and outstanding views are among the attractions to be enjoyed here. (The route can be done as a car shuttle by leaving a car at one of the many parking areas along 17-Mile Drive.)
Directions:	Same as for "Dune Boardwalk" on p. 24.
Facilities:	Phone at the trailhead; nearby Asilomar Conference Grounds has water, rest rooms, store, dining hall, and lodging.
Trailhead:	South side of Sunset Dr., several hundred feet southeast of the entrance to Asilomar State Beach.

The Bay Trail, closed to bikes, leads you on a level course southwest from the trailhead, and in about 150 feet you come to a bridge over a small creek lined with willows and cattails. From here you have a fine view of the Inn at Spanish Bay and the adjacent golf links. Early in the 20th Century, a mining operation extracted high-quality sand from the dunes near Spanish Bay, as the near-shore water between here and Point Joe is called. Some of the sand was used to make glass, and some was sent to Hawaii to augment beaches at Waikiki. The dunes you see now have been restored by removing invasive non-native plants and planting native species.

The trail bends right and heads toward the beach through a corridor of vegetation, including willow, coyote brush, blackberry vines, and young Monterey pines. Soon you reach the start of a boardwalk that runs over the dunes, parallel to the shoreline. This is a perfect place to study some of the common coastal plants, including beach sagewort, sand-verbena, lupine, seaside daisy, and sea rocket. A sign reading BALLS IN PLAY reminds you that a busy golf course is nearby. A sandy path through low dunes, right, leads to Asilomar State Beach, a lovely crescent of sand and surf shown on some maps as North Moss Beach.

The gently undulating boardwalk runs between the golf course, left, and the beach, a few hundred feet to your right. Sprouting from the sand

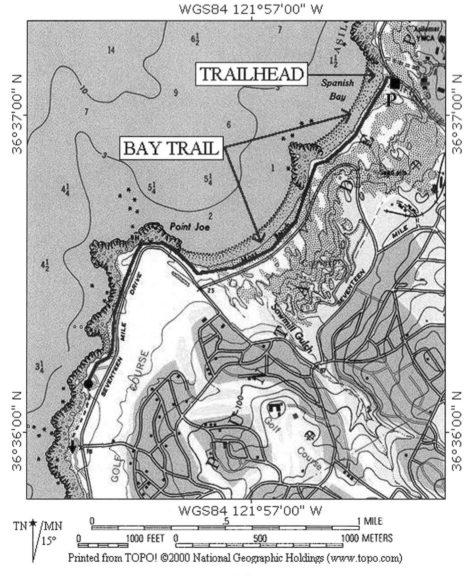

2. Spanish Bay

are mock heather, paintbrush, milk vetch, and sea pink, also called thrift. A path to the beach heads sharply right, but you continue straight, passing a rest bench, also on the right. The shoreline abruptly becomes rocky and rugged, but only for a short distance. Ahead is sandy South Moss Beach, almost a replica of its cousin just to the north. Staying right at a fork, you soon reach a picnic site and a parking area for Spanish Bay, which is stop 5 on 17-Mile Drive. This scenic spot, with its gently sloping sandy beach, draws crowds of tourists, and it's easy to see why—it is one of the loveliest beaches on the Monterey coast. (Although Spanish Bay is named for the early explorers who ventured here by sea and by land, the name itself does not appear in the authoritative book, *California Place Names*.)

The boardwalk ends at the parking area, and you continue on a trail of firm sand between the beach, right, and 17-Mile Drive, left. Now the trail swings away from the road, crosses a creek that drains through a culvert, and then dips into a hollow filled with mock heather, coyote brush, lupine, and California sagebrush. A large Monterey cypress, left, looks right at home here, but these ubiquitous trees are actually native to only two spots on the California coast—Point Lobos, and the Cypress Point/Crocker Grove area several miles ahead on 17-Mile Drive.

The trail crosses a driveway and parking area, and then bends right on its way toward Point Joe, named for a Chinese man who lived in a driftwood house here in the 1890s and early 1900s. Before you reach the point, you pass an information board, right, describing some features of this fascinating area. The wild sea just west is probably caused by submerged rocks, which spelled doom for mariners bound for Monterey Bay. To the north, past Asilomar and Pacific Grove, you may see the distant Santa Cruz Mountains. Huckleberry Hill, the high ground to the east, holds the S. F. B. Morse Botanical Reserve, home to bishop pines and rare Gowen cypress trees.

When you reach Point Joe itself, take a moment to imagine the imperceptible (except during earthquakes) but relentless movement of the earth's crust that brought this granitic outcrop north along the San Andreas fault from southern California. The promontory here is a great vantage point from which to look during winter for migrating gray whales. The offshore rocks provide roosts for pelagic (ocean-going) birds, including Brandt's cormorant, a black bird with a snake-like neck. Other birds to look for nearby are shorebirds such as killdeer, which despite their classification are often found inland, and whimbrels, denizens of open beaches and rocky coasts.

Your route is right beside 17-Mile Drive and, as you round Point Joe and head south, you cross a golf-cart path—a tee is just right—and then veer right onto a dirt trail. After crossing the next golf-cart path, you traverse a grassy area dotted with brass buttons and footsteps of spring, both of which produce yellow flowers. More brass buttons, when in bloom, give a yellow border to a pond, left. Where iceplant (a non-native) has been removed as part of a restoration effort, you walk beside clumps of lizard tail, saltbush, and seaside daisy. Here you also find salt grass— tolerant, as its name implies, of high salinity.

Now you pass a parking area, right, for China Rock, which is stop 8 on 17-Mile Drive. Like other coastal California names prefaced by "China," this one refers to Chinese fishing villages that thrived nearby during the late 1800s and early 1900s. Just past China Rock is another parking area, which the trail skirts. With 17-Mile Drive just left, you continue south to the next parking area, where the trail swings right to the edge of sheer coastal cliffs. The scene here is stunning, with a view extending south to Bird Rock, about a mile away. There are picnic tables, and some say this is one of the best places on the Monterey coast to watch the sunset. After enjoying this wonderful spot, retrace your steps to the parking area.

Seaside daisies blanket the rocky shore near Spanish Bay.

Carmel River State Beach
BLUFF TO BEACH

Length: 1.8 miles

Time: About 1 hour

Rating: Easy

Regulations: CSP; dogs on 6-foot or shorter leash.

Phone: (831) 649-2836

Web site: *http://parks.ca.gov*

Highlights: This mostly out-and-back hike starts on a lovely bluff overlooking Carmel River State Beach, then descends to a dirt road that runs along the scenic shoreline to the mouth of the Carmel River. From there, a short trail leads up and over a hill from where members of the 1769 Portolá expedition tried to signal their overdue supply ship, the *San Jose*, which never arrived.

Directions: From the junction of Hwy. 1 and Rio Rd. just southeast of Carmel, go south 0.8 mile to Ribera Rd. and turn right. Go 0.7 mile to a small parking area at the end of the road.

Facilities: None

Trailhead: South side of parking area.

Nestled in a residential area at the end of Ribera Rd., on a bluff overlooking the Pacific, is the trailhead for two trails. One, which you will use at the end of this hike, connects the bluff with a beautiful beach directly below and west. The other, a single track which you begin walking on now, takes a more leisurely route south through a scrubby area punctuated by stands of Monterey cypress, clusters of coyote brush—where hummingbirds may perch for an instant before again taking flight—and tangles of blackberry vines. Overhead you may be lucky enough to see swifts cavorting on the ocean breezes.

On the California coast in spring, large shorebirds called whimbrels gather to feed and fatten themselves before flying north to their Arctic breeding grounds. You may see these tawny birds on the beach below, probing with decurved bills for food in the wrack line. Some common land birds to watch for here are spotted towhee, song sparrow, and California quail, each often heard first and then seen. Another species of towhee, California towhee, may also appear in nearby thickets.

A formation of rock pinnacles just off the right side of the trail is mirrored by a set of similar rocks on the beach below. Seaside daisies, suncups, checkerbloom, wild mustard, and a species of paintbrush called seaside painted cup provide the foreground for this lovely scene. Staying right at a fork, as directed by an arrow on a trail post, you pass a rest bench and then a junction with a trail, right, leading down to the beach. Just past the junction, the other branch of the previous fork joins sharply from the left. At a four-way junction you again follow an arrow's advice and turn left, descending gently on a course that bends right through grassy fields dotted with red maids and lupine. The lovely crescent beach ahead, called Monastery Beach for the nearby Carmelite Monastery, and also San Jose Creek Beach for an adjacent creek, is part of Carmel River State Beach.

Passing straight through another four-way junction, you soon reach a **T**-junction with a dirt road, shown on the Point Lobos State Reserve map as Service Road & Trail, that runs along the coast. From this junction a beautiful vista encompasses the rocky headlands of Point Lobos State Reserve, rising out of the surf to the southwest. Here you turn right, and soon pass a trail going left to the shoreline pinnacles you saw from atop the bluff. The spring wildflower display here can be stunning, with paintbrush and seaside daisies competing for your attention.

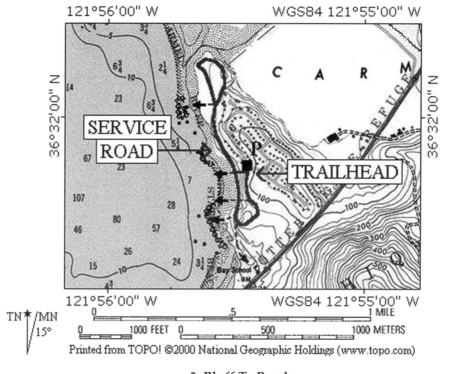

3. Bluff To Beach

Easy walking on a level road brings you to a four-way junction. Here a trail goes right and uphill, and another goes left to a lovely expanse of white-sand beach. You continue straight. Just back from the beach, ice-plant and lizard tail carpet the ground. Iceplant, an invasive non-native, is being removed from some locations on the coast, and lizard tail, a native member of the sunflower family, is sometimes planted in dune-restoration projects. At the next four-way junction, a trail, which you will use later to return to the parking area, rises steeply right, aided by steps, and another descends a set of steps to the beach, left.

Passing several homes set just above the road on a slope festooned with masses of purple-flowering pride of Madeira, you soon reach a fork where you stay left. On a hillside ahead and right stands a large, white, memorial cross, marking the spot where, on December 10, 1769, the Portolá expedition from Mexico erected a cross to signal its long-overdue supply ship, the *San Jose*. The expedition then headed south to San Diego, but the ship never arrived, presumably having been lost at sea.

At about the 1-mile point, you come to another four-way junction, with a trail leading left to the beach and a path going right. The sandy soil just back from the beach is perfect for beach primrose and yellow sand-verbena, both low, spreading plants with fleshy leaves. Also, here beach burr and mock heather compete with the ubiquitous iceplant. After per-haps a detour to study the dune plants more carefully, you continue straight to a turn-around at the road's end on a bluff overlooking the mouth of the Carmel River. A seasonal sandbar usually forms during summer and fall across the river mouth, creating a large lagoon and marshy area behind it. This area, the Carmel River Lagoon and Wetlands Preserve, offers fine habitat for waterfowl, waders, shorebirds, and gulls.

From the turn-around, steps lead down to the river's edge, and a sin-gle-track trail veers right and heads away from the beach. To follow it, you turn right and walk through a field of mustard and wild radish, pass-ing a rest bench and beginning a short climb up the cross-topped hill. Just before reaching the cross, you follow a trail going right and downhill, passing another rest bench, through a scrubby area of lupine and California sagebrush. At a four-way junction, where a plaque on a rock gives information about the memorial cross, you continue straight and soon merge with the Service Road & Trail.

Now you retrace your steps to the four-way junction where the trail rises steeply to the parking area. Turning left, you climb on steps cut from the hillside and reinforced with large blocks of wood. Pause and turn for one last glimpse of Carmel Bay and the Pacific Ocean.

4

Elkhorn Slough National Estuarine Research Reserve
FIVE FINGERS LOOP

Length: 2.5 miles

Time: 1 to 2 hours

Rating: Easy

Regulations: California Department of Fish and Game; open Wednesday through Sunday, 9 A.M. to 5 P.M.; entrance fee; foot traffic only; no dogs.

Phone: Visitor center and offices, (831) 728-2822; Elkhorn Slough Foundation, (831) 728-5939.

Web site: *www.elkhornslough.org*

Highlights: This easy and enjoyable semi-loop uses the main trail from the visitor center, and the Long Valley and Five Fingers loop trails to explore Parsons Slough and one of The Five Fingers at its upper reaches. Birders especially will enjoy this trip—be sure to bring binoculars and a spotting scope, as many of the birds are far away on mud flats. Birders will also want to visit the lagoon at nearby Moss Landing State Beach for shorebirds and waders. Another way to explore the slough is by kayak, which can be rented in the town of Moss Landing. The Monterey Bay Bird Festival, held the first weekend in October, is presented by the Elkhorn Slough Foundation and local birding organizations.

Directions: From Hwy. 1 in Moss Landing, take Dolan Rd. east 3.5 miles to Castroville Blvd., which joins from the right. Continue straight, now on Castroville Blvd., 0.2 mile to Elkhorn Rd. and turn left. Go 2 miles to the reserve entrance, turn left, and go 0.1 mile to a large, paved parking area.

                   From Hwy. 101 in Prunedale, exit at San Miguel Canyon Rd. and take it northwest 0.8 mile to Castroville Blvd. Turn left, go 3 miles to Elkhorn Rd., and turn right. Go 2 miles to the reserve entrance, turn left, and go 0.1 mile to a large, paved parking area.

Facilities: Visitor center with displays, books, maps, and helpful staff; rest rooms, water, phone, picnic tables.

Trailhead: South side of visitor center.

Before starting off on the trails, be sure to check out the wonderful visitor center, where you can pick up a map and view the natural-history displays, some of them interactive and great for children. Here you pay your entrance fee, which is waived if you are 16 or under, or have a California fishing or hunting license or a California Wildlife Campaign membership. For a small fee, you can purchase an annual pass, which gives you access to all California Wildlife Campaign sites, including Elkhorn Slough.

According to *A Natural History of the Monterey Bay National Marine Sanctuary*, Elkhorn Slough is the largest coastal wetland between San Francisco and Morro bays. A slough is "a narrow, winding waterway edged with muddy and marshy ground." Although it resembles a river and lies in an ancient riverbed, Elkhorn Slough, 7 miles long, has a flow of freshwater only in winter, when rainwater drains into it from surrounding hills. During this time, the slough becomes an estuary, a place where freshwater and saltwater meet. In the summer, when no freshwater enters the slough, evaporation concentrates the salinity in its upper reaches to levels greater than seawater.

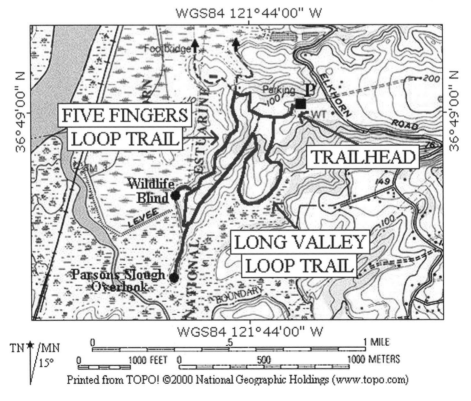

4. Five Fingers Loop

Daily tidal action in Elkhorn Slough creates a strong current, up to three knots, and also a rise and fall in water level. There are four habitats associated with the slough: waterways, mud flats, salt marsh, and uplands. Because of its strategic position on the Pacific Flyway, a migratory route for birds, the slough and nearby areas attract more than 260 species of songbirds, shorebirds, waders, raptors, and waterfowl. Human use of the slough, starting with the Ohlone Indians, goes back thousands of years. Recent human intervention has altered the slough's environment, including dredging, diking, cattle grazing, the extension of the Southern Pacific Railroad in the 1870s, and the opening of Moss Landing Harbor in the 1940s.

On the south side of the visitor center, you find a paved path heading southwest and follow it for about 100 feet, where a dirt-and-gravel road joins it from the left. Here you stay on the paved path as it bends right, giving you a view of Elkhorn Slough and the large power plant at Moss Landing. Surrounding you are weedy fields of poison hemlock, wild radish, mustard, and thistle. Soon you reach a junction with the Long Valley Loop Trail, a dirt road, where you turn left. Now the road curves left and begins to descend on a moderate grade through stands of coast live oak, passing a rest bench, right.

The upper reaches of Parsons Slough, which flows into Elkhorn Slough, divide into five branches, called The Five Fingers. One of these lies just ahead; through a break in the weedy screen of poison oak and blackberry vines you may be able to spot shorebirds, such as greater yellowlegs, marbled godwits, dowitchers, willets, and sandpipers, feeding on exposed mud flats and in shallow water. Now the route swings right and follows the shoreline, soon reaching a boardwalk jutting southwest over the water. Pickleweed, a salt-marsh plant adapted to occasional flooding by the tide, grows nearby.

Leaving the boardwalk behind, you climb on a gentle and then moderate grade, passing a rest bench, right, and arriving at a **T**-junction with the Five Fingers Loop Trail. Here you turn left and enjoy a level walk past stands of tall eucalyptus trees, stopping to scan the skies for hawks, falcons, and possibly a golden eagle. At about the 1-mile point, you reach a junction where the Five Fingers Loop Trail veers right, and a trail to Parsons Slough Overlook, about 0.3 mile, goes straight. Birders will want to visit the overlook, especially in fall. Here, on October 31, 1982, the record for spotting the most bird species in a single day from one location was set at 116.

Even on a non-record day, especially from fall through spring, you are likely to see pelicans, egrets, shorebirds, and waterfowl from the overlook. Flocks of shorebirds and waterfowl often attract aerial predators, especially merlins and peregrine falcons. Shorebirds or waterfowl taking off in a frenzy, may be reacting to a raptor cruising overhead. If you have binoculars handy, check the nearby powerline towers, where hawks and falcons perch while scanning for prey.

If you have walked to Parsons Slough Overlook, retrace your steps to the previous junction and turn left. Otherwise, stay on the Five Fingers Loop Trail by turning right and then passing a rest bench and a trail, signed WILDLIFE BLIND, veering sharply left. The blind is a small building with openings for camera lenses and spotting scopes. It offers another vantage point for Parsons Slough and protection from the wind. Now you descend on a gentle grade through a large grove of eucalyptus, trees imported from Australia and planted in the mid 1800s. Chestnut-backed chickadees may be flitting among the sickle-shaped eucalyptus leaves, which rustle noisily in the breeze.

At about the 2-mile point, you pass a closed service road, left, and approach the barns of the old Elkhorn Dairy, which operated from 1922 to the early 1970s. The barns have been home to barn owls, and you may also spot a white-tailed kite on patrol, hovering over some unsuspecting rodent in the field. At a four-way junction with the South Marsh Loop Trail, you turn sharply right onto a dirt-and-gravel road and begin to climb, soon passing an observation platform with several spotting scopes for viewing the slough. With a rest bench on your right, you now reach a paved path and a junction with the Five Fingers Loop Trail. About 200 feet ahead is the junction with the Long Valley Loop Trail, where you began this loop. From there, retrace your steps to the parking area.

Two old barns are the remains of former dairy operations in the Elkhorn Slough area.

5

Elkhorn Slough National Estuarine Research Reserve
SOUTH MARSH AND HUMMINGBIRD ISLAND

Length: 2.8 miles

Time: 2 hours

Rating: Easy

Regulations: California Department of Fish and Game; open Wednesday through Sunday, 9 A.M. to 5 P.M.; entrance fee; foot traffic only; no dogs.

Phone: Visitor center and offices, (831) 728-2822; Elkhorn Slough Foundation, (831) 728-5939.

Web site: *www.elkhornslough.org*

Highlights: Using the South Marsh Loop Trail, along with main trail from the visitor center and a short trail to Hummingbird Island, this easy and scenic semi-loop lets you visit a rookery for herons and egrets and an art-in-nature project honoring the Native Americans who called this area home for thousands of years.

Directions: Same as for "Five Fingers Loop" on p. 34.

Facilities: Visitor center with displays, books, maps, and helpful staff; rest rooms, water, phone, picnic tables.

Trailhead: South side of visitors center.

Follow the route description for "Five Fingers Loop" on p. 34 to the junction with the Long Valley Loop Trail. From here you continue straight on the paved path, soon passing the Five Fingers Loop Trail, left, and then an observation platform with spotting scopes for viewing the slough. In the distance are Moss Landing State Beach, the wetlands behind it, which harbor many shorebirds and waders, and the towers of the power-generating station in Moss Landing.

Just past the platform, the route changes to a dirt-and-gravel road, curves right, and descends. The two barns nearby were part of the Elkhorn Farm Dairy, which operated here from 1922 until the early 1970s. Barn owls have nested here, and you may also see a great blue heron or an egret flying between the slough and its roosting area at Rookery Pond, which you will visit later on this route. Soon you reach a four-way junction with a rest bench on the right. Here the Five Fingers Loop Trail joins sharply from the left, and the South Marsh Loop Trail angles left and also straight.

You bear left and pass through a weedy area thick with poison hemlock, milk thistle, mustard, and wild radish. Directly in front of you is the larger of the two barns, signed ELKHORN FARM. A trail to it veers right, but the main route curves left around the barn's south side. This is a good place to look for white-tailed kites, crow-sized raptors that hover over open fields in search of rodents. Passing under a set of powerlines, you descend to the level of the slough, with its many convoluted channels, and reach a long boardwalk stretching out over a marshy area. This area, like many California wetlands, was diked and used for pasture to support the dairy industry. In October, 1983, the diked area was opened to the flow of the tides as part of a wetland-restoration project.

A lovely hillside, rising right, supports California poppies and clumps of lupine. To your left, a boardwalk extends west over an area of salt marsh, affording a closer look at wading birds and shorebirds. Passing a power-line tower, the route soon comes to a bridge that spans open water. If you look to the right while crossing the bridge, you may see egrets roosting in trees around Rookery Pond. From here, they look like white flecks, but you will have a closer look in a little while. Closer to you, cor-

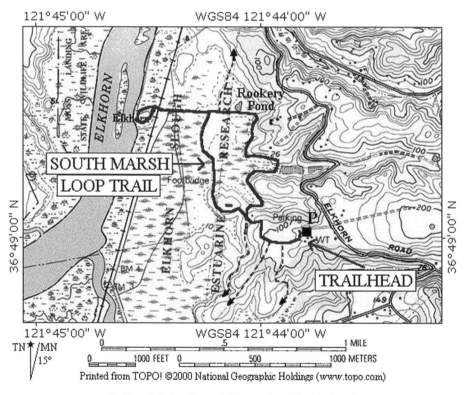

5. South Marsh and Hummingbird Island

morants and western grebes may appear on the water. Once across the bridge, you pass a rest bench, right, and follow a trail that bends left. A weedy field of coyote brush and poison hemlock is right, and on your left, a small salt marsh forms a border between land and open water. A plant called pineapple weed, which produces little yellow flowers, carpets the trail in places.

Just shy of the 1-mile point, you reach a **T**-junction with a dirt road. Here you turn left to visit Hummingbird Island (or, if you want a shorter hike, you can turn right and stay on the South Marsh Loop Trail). Turning left, you follow a dike that divides South Marsh from Whistle Stop Lagoon, which takes its name from the nearby railroad right-of-way. One of the land birds associated with marshes is the red-winged blackbird. You may see them here, defending their territories and flashing their red epaulets.

As you reach the far end of the dike you are now on Hummingbird Island. A trail post with a sign directs you to the right, and there is a toilet, left. Ahead, a barbed-wire fence guards the railroad tracks. To cross the tracks, you pass through a gap in the fence, watching carefully for trains. About 30 feet past the tracks is a junction, unsigned, with a trail going left and then up a set of wooden steps. This is the return part of a loop trail which you will follow on Hummingbird Island. By continuing straight, past venerable coast live oaks, you soon reach the edge of Elkhorn Slough.

This area was used at the turn of the last century by the Empire Gun Club, one of many private California hunting organizations, situated near marshes and wetlands. The island was used for thousands of years by Native Americans, and now is home to a special art-in-nature project, created in 1989 by John Roloff and Heather McGill, to honor the Ohlone Indians. At the edge of the slough, here a broad expanse of water, eucalyptus trees shade a rest bench, giving you a perfect vantage point from

The expanse of Elkhorn Slough provides ample opportunity for spotting shorebirds, waders, and other birds.

which to study whatever waterfowl and shorebirds may be present. Beneath the slough's calm surface glide many species of fish, and on its muddy banks marine mammals such as sea otters and harbor seals may be seen. At the rest bench the trail turns left, and you follow it past a large clearing, left, where vetch and blue-eyed grass may add bright flecks of blue and magenta to complement the green grass.

Bearing left at a fork, you come to the first art project, called "Midden Sculpture," made with oyster shells and rocks, and featuring a pool teeming with fish. The second project consists of wire frames placed around tree trunks to resemble Native American dwellings. The third project is a concrete bench inscribed with the names of North and South American Indian tribes, and also the scientific names of many species of hummingbirds. Monterey cypress lend their stately presence to the area. Bearing left at the bench, you enter a beautiful, shady grove of coast live oak and a few coast redwood trees, and then descend a set of wooden steps. Ahead about 150 feet, you rejoin the first part of the trail at a **T**-junction, where you turn right.

Now you retrace your steps to the junction with the South Marsh Loop Trail, and then continue straight. Just past a powerline, you come to a large grove of eucalyptus trees, which in spring are festooned with brushy, white flowers, and then pass a junction with a trail to the North Marsh Overlook, left. Ahead is Rookery Pond, and when you reach it, you will have a good view of the tall Monterey pines in which the egrets and herons prefer to roost. From a boardwalk on the pond's south edge, you can watch these large birds—a great blue heron has a 6-foot wingspan—maneuver above the treetops and then glide in for a perfect landing.

Just past the pond, the route gains elevation on a gentle grade and curves right. Here, oaks and pines provide perfect habitat for acorn woodpeckers, and in the bark of selected trees you may see the many holes they drill to store acorns. Low brush beneath the trees may shelter a covey of California quail, and the branches above may be teeming with bushtits, chickadee-like birds that feed on insects. Now on a curving course, you follow the contours of a marshy wetland, right, passing several closed service roads, a rest bench, and an unofficial trail that goes left to Cattail Swale. Poppies and yellow bush lupine add color to the scene.

Once past the trail to Cattail Swale, the route curves right through a shady area thick with coffeeberry, western creek dogwood, blackberry vines, ferns, and miners lettuce. A drinking fountain, left, offers refreshment, and soon you see the larger of the two Elkhorn Farm Dairy barns ahead. Out in the open now, you pass a rest bench, right, make a final curve around a finger of marsh, and then reach a fork, where you stay left. Drawing abreast of the smaller barn, left, you come to the four-way junction where you joined the South Marsh Loop Trail. From here you bear left and retrace your steps to the parking area.

Fort Ord Public Lands
CHAPARRAL LOOP

Length: 6 miles

Time: 3 to 4 hours

Rating: Difficult

Regulations: BLM; travel only on signed roads and trails; no shooting or hunting; no overnight camping, fires, or woodcutting. **Warning:** Because this area was used by the military for more than 60 years, live rounds and explosives remain in public areas as well as in posted areas; do not touch unfamiliar objects, especially metal. Mark the location and call the federal police at (831) 242-7851 or (831) 242-7924.

Phone: BLM, (831) 394-8314

Web site: *www.ca.blm.gov/hollister*

Highlights: This rugged and scenic loop, which uses Old Reservation, Jack's, and Engineer Canyon roads, and Trails 02, 41, 36, and 03, lets you sample some of the features, including beautiful oak groves, lush grasslands dotted with wildflowers, and sunny hillsides of chaparral, this fascinating area, which is in the process of being reclaimed from many years of military use, has to offer.

Directions: From Hwy. 68 eastbound between Monterey and Salinas, take the Reservation Rd./River Rd. exit. After exiting and coming to a traffic signal, go left under the highway on Reservation Rd., and after several hundred feet turn left onto Portola Dr. After 0.2 mile Portola Dr. turns sharply left, but you continue straight, now on Creekside Terrace. After 0.1 mile you come to a small dirt parking area, left.

From Hwy. 68 westbound between Monterey and Salinas, take the Reservation Rd./River Rd. exit. After exiting, turn right at a stop sign onto Reservation Rd., and then immediately left onto Portola Dr. After 0.2 mile Portola Dr. turns sharply left, but you continue straight, now on Creekside Terrace. After 0.1 mile you come to a small dirt parking area, left.

Facilities: None

Trailhead: Northwest end of parking area.

The Fort Ord Public Lands were once part of the 44-square-mile Fort Ord Military Reservation near Monterey Bay, which served during World War II as a staging area for army troops heading to the Pacific, and then, during the Vietnam War, as a basic-training center. Fort Ord is named for Edward Ortho Cresap Ord, who as a lieutenant in 1847 was stationed in Monterey, distinguished himself as a general in the Civil War, and later became commander of the Department of the Pacific. After the base closed in 1991 and the last personnel departed in 1994, the U.S. Army gave about 7,000 acres to the Bureau of Land Management (BLM). Other lands were used to establish the campus of California State University, Monterey Bay. The Army is in the process of clearing dangerous materials from the remaining 8,000 acres, which will then be transferred to the BLM.

From the parking area, you head northwest, past a large metal gate, on the continuation of Creekside Terrace, here called Old Reservation Road. This paved route soon crosses a bridge over El Toro Creek, a sandy arroyo where you will find willow and black cottonwood, and then passes an information board and a holder for maps, which may be empty. The nearby hillsides are cloaked in chaparral, mostly chamise, coyote brush, poi-

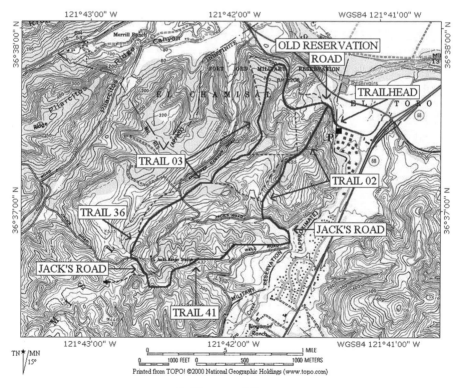

6. Chaparral Loop

son oak, and toyon. As the road curves left, you pass Trail 30, a single track heading right, and then come to a junction with Trail 02, a sandy path going left.

Here you turn left and begin to climb on a gentle grade that soon becomes steep. Stay alert for bikes and horses on this multi-use trail, in places rough and eroded. The sticky, fragrant plant with yellow flowers growing beside the trail is telegraph weed, a common member of the sunflower family. Other trailside plants here include bush monkeyflower, blackberry, fennel, and mustard. Welcome shade is provided in places by venerable coast live oaks, their limbs draped with lice lichen, known locally as old man's beard. As you struggle uphill, take time to rest and admire the view east to the checkerboard lands—light and dark green alternating with freshly plowed brown—of the agriculturally rich Salinas Valley.

Finally reaching a flat spot in a clearing, just before the 1-mile point, you are faced with a confusing five-way junction. Trail 02 bends left and continues uphill. Trail 31 takes off directly across the clearing and bends sharply right. Trail 34 veers right at a gentler angle and climbs. From this clearing you have a wonderful view west into the heart of the Fort Ord Public Lands, a vast and rolling array of chaparral-clad hills cut by rugged canyons. You stay on Trail 02, now a dirt road bordered by California sagebrush and black sage. Cresting a rise and bending sharply right, the road begins a long descent on a moderate grade. Listen here for the wrentit, whose call sounds like someone trying to start a reluctant car, and scan the sky every once in a while for birds of prey.

Beside the trail are remnants of a log cabin that once belonged to a Boy Scout camp. Now the road winds its way gently downhill and parallel to a valley, which is on your right. At a junction signed for Trails 04 and 31, you continue descending on Trail 02, soon reaching a **T**-junction with Jack's Road. You turn left and proceed, enjoying a vista that takes in open, grassy hills and Boy Scout Pond, a small body of water surrounded by freshwater marsh. A sign points ahead to Oil Well Road, but before reaching the road you turn right onto Trail 41, a single track that meanders around the pond through a shady grove of coast live oak. A rolling climb with some steep pitches takes you west, leaving the pond behind.

A dark shape flying fast through the trees could be a Cooper's hawk, a crow-sized raptor that preys on songbirds and small mammals. Now the oaks are joined by California buckeyes, many of them doing poorly here. A large field of sedges, tall grass-like plants with triangular stems and brown flower heads, indicates residual moisture in a low-lying area. In places, unofficial trails diverge from the main route; avoid taking them. Your trail curves south and works its way up the side of a ridge on what becomes, near its crest, very steep and eroded ground. Pausing to rest, you are rewarded by a fine view east: through a notch where two ridges come together, you will see the 3,000-foot summits of the distant Gabilan Range.

Curving left, you stay just below the ridgecrest, but soon the trail swings right and climbs. Once atop the crest, you can detour left to the summit of a knoll that provides spectacular 360° views. Now back on the trail, you cross to the west side of the ridge, and then head southwest through beautiful open country where a restoration project is underway to encourage the growth of native grasses. The trail descends to a saddle, crosses it, and then heads west and steeply uphill, following a ridgecrest. At about the 3-mile point, where the trail swings right and begins to descend, you can follow a short spur trail to the summit of another knoll. Views southwest of the Santa Lucia Mountains on the far side of Carmel Valley enhance the top-of-the-world feeling.

When you are ready to leave this scenic perch, descend on a gentle and then moderate grade to a **T**-junction. Here, Trail 41 goes left, but you turn right onto a short trail that goes several hundred feet to Jack's Road. Once on the road, which is paved, you turn left and begin a gentle climb. After several hundred yards, you reach a junction with Trail 36, where you turn right. This rolling, ridgetop route takes you northeast through a treasure

Birders on Ford Ord Public Lands listen for songbirds and keep an eye out for raptors above these hills.

Look for these rock formations on Old Reservation Road.

trove of chaparral—plants such as manzanita, chamise, toyon, and various species of *Ceanothus*, which thrive in the sandy soil and are adapted to drought and fire.

Passing Trail 38, left, you soon begin a long, gentle descent on a rocky, eroded track that brings you to a four-way junction with Engineer Canyon Road. Walking directly across this dirt road, you find Trail 03 and, to its right, Trail 33. Choosing Trail 03, a dirt road, you climb a short, steep pitch through a road-cut that exposes layer upon layer of coastal rocks. As the road rises toward the sky and then levels off, you enjoy expansive views southeast across Highway 68 and Toro County Park to Mt. Toro (3560'), part of the Sierra de Salinas.

Where Trails 33 and 04 go right, you stay on Trail 03 as it curves left. At the next junction, Trail 32 goes left, and Trail 33 heads right, but you continue straight on Trail 03, here mostly level and sandy. Purple asters, which continue to bloom from summer into fall, may provide dots of color in the otherwise monochromatic landscape. Passing a junction, right, with Trails 33 and 34, the road swings north and begins to descend, with an extremely steep drop to the right, and a gentler slope falling away left. At about the 5-mile point, Trail 33 veers left, but you continue descending on Trail 03. Where Trail 33 rejoins from the left, your route makes a big bend to the right and soon merges with Old Reservation Road.

Bearing to the right on Old Reservation Road, you pass a junction, left, with Trail 30. The steep embankments of a road-cut show evidence of landslides, and the soft dirt and red-colored rock have been eroded into weird formations. As the road bends left, Trail 31 takes off to the right. Staying on Old Reservation Road, you soon reach the junction with Trail 02, right, where you began this loop. From here, retrace your steps to the parking area.

Fort Ord Public Lands
GRASSLANDS LOOP

Length: 5.7 miles

Time: 3 to 4 hours

Rating: Moderate

Regulations: BLM; travel only on signed roads and trails; no shooting or hunting; no overnight camping, fires, or woodcutting. **Warning:** Because this area was used by the military for more than 60 years, live rounds and explosives remain in public areas as well as in posted areas; do not touch unfamiliar objects, especially metal. Mark the location and call the federal police at (831) 242-7851 or (831) 242-7924.

Phone: BLM, (831) 394-8314

Web site: *www.ca.blm.gov/hollister*

Highlights: This athletic loop, best done on a cool day with good visibility, uses Toro Creek, Guidotti, Skyline, and Oil Well roads to reach the high, rolling hills that form the backbone of Fort Ord Public Lands. Fine views from the ridgetops reward your efforts. During fall migration, birds of prey patrol the skies, and in spring, wildflowers decorate the grassy slopes.

Directions: From the junction of Hwy. 1 and Hwy. 68 in Monterey, take Hwy. 68 east 10.4 miles to a large dirt parking area on the north side of the highway (be careful of oncoming traffic).

Facilities: None

Trailhead: West side of parking area.

The parking area for this hike is sandwiched between busy Hwy. 68 and a housing development called Toro Creek Estates. A large orange metal gate marks the entrance to Fort Ord Public Lands, managed by the BLM in partnership with the communities of the Monterey region. Just past the gate is an information board with a map and a notice about unexploded ordnance, reminding you of the area's military past. Your route, a dirt road, angles right, and there are also several unofficial trails beside it— one left, the other right.

Tall sycamores and eucalyptus trees offer shade, and beautiful, grassy hills rise to the north. This part of Fort Ord Public Lands consists mostly of open grassland and rolling hills, in contrast to the deeply cut canyons and chaparral-clad ridges in the park's northeast corner, described in Trip 6, "Chaparral Loop." After about 100 yards, you reach a **T**-junction, marked by a trail post, with Toro Creek Road. Ahead is a wide, sandy arroyo, the channel of El Toro Creek, which eventually leads to the Salinas River. Turning left, you walk parallel to the arroyo, which is bordered by willows and clumps of California sagebrush, mustard, and poison oak.

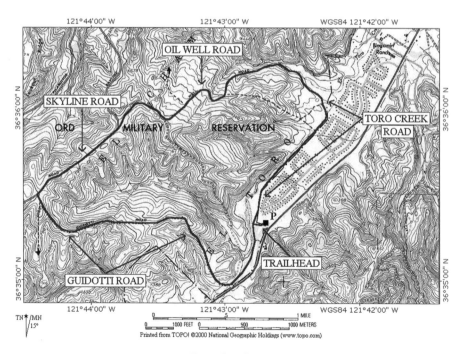

7. Grasslands Loop

Now you merge with Guidotti Road, which goes left to a gate beside Hwy. 68, and also right, crossing El Toro Creek via a cement bridge. Bearing right, you cross the creek and then begin to climb on a moderate grade through a savanna dotted with wonderful valley oaks, identified by their deeply lobed leaves, checkered bark, and large, egg-shaped acorns. As you ascend the eroded dirt track, pause now and again to admire the sweeping view that takes in the Salinas Valley and the Gabilan Range to the east, and the oak-studded hills of Toro County Park and the Sierra de Salinas to the southeast.

Now atop a ridge, scan the sky for raptors, especially during fall migration, when red-tailed hawks, red-shouldered hawks, American kestrels, and northern harriers commonly appear. Also in fall, look for migrating monarch butterflies—their winter home in Pacific Grove is not far away. Horehound, mullein, and yellow-flowering telegraph weed line the road. Look here for stands of native bunchgrasses such as purple needlegrass. And be sure to watch out for star thistle, one of California's most invasive plants. Seeds from this pesky invader will attach themselves to your socks, pants, or bicycle tires, making you an unwitting accomplice in its spread.

Your climb to the high ridge ahead is relieved by short stretches of level ground, and soon you reach a saddle where a dirt road, not shown on the park map, joins from the left. As you crest a rise just past the 2-mile point, Trail 47 joins sharply from the left, and about 200 feet ahead you reach a **T**-junction with Skyline Road. From here you have a stunning view north along the Monterey coast all the way to the Santa Cruz Mountains. Turning right, you begin a gentle and then moderate descent, with Fremont Peak ahead in the hazy distance. To your left is a deep canyon that holds Pilarcitos Creek and Pilarcitos Canyon Road. When you reach a fork marked by a trail post, you continue straight, now on Oil Well Road, and soon your route drops below the ridgetop, now on your left. To your right, and far below, is Hwy. 68, and across it are the enticing hills of Toro County Park, described in Trip 29.

A steady, winding descent on a gentle grade takes you past a junction with Trail 10, left, and soon you enter the pleasant realm of coast live oaks and willows. Here you may find western scrub-jays, Savannah sparrows, and Say's phoebe, a member of the flycatcher family. At about the 4-mile point, you pass a dirt road, right, signed for Trails 45 and 46, but you continue to descend, now on a moderate grade. A valley lined with trees and shrubs, indicating a creek, is to your left. Soon you reach a fork, marked by a trail post, where Oil Well Road veers left, and Toro Creek Road goes right.

Turning right, you follow a dirt-and-gravel road through an area of grass and coyote brush. Passing a closed trail, left, your route climbs gently and winds its way toward El Toro Creek and Toro Creek Estates. You may find Black phoebe, another member of the flycatcher family, and

California towhee, a ground-feeder, here. Where a dirt road joins sharply from the left, you continue to follow Toro Creek Road as it bends right and then runs parallel to El Toro Creek, which is on your left.

At about the 5-mile point, Trails 45 and 46 join here from the right. Soon the road drops into the arroyo holding El Toro Creek, which is dry for much of the year, and crosses to the other side. A large school with a playground and sports fields is behind a fence to your left. Here the road margins are decorated with lupine and California poppies. Towering Monterey pines form a shady corridor that leads you to the southwest edge of Toro Creek Estates, where an unofficial trail departs left. Several hundred feet ahead is the junction where you began this loop; from here you turn left and retrace your steps to the parking area.

✦ Garland Ranch Regional Park ✦

Garland Ranch Regional Park, operated by the Monterey Peninsula Regional Park District, is a magnificent, sprawling open space located along Carmel Valley Road about 9 miles east of Hwy. 1. The park's more than 4,400 acres of floodplain, wooded canyons, redwood groves, oak savannas, and chaparral-cloaked hillsides are bordered on the northeast by the Carmel River and on the southwest by the steep and rugged north wall of the Santa Lucia Range. Trails run the gamut from easy to challenging and provide something for everyone—solitude, exercise, spring-wildflower viewing, birding, and great views of the Monterey peninsula. Lovely Garzas Creek, a tributary of the Carmel River, runs through the middle of the park

Named for William M. Garland, whose 541-acre ranch was the district's first open-space acquisition, the park was opened in 1975 and has since grown to its present size through gifts and purchased additions. Prior to becoming a park, the area was last used for ranching and logging, and even earlier was an important habitation site for local Rumsen Indians. Today, hikers, joggers, equestrians, and other nature lovers enjoy Garland Ranch. Limited mountain biking is available in the Cooper Ranch area on the park's west corner. Several areas in the park are open for limited use by permit only; call the park district (see below) for information and permits.

Near the main park entrance off Carmel Valley Road is a small visitor center which has books, displays, posters, and lists of the park's common plants and animals. There are rangers, naturalists, and docents to help you enjoy your visit and to respond to emergencies. The district provides both in-class environmental education programs and outdoor interpretive hikes for all ages. Events and outings are posted at the park and also on the park district's Web site: *www.mprpd.org/parks/garland.html*. The park, which is open year-round from sunrise to sunset, is served by public transit.

Though Garland Ranch Regional Park is one of the few public parks where dogs are welcome on the hiking trails, the park district asks for your cooperation. Please be responsible. Keep your dog on a leash not over 7 feet long, or under *immediate* voice control. Allowing your dog to run far ahead of, or behind, you can create a situation of conflict or mishap. Dog owners must clean up after their pets. Smoking is prohibited on the park's trails.

VISITOR CENTER: (831) 659-6065

RANGER STATION: (831) 659-6063

MONTEREY PENINSULA REGIONAL PARK DISTRICT: (831) 659-4488

FRIENDS OF THE PARK DISTRICT: (831) 659-6062

MONTEREY—SALINAS TRANSIT: (831) 899-2555

Garland Ranch Regional Park
BUCKEYE NATURE TRAIL

Length:	2 miles
Time:	1 to 2 hours
Rating:	Easy
Regulations:	MPRPD; no horses; dogs under immediate voice command or on a leash not more than 7 feet.
Phone:	MPRPD, (831) 659-6063
Web site:	*www.mprpd.org/parks/garland/html*
Highlights:	Using the Lupine Loop, Buckeye, and Mesa trails, this enjoyable semi-loop is a fine introduction to one of Monterey County's best parks. Along the way, you follow the self-guiding Buckeye Nature Trail, where descriptive signs provide information about the area's natural and human history.
Directions:	From the junction of Hwy. 1 and Carmel Valley Rd. just east of Carmel, take Carmel Valley Rd. east 8.7 miles to a large dirt parking area, right.
Facilities:	Visitor center with maps, pamphlets, and helpful staff; rest rooms, telephone, picnic tables.
Trailhead:	South side of the permanent bridge over the Carmel River.

From the parking area, walk west along a path that parallels the Carmel River, the lovely stream on your left. When you reach a dirt road joining from the right, you turn left and cross a large, permanent bridge. Another bridge, removed during the winter, is located several hundred yards upstream. Once across the bridge, you reach the trailhead. Here the Cooper Trail, closed to horses, heads straight, but you turn left toward the informative Garland Ranch Visitor Center. This trail, a wide dirt path, is closed to bikes. After about 125 feet, you come to a junction with the

Lupine Loop, going both straight and right. (To get to the visitor center, which is certainly worth a visit, continue straight for several hundred yards.)

Here you turn right and follow the Lupine Loop, a level, sandy path through a grassy meadow dotted with its namesake plant, and also with California poppies, fiddleneck, and red maids. The trail is bordered by eucalyptus, sycamore, and black cottonwood. Snivleys Ridge, the northern crest of the Santa Lucia Range, rises steeply to the south. Standing amid these open fields, scan the sky for raptors—among the common ones here are red-tailed hawk, red-shouldered hawk, white-tailed kite, and American kestrel. Golden eagles and peregrine falcons have also been seen in the park.

Soon an unofficial trail from the visitor center joins from the left, and then you reach a four-way junction marked by a trail post. Here, an

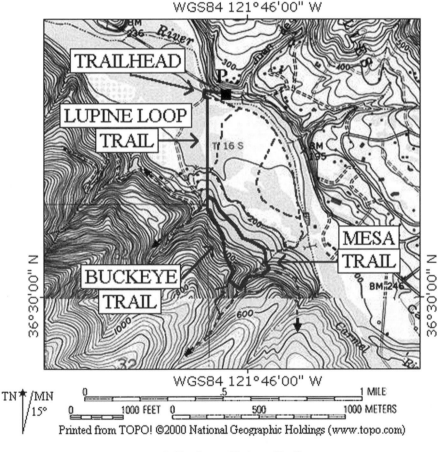

8. Buckeye Nature Trail

unsigned trail from the visitor center joins sharply from the left. Veering left is the Cottonwood Trail, and straight ahead is the continuation of the Lupine Loop and access to the Mesa, Maple Canyon, and Buckeye trails. Shade here is provided by Monterey pines, coast live oaks, and California buckeyes, their limbs arching above an understory of California sagebrush, snowberry, blackberry, and poison oak. About 100 yards and uphill from the previous junction is another four-way junction.

The Lupine Loop here turns left, and the Live Oak Trail is right, but you continue straight, now on the Buckeye Trail. In spring, this area may be beautifully decorated with wildflowers, including bluedicks, Chinesehouses, fiesta flower, wild geranium, California buttercup, and milkmaids. Soon you pass a junction with the Maple Canyon Trail, right, and then come to a wood fence with a narrow gap, which marks the beginning of the self-guiding Buckeye Nature Trail. Along the way, signs beside the trail explain features of the natural environment and human interaction with it. The trail, here a single track, rises gently through dense forest, mostly of coast live oak, California bay, toyon, and buckeye. Some of the trees are draped with strands of lace lichen, which resembles Spanish moss found in the southeastern U.S.

Now the route levels and you traverse a hillside that falls away left, passing a sign that explains the value of coast live oaks to the Native Americans who lived in this area for thousands of years. The next sign is about lichens, which are actually two life forms—fungi and algae—living together. Several hundred feet ahead you climb several steps and then switchback sharply right. At a junction marked by a trail post, the Siesta Point Trail goes straight, but you stay on the Buckeye Nature Trail by turning left. Just uphill from the junction is a sign about ferns, four species of which—maidenhair, golden-back fern, polypody, and wood fern—are found nearby.

Where a rock cliff rises right, the trail emerges briefly from forest into full sun, and here a sign provides information about the area's geology. Now back in the forest, you descend a set of wood steps, cross a plank bridge over a small creek, and reach the Mesa Trail, one of the park's main thoroughfares. Here you turn left, and immediately pass the Cliff Trail, right. After a couple of hundred feet, in an area that may be wet and muddy, you turn right onto the continuation of the Buckeye Nature Trail, signed TO INDIAN ROCK AND THE WATERFALL TRAIL.

With luck, you will encounter dry ground as you follow a single track as it rises on a gentle grade, with a steep hillside to your right. A sign explains the various uses Native Americans made of poison oak, a plant most of us shun. As the trail begins to descend, you pass a massive boulder and then several smaller ones, left. If you look at these carefully, you will find circular depressions in the rock surface, formed where Native Americans ground acorns. These boulders are shown on the park map as Rumsen Grinding Rock, a name that refers to the local Indians. A nearby sign describes in detail the process of drying, grinding, leaching, and cooking acorns. Park rangers say Native Americans consider the largest of all the rocks to be a "birthing rock." On its north side are many depressions thought to represent generations of women in labor.

Continuing downhill, you soon reach a wooden fence with a gap, which you pass through. About 50 feet past the fence is a junction where you turn sharply left and, in a few hundred feet, regain the Mesa Trail. Veering right onto it, you walk about 100 feet on level ground to a fork, where you bear left and immediately reach a junction with the Lupine Loop, which goes left and right. Here, at about the 1-mile point, you turn left and begin a gentle ascent on a wide, rocky path. Soon the grade levels, and you may begin to hear traffic noise from busy Carmel Valley Road in the distance downhill and right. The spring wildflowers in this park usually put on a fine show, so look beside the trail for lupine, California buttercup, blue-eyed grass, Chinesehouses, and shooting stars. Passing a rest bench, right, you reach the four-way junction where you began this loop. From here, you bear right and retrace your steps to the parking area.

Garland Ranch Regional Park
EAST RIDGE

Length:	4 miles
Time:	4 to 5 hours
Rating:	Difficult
Regulations:	MPRPD; no bikes, no horses; dogs under immediate voice command or on a leash not more than 7 feet long.
Phone:	MPRPD, (831) 659-6063
Web site:	*www.mprpd.org/parks/garland.html*
Highlights:	This rugged but rewarding semi-loop uses the Garzas Canyon, Veeder, East Ridge, Saddle, Vasquez, and Terrace trails to explore the high ground south of Garzas Creek in a remote and secluded part of this popular park. There are few better places to enjoy spring wildflowers and fabulous views of Carmel Valley and its neighboring hills; pick a clear day and avoid hot weather.
Directions:	From the junction of Hwy. 1 and Carmel Valley Rd. just east of Carmel, take Carmel Valley Rd. east 10.4 miles to Boronda Rd. Turn right, go 0.5 mile, and turn left onto East

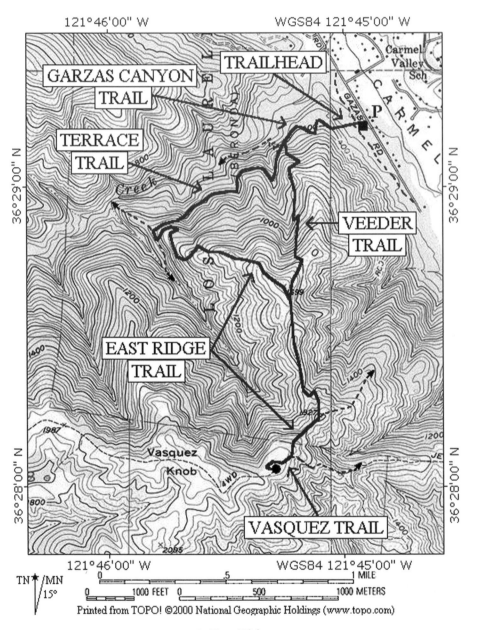

9. East Ridge

Garzas Rd. Go 0.2 mile and park along the road's right shoulder.

Facilities: None

Trailhead: Southwest side of road.

From the trailhead, you follow the Garzas Canyon Trail, here a wide dirt path, and head uphill on a gentle grade through a dense forest of coast live oak. The understory here, as in many coastal areas, is made up of blackberry vines, poison oak, snowberry, and hedge-nettle. After several hundred feet, you pass a branch of the River Trail going right, and then, in another 50 feet, reach a junction where another branch of the River Trail veers sharply left. Here your route curves right and continues uphill.

Now the oaks, some draped with strands of lace lichen, are joined by California buckeyes, and you may find shrubs such as bush lupine, California sagebrush, redberry, and bush monkeyflower. Lovely spring wildflowers here include Chinesehouses, fiesta flower, and California buttercup. A few steep sections punctuate the moderate uphill trail. Soon you come to a junction with the Veeder Trail, closed to horses. Here you turn left onto a single track and continue moderately uphill, aided by several switchbacks. The riot of vegetation is amazing, and you can add to your list another tree, California bay, along with wildflowers such as fiddleneck and woodland star.

Coming out onto a weedy hillside that falls away left, you have a fine view across the Carmel Valley, checkered with housing developments, and east to the Sierra de Salinas, the range dividing the Carmel and Salinas valleys. As you steadily gain elevation, you reach an area of coastal scrub and chaparral, with California sagebrush, coffeeberry, black sage, coast silk-tassel, toyon, and fuchsia-flowered gooseberry. After a rainy winter, the wildflower display at the higher elevations of this park can be superb, and you may find paintbrush, cream cups, shooting stars, blue-eyed grass, and buttercups dappling the landscape with color. This is certainly one of the park's finest trails for wildflower viewing.

Now the route bends left and enters a grassy meadow, where a welcome rest bench awaits. Underway again, you make a rising traverse that soon becomes a steep climb across a scrubby hillside. To the northwest, beyond the canyon holding Garzas Creek, you can see a large, flat area called La Mesa and the high ground of Snivleys Ridge (see Trip 11 for trails up Snivleys). Now on a

Fiddleneck

ledge above a hillside that falls away left, you may find yourself gazing over masses of bush lupine, observed from above by darting swallows. Cresting a low rise, the grade finally eases, and you arrive at a flat spot near a lovely seasonal pond and a junction with the East Ridge Trail.

At this four-way junction, the East Ridge Trail goes left and right, and a short trail goes straight and then curves around the pond to a rest bench in the shade of a craggy old oak. The north-facing bench is an ideal spot for a picnic or perhaps just a breath-catching respite. (A shorter version of this route can be made by turning right onto the East Ridge Trail and then following the route description below.) When you are ready to resume climbing, head southeast on the East Ridge Trail by keeping the pond on your right. The grade is moderate, and your way is shaded by coast live oaks and madrones.

As you ascend, the views get better and better—east is the Carmel Valley, west are rugged canyons, and in the distance northwest is a fire lookout that crowns Pinyon Peak (2248'). A cooling breeze from the Pacific will be welcome on a warm day. Now atop a ridge on an eroded track, you work your way up a steep grade that takes you through an area of chaparral, mostly chamise. At about the 2-mile point, you reach a four-way junction. Here the Saddle Trail goes left and right, and a short trail continues straight.

Now you turn right and enjoy an almost-level walk, which a fantastic display of California poppies and bush lupine may enliven in spring. Climbing again, you soon reach a **T**-junction, shown incorrectly on the park map, with the Vasquez Trail. Turning right, you continue climbing on a moderate grade, spurred on by gorgeous views and perhaps equally fine wildflower displays. Above you and on your left is an open, grassy meadow topped by a lone oak with fantastically twisted limbs. Look here for a low, almost flattened plant with yellow flowers called footsteps of spring, an early blooming member of the carrot family.

The trail soon veers left, crosses the meadow, and reaches a fence that marks the park boundary. (The park map indicates a rest bench here, but I found none.) From this wonderful spot, inviting for a picnic or a well-deserved break, you have stunning 360° views—on a clear day you will be amply rewarded for your efforts! When you have finished enjoying this fine spot, retrace your steps to the junction with the Veeder Trail.

With the seasonal pond on your left, stay on the East Ridge Trail as it carries you over a grassy hill covered with lupine, California poppies, purple owl's-clover, and pearly everlasting. Once past the hill, you make a steep descent on a narrow ledge cut from a hillside. The deep canyon, left, holds the Redwood Canyon Trail. In a good year, the spring flowers continue their colorful blaze, mixing blues, yellows, and purples, and attracting equally colorful butterflies. After curving right, the trail switchbacks left and soon brings you to a junction with the Redwood Canyon Trail, left.

Your route, still the East Ridge Trail, jogs sharply right, and in a couple of hundred feet meets the Terrace Trail, right. Here you turn right and descend on a narrow track through a forest of bay, coast live oak, and even a few coast redwoods. Keep a wary eye on the steep drop to Garzas Creek. Some of the plants associated with the coast redwood region are here, including creambush, snowberry, poison oak, trillium, Solomon's seal, and larkspur. Now your descent is aided by a few tight switchbacks, and then a rolling course takes you into the first of two ravines jutting a short distance southeast from Garzas Creek canyon.

The trail really earns its name as you approach the second ravine, with an almost-vertical drop left. After emerging from this ravine, you climb on a moderate grade—in one place you are on dirt steps held in place by wooden blocks—past a hillside brightened by California poppies, Chinesehouses, and bush lupine. The Terrace Trail ends at a junction with the Garzas Canyon Trail, marked by a trail post and a rest bench. Here you go straight on the Garzas Canyon Trail, climbing through dense forest on a moderate grade, cresting a rise, and then making a moderate descent. After about 150 yards, you come to the junction with the Veeder Trail where you began this loop. From here, retrace your steps to the parking area.

Garland Ranch Regional Park
REDWOOD CANYON

Length:	3.5 miles
Time:	3 to 4 hours
Rating:	Moderate
Regulations:	MPRPD; no bikes, no horses; dogs under immediate voice command or on a leash not more than 7 feet long.
Phone:	MPRPD, (831) 659-6063
Web site:	*www.mprpd.org/parks/garland.html*
Highlights:	This tranquil semi-loop uses the Garzas Canyon, East Ridge, Redwood Canyon, and Terrace trails to explore the riparian habitat along Garzas Creek, and then a secluded coast redwood forest along one of the creek's tributaries. Above its junction with the East Ridge Trail, the Redwood Canyon Trail makes four tricky crossings of Garzas Creek. Removable bridges span three of these from April or May through October or November. During spring and fall, call

the park to make sure the bridges are in; the crossings may be dangerous without them. Carry a walking stick or a trekking pole to aid with any unbridged crossing.

Directions: Same as for "East Ridge" on pages 55–57.

Facilities: None

Trailhead: Southwest side of road.

Follow the route description for "East Ridge" on pages 55–57 to the junction with the Veeder Trail. Here you continue straight on the Garzas Canyon Trail, soon reaching a junction with the Terrace Trail, which goes straight. Making a sharp switchback right, you begin a long, zigzag descent, alternating between moderate and steep, to Garzas Creek. The plant life beside the creek is rich and varied, and this is a wonderful area to study ferns, including bracken, maidenhair, wood fern, golden-back fern, and polypody. Among the spring wildflowers putting on a show here may be Solomon's seal, white globe lily, paintbrush, and woodland star. The creek itself, rocky and narrow with clear, deep pools, is bordered by willow, alder, sycamore, bigleaf maple, and toyon.

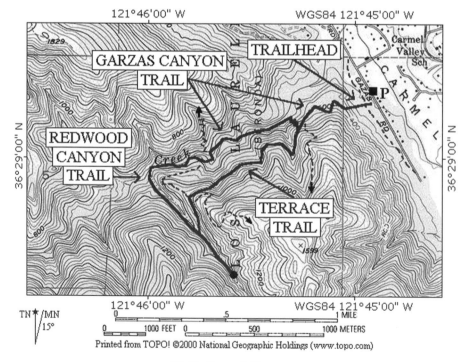

10. Redwood Canyon

A wood bridge takes you across Garzas Creek, which now is on your left. The trail, a single track, soon turns away from the creek and begins a rolling course that leads eventually to a fork with a trail post in the middle. Here the Garzas Canyon Trail goes right and uphill, but your route, the East Ridge Trail, goes left and descends to the creek. After about 100 yards, you reach another bridge, and once across it, you veer right, walking upstream with the creek on your right. Look here for thimbleberry, which has white, rose-like flowers, and larkspur, which sports purple flowers that are pointed at one end. At the next fork, the East Ridge Trail heads left, but you follow the Redwood Canyon Trail, right, which is closed to horses.

The trail descends through a small meadow and reaches the first of four crossings of Garzas Creek, only two of which appear on the park map. Three of these—the first, third, and fourth—have removable bridges that are in place usually from April or May through October or November, depending on water level. Without these bridges, the crossings may be dangerous! Once across the creek and its adjacent flood channel, rejoin the trail at a trail post, bear left, and continue walking upstream. At the next crossing, which is unbridged, carefully pick your way across on large rocks and then resume hiking upstream with the creek on your right.

A very rocky area marks another flood channel. When the bridges are in, the park district improves this area with a path of gravel and stones. Follow this path to the third crossing, which puts you on the north side of Garzas Creek. Veering left and uphill, you cross the mouth of a narrow gully that descends from the right and then make your way on a narrow ledge carved from a hillside that falls away left to Garzas Creek. Look here in spring for wallflower, a tall, rangy plant with lance-shaped leaves and clusters of orange-yellow flowers. Descending again to the creek, you cross another rocky flood channel before reaching the fourth and final crossing.

Now on the south side of Garzas Creek, the trail turns southeast and climbs gently into the mouth of a steep-walled canyon that holds a small stream, which is on your right. Soon you pass the first of many coast redwoods tucked away in this hidden enclave. Associated with coast redwood forests are some plants you may see here—sword fern, wild rose, and colt's-foot, which has a large, deeply cut, almost circular leaf held low to the ground on a single reddish stem. A soft carpet of redwood twigs and needles cushions your feet.

The stillness of the forest makes this a good place to practice "birding by ear," the technique of identifying birds by their songs and call notes, which are most often heard during breeding season in spring and early summer. Among the songsters that breed in the park are olive-sided flycatcher, black phoebe, Bewick's wren, and Hutton's vireo. Crossing the stream, which may be dry, on a short plank, you follow the trail, here a narrow track, as it takes you moderately uphill across a hillside that rises right. Soon the route curves left and, at about the 2-mile point, comes back to the stream, spanned by a plank. Here the trail splits. The way across the stream is a connector to the East Ridge Trail. To explore farther into the redwood-filled canyon, stay on this side and continue walking upstream about 0.25 mile to where the trail dead-ends in a lovely, secluded grove of giants.

When you finish enjoying a rest and perhaps a picnic in this magical place, retrace your steps to the previous junction, cross the stream, and begin climbing. As you rise out of the canyon, you leave the redwoods behind and enter a brighter realm of coast live oak, bay, and buckeye trees. A sunny hillside, right, may be decorated with California poppies, bush lupine, Chinesehouses, and bluedicks. At a junction with the East Ridge Trail, follow the route description for "East Ridge" on p. 59 back to the parking area.

11 Garland Ranch Regional Park
SNIVLEYS RIDGE

Length: 6 miles

Time: 3 to 5 hours

Rating: Difficult

Regulations: MPRPD; dogs under immediate voice command or on a leash not more than 7 feet long.

Phone: MPRPD, (831) 659-6063

Web site: *www.mprpd.org/parks.garland.html*

Highlights: Climbing steadily from the Carmel Valley floor, this athletic semi-loop eventually rewards you with stunning vistas from atop Snivleys Ridge, the northernmost rampart of the Santa Lucia Range. Using the Lupine Loop, Maple Canyon, Sage, Sky, Snivleys Ridge, and Mesa trails, this route samples many of the park's varied habitats, including riparian woodland, coastal forest, and chaparral.

Directions: Same as for "Buckeye Nature Trail" on p. 52.

Facilities: Visitor center with maps, pamphlets, and helpful staff; rest rooms, telephone, picnic tables.

Trailhead: South side of the permanent bridge over the Carmel River.

Follow the route description for "Buckeye Nature Trail" to the junction of the Buckeye and Maple Canyon trails (shown incorrectly on the park map). You veer right onto the Maple Canyon Trail and begin a moderate climb, passing through a gap in a barbed-wire fence. Approaching a ravine that holds a seasonal creek, the trail bends right and brings you to a **T**-junction with a short connector to the Live Oak Trail, closed to horses. Turning left, you follow the creek upstream on a moderate climb, keeping it on your right. The trail swings right to cross the creek, and

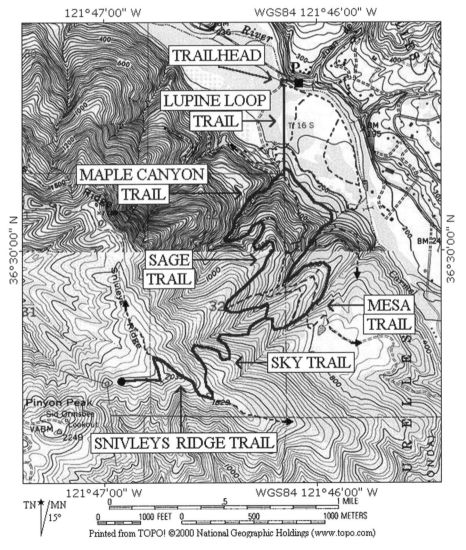

11. Snivleys Ridge

then resumes its upstream direction. Soon, an unmaintained trail departs left across the creek. Overgrown and jungle-like, the ravine, here steep-walled, feels remote, even though busy Carmel Valley is less than a mile away.

At about the 1 mile point, you pass a junction with the Live Oak Trail, and just ahead your trail swings sharply left, crosses the creek, which flows through a culvert, and begins a strenuous climb out of the ravine. Traversing a steep hillside, you pass thorough a beautiful grove of euca-lyptus and Monterey cypress, some draped with folds of lace lichen. A homestead site, marked on the park map, is uphill and right—parts of a brick chimney are all that remain. Where the grade eases, you have your first view northeast to Carmel Valley. Now on a level course, you soon reach a junction with the Sage Trail, where you turn right and resume climbing.

This is an area of coastal scrub, consisting here of California sagebrush, coffeeberry, creambush, and bush monkeyflower. As its name indicates, coastal scrub is a collection of plants often found growing near the coast. The rugged hills of this park, which lies on the north edge of the Santa Lucia Range about 10 miles from the Pacific Ocean, are perfect for this type of plant community. Now the route, perched on a narrow shelf with a steep drop left, levels and passes through stands of coast live oak, which offer welcome shade on a hot day. Turning southeast, you enter an area of chaparral, mostly chamise and black sage, plants that love sunny, open slopes.

Descending to the head of a deep ravine, left, you reach a junction with the Fern Trail, descending left, a rest bench, and a watering trough for horses—actually an old bathtub filled by a spring. This shady spot is a perfect place to rest before tackling the heights ahead. From here, the Sage Trail climbs steeply out of the ravine, bends right, and, at about the 2-mile point, ends at a junction with the Sky Trail. To the east and far downhill is a large clearing called La Mesa, and a dot of water called La Mesa Pond, marked on the park map as a wildlife habitat. Amphibians that may be found near the pond include California newts, Pacific treefrogs, and bullfrogs.

You continue straight, now on the Sky Trail, which climbs through a forest of coast live oak on a grade alternating between moderate and steep. Aided by several switchbacks, you steadily gain elevation. With a few welcome level places, the views improve. After a relentless trek, most of it uphill, you arrive at a junction marked by a trail post and a rest bench. Here, at about the 3-mile point, the Sky Trail ends at the Snivleys Ridge Trail, a dirt road. You are atop the northernmost wall of the Santa Lucia Range, on a ridge that forms the southwest side of Carmel Valley. From here, the views on a clear day are spectacular. To the northeast is the valley's other side, formed by the Sierra de Salinas. To the south is the continuation of the Santa Lucia Range, home of Los Padres National

Forest and the Ventana Wilderness, with peaks nearly 5,000 feet high. And to the west rises Pinyon Peak (2248'), crowned by a fire lookout.

Your goal is a lower summit, also west, just above 2,000 feet. To reach it, you turn right onto the Snivleys Ridge Trail, and then stay right at a fork where an unofficial trail climbs steeply uphill. Alternating between gentle and moderate, the rising route traverses a hillside that falls away right, passing stands of madrone and valley oak. At a junction, you veer left onto a dirt road and walk through a weedy clearing of coyote brush, bracken, and chamise. Soon the road ends, but you turn right onto a single-track trail that heads west about 100 yards along a ridgetop to a rock outcrop where a rest bench awaits. (The trail continues another 100 yards or so to a large grove of coast live oaks, but the views are no better from there.) After enjoying this magnificent vantage point, retrace your steps to the junction of the Sky and Sage trails.

The difficult Snivelys Ridge route is worth the effort: it rewards you with spectacular views of Carmel Valley.

Here, at about the 5-mile point, you continue straight on the Sky Trail, descending on grade that alternates between moderate and gentle. La Mesa and its pond are downhill and right. The well-graded trail makes a series of **S**-bends in the shade of coast live oaks. Soon you pass the Deer Trail, left, and then another trail, signed TO FERN TRAIL, going left and uphill. Just past it, the Sky Trail ends at a junction with the Mesa Trail, a dirt road that goes straight and also sharply right. You go straight, and after about 60 feet pass a junction with the Hawk Trail, left. Here the Mesa Trail, which gets heavy use from equestrians, is signed LA MESA TRAIL, but on the park map it keeps its former name. Another branch of the Hawk Trail soon takes off uphill and left, and then, in a shady forest of bigleaf maple and California bay, you come to a wet area and a junction with the Fern Trail.

With a rest bench conveniently placed in the shade, the Fern Trail goes left and steeply uphill, but you stay on the Mesa Trail, crossing a creek that flows across the road in a shallow ditch. Beside the creek are a few young coast redwoods and stands of western creek dogwood, a large-leaved shrub that produces white flowers in spring and small white fruits in fall. Still on a downhill course, you pass a junction with a trail, left, signed TO SIESTA POINT. With a small stream perhaps flowing across the trail about 100 yards ahead, you come to a four-way junction: here the Buckeye Nature Trail goes left, and the Cliff Trail climbs a set of wooden steps, right. You soon meet the Buckeye Nature Trail again, as it departs right for Indian Rock (shown on the park map as Rumsen Grinding Rock, after the local Native Americans) and the Waterfall Trail. Then, after passing another connector to the Waterfall Trail, right, you veer left at a fork and come to a junction with the Lupine Loop. From here, follow the route description for "Buckeye Nature Trail" on p. 55 back to the parking area.

12   Garrapata State Park
SOBERANES CANYON

Length:	3 miles
Time:	2 to 3 hours
Rating:	Moderate
Regulations:	CSP; no bikes, no dogs.
Phone:	(831) 624-4909
Web site:	*http://parks.ca.gov*
Highlights:	This out-and-back route uses the Soberanes Canyon Trail to explore the wonderful variety of plant communities found along Soberanes Creek, which range from coastal scrub to cactus garden to redwood forest. Spring brings the wildflowers to their peak, but the park is really a year-round treasure. A walking stick is helpful for the many creek crossings.
Directions:	From the junction of Hwy. 1 and Rio Rd. just southeast of Carmel, take Hwy. 1 south 7 miles and park on the road shoulder, well off the highway. (A line of cypress standing on the road's east side marks the trailhead.)
Facilities:	Toilet about 0.25 mile south on the trail to Soberanes Point, on west side of highway.
Trailhead:	On east side of highway.

Hillside mission cactus garden in Soberanes Canyon delights hikers in Garrapata State Park at any time of the year.

A dirt road, gated but with a gap on the left, leads you away from busy Hwy. 1 and into a field of mustard and wild radish, which, although they are invasive non-natives, are colorful when in bloom. A historic farm building of corrugated metal and a garden of calla lilies, escaped from cultivation, add to the scene, and soon you come to a **T**-junction, where you turn left. Passing the metal building, you immediately turn right, perhaps noting the sign listing the trail name as SOBRANES CANYON TRAIL. This spelling appears on other signs in the park, but the park map uses Soberanes, the name of a prominent Monterey family, probably descended from José Maria Soberanes, one of the Spanish soldiers who explored Alta California with the Portolá expedition in 1769–1770. The name of the park itself, Garrapata, is the Spanish word for "tick," a pest the early explorers of this area probably encountered.

Descend to Soberanes Creek, a lovely stream nestled in a valley that is filled with wildflowers in the spring. You cross the creek on a wooden bridge and arrive at a junction with the Rocky Ridge Trail, left. Continuing straight, you enjoy a gentle climb amid bush lupine, California poppies, paintbrush, nightshade, morning glory, and lizard

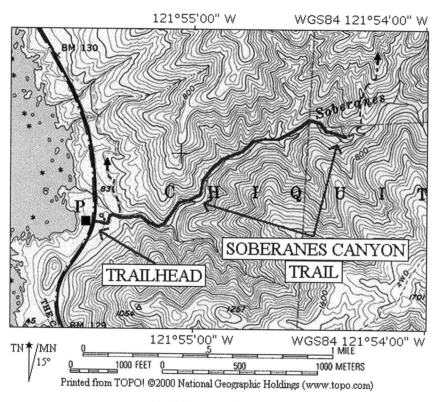

Printed from TOPO! ©2000 National Geographic Holdings (www.topo.com)

12. Soberanes Canyon

The Soberanes Canyon trip takes you back and forth across lovely Soberanes Creek and leads you through a variety of plant communities.

tail. Although the wildflowers may dazzle you in spring, a year-round attraction lies just ahead—a hillside covered with mission cactus, a cultivated variety that is now naturalized in a few areas in Monterey County.

The sandy single track now finds a level course beside the creek, right, and soon brings you to another bridge, this one across a marshy area that floods in winter. With the creek now on your left, you resume climbing on a gentle grade past stands of willow and blue blossom, whose branches arch over clumps of monkeyflower, yarrow, and fiesta flower. The next bridge takes you back to the north side of the creek. After following a winding route, and only about 0.5 mile from the hillside of cactus, you enter another unique botanic area, a coast redwood forest. Here too are such redwood companions as California bay, sword fern, redwood sorrel, gooseberry, thimbleberry, and coffeeberry.

Using logs to cross the creek, you follow a ledge that rises to about 20 feet above its plashing pools, which are below and left. The next crossing, also on logs, puts you back on the creek's north side, where dirt steps held in place with logs aid you in a moderate ascent. Two more crossings, also on logs, bring you to a fork with a trail post in the middle. Here, an old trail goes right to cross the creek once again, but a better choice is to bear left onto a newer trail and make a rising traverse on a moderate grade, aided again by steps. A hillside of coastal scrub rises left, and giant redwoods line the creek, right and downhill.

Now the route levels and then descends to a tributary of Soberanes Creek that may be trickling across the trail from left to right. A gentle climb brings you to a junction with the old trail joining from the right. Ahead, the trail deteriorates and the going gets rough, as the narrow, overgrown track steeply rises and falls. You are rewarded, however, by the sight of a massive cliff, which may be dripping wet, holding a hanging garden of ferns. After a set of switchbacks brings you down to Soberanes Creek, you can take a well-deserved break in a clearing surrounded by redwoods. (From here, the poorly maintained trail climbs steeply up the north wall of Soberanes Canyon, eventually meeting the Rocky Ridge Trail.) When you have finished enjoying this secluded spot, retrace your steps to the parking area.

| 13 | Garrapata State Park
SOBERANES POINT AND WHALE PEAK |

Length: 1.5 miles

Time: 1 to 2 hours

Rating: Easy

Regulations: CSP; no bikes, no dogs.

Phone: (831) 624-4909

Web site: *http://parks.ca.gov*

Highlights: This scenic semi-loop uses a trail that wanders out to Soberanes Point and then circles Whale Peak, which you can climb via a spur trail. Along the way you pass vantage points with great views up and down the coast, and in spring you may be surrounded by colorful displays of wildflowers. Bring binoculars to check out the birds and marine mammals at sea, on nearby rocks, and in protected coves along the shoreline. Please use caution near the coastal cliffs.

Directions: Same as for "Soberanes Canyon" on p. 67.

Facilities: Toilet about 0.25 mile south on the trail to Soberanes Point.

Trailhead: West side of highway

Two trails depart from this trailhead, which is marked by a metal gate with a gap you can pass through. You take the left one, which meanders through an area of coastal scrub—coyote brush, California sagebrush, poison oak—and soon reaches a large grove of Monterey cypress. On the right, a hillside full of mustard, blazing yellow in spring, drops steeply to a wave-washed beach below. The trail now works its way through a tree-less field carpeted with hedge-nettle, lizard tail, iceplant, and deer lotus. Clumps of blue blossom may be putting on a showy display.

Where a trail post marks the junction with the return part of your loop, left, you continue straight, enjoying a level walk with a fine view of the rugged, rocky coastline. Two offshore rocks, colored white by guano, are used as resting spots for birds and seals. Where the trail begins to climb, you pass through a fantastic wildflower garden, decorated in spring and summer with California poppies, seaside daisies, paintbrush, and wild iris. Low-growing coffeeberry and blackberry provide patchy ground cover.

Bearing right at a fork, you aim for Soberanes Point, a rocky promon-tory jutting out into the Pacific Ocean. Bush lupine and the cream-colored flowers of milk vetch form a lovely foreground for the magnificent rock formations that are periodically showered with foamy spray from the waves. The trail hugs the cliff edge, giving you the opportunity to study the gulls, cormorants, and other sea birds that collect on the nearby rocks and in the somewhat sheltered coves below the point.

Several unofficial trails branch left and right from your route, which continues roughly parallel to the coastline. The rock cliffs that rise from the ocean are divided into colored bands—dark gray nearest the water,

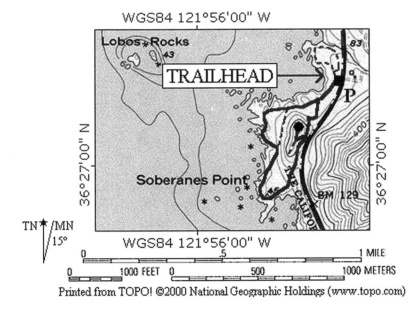

Printed from TOPO! ©2000 National Geographic Holdings (www.topo.com)

13. Soberanes Point and Whale Peak

fading to light tan higher up. The twin-humped hill rising left is Whale Peak, and a trail up it is part of this route. A dense carpet of morning glory cloaks the ground beside the trail. At a **T**-junction you turn right, rejoining the trail you forsook at the previous junction. Use caution when near the cliffs.

Now descending on a gentle grade, not too far above sea level, you reach a fork with an unofficial trail; here you stay right. As the trail nears the end of a south-facing promontory, you have a stunning view down the coast all the way to Point Sur. The near-shore waters from the mouth of the Carmel River to the Monterey–San Luis Obispo county line are designated as the California Sea Otter Game Refuge. As the trail bends left, you may see some of these delightful creatures in a kelp-filled cove to your right.

Heading north, you soon near busy Hwy. 1, which is on your right. Before beginning a climb of Whale Peak's east shoulder, you pass a gate and a dirt parking area, both right. Now making a moderate ascent on an eroded track, you quickly reach a junction: left is the trail to the summit of Whale Peak, and right is the trail back to your parking area. Turning left, you make a rising traverse across a brushy hillside of coastal scrub. A couple of young pines cling to precarious ledges amid clumps of chamise and buckbrush.

Whale Peak has two summits, the north one being slightly higher. At a **T**-junction on a saddle between them, you turn right and work your way over rocky ground about 100 yards to the north summit. Here, when wildflowers are in bloom, you will be treated to a wonderful display of bluedicks, yarrow, blue blossom, and paintbrush. The 360° views are spectacular. After enjoying this fine spot, return to the junction with the main trail around Whale Peak, and bear left.

Now descending via tight **S**-bends, a long traverse, and finally a switchback, you reach a field overgrown with mustard and poison oak. An unofficial trail joins sharply from the right, and your route bends left through an area that may be wet during the rainy season, as evidenced by stands of rushes jutting up from the packed dirt. Soon you come to the junction you passed at the beginning of this loop. From here, you turn right and retrace your steps to the parking area.

Huckleberry Hill Nature Preserve
WILD BOAR OVERLOOK

Length: 1.6 miles

Time: 1 to 2 hours

Rating: Moderate

Regulations: City of Monterey

Phone: (831) 646-3866

Web site: *www.monterey.org/rec*

Highlights: Using Summit and Water Tank roads, and the Presidio View and Wild Boar trails, this short but enjoyable semi-loop takes you atop Presidio Knoll and into the realm of Monterey pine and evergreen huckleberry. Despite the dense forest, there are fine views to be had along the way, especially from an overlook at the end of the Wild Boar Trail.

Directions: From the junction of Hwy. 1 and Hwy. 68 just south of Monterey, take Hwy. 68 west 0.9 mile to Skyline Forest Dr. and turn right. Go 0.2 mile to Skyline Dr., turn left, and go 1 mile to a stop sign at Veterans Dr. and Chatswood Pl. Turn right, go about 150 feet, and turn left into a small, paved parking area.

Facilities: None at trailhead, but in Veterans Memorial Park, adjacent to the parking area, there are rest rooms, water, picnic tables, phone, and campsites.

Trailhead: North side of parking area.

This 81-acre preserve, established in 1988 through a long-term lease from the U.S. Army, is one of those jewels that delight guidebook authors. Sandwiched between the Presidio of Monterey and a housing development, and within earshot of the barking sea lions of Fisherman's Wharf, the trails here offer hikers, walkers, and joggers a tranquil sanctuary in the middle of the busy Monterey peninsula. Atop Presidio Knoll, the main feature of the preserve, you will pass through a vast stand of Monterey pines, an impressive collection of these familiar trees, which are grown worldwide but are native to only a few locations on the California coast.

The Presidio View Trail, carpeted with pine needles, leads you north on a level course from the parking area. On your left is a residential area, and on your right is Veterans Memorial Park and campground. Coast live

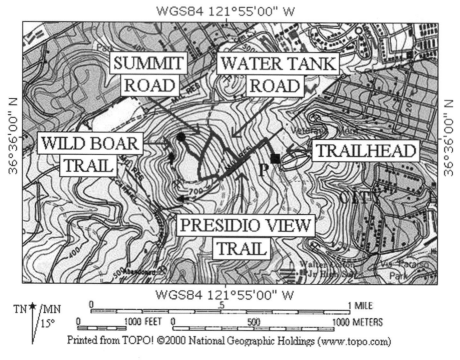

WGS84 121°55'00" W

TN ↑ /MN
  /15°

Printed from TOPO! ©2000 National Geographic Holdings (www.topo.com)

14. Wild Boar Overlook

oaks are scattered among the pines, and you can just see the outline of Monterey Bay and its surrounding hills through the trees. Soon you pass a trail merging from the right, and about 100 feet ahead, you turn sharply left and begin to climb, still on the Presidio View Trail.

At first the grade is gentle, but where it changes to steep you are aided by wood steps. Beside the trail grow manzanita, toyon, bush mon-keyflower, and evergreen huckleberry, which lends the preserve its name (although Huckleberry Hill itself is about 1 mile south in the Del Monte Forest of Pebble Beach). The pines towering overhead may be alive with birds and birdsong—among the common species here are acorn wood-pecker, northern flicker, scrub jay, Steller's jay, cedar waxwing, red-breasted nuthatch, and golden-crowned kinglet. About halfway up the steps, linger for a moment to admire the view, less obstructed by trees here. You will see Monterey Bay's sweeping, sandy curve, and of the Gabilan Range, east, on the far side of the Salinas Valley.

At the top of the steps, the route, here a wide dirt path, levels briefly but then resumes its steep rise. Passing a junction with Water Tank Road, right, you continue uphill to the next junction, where you turn right onto

Summit Road. After several hundred feet, you reach an unsigned **T**-junction, where you turn left. You are still following Summit Road and now are on the crest of Presidio Knoll. The surrounding huckleberry forms a dense, widespread understory. You may also see a few madrones and some stands of manzanita. Rising above all are the native Monterey pines, some stout but most slender, even spindly.

The route follows a gently rolling course to the next junction, where Opossum Road goes left and downhill. Here you stay on Summit Road as it swings right and across the top of Presidio Knoll. To the left, you begin to glimpse the Pacific Ocean, a blue glimmer through the trees. With the first of two water tanks on your right, you turn left onto the Wild Boar Trail, and begin to descend on a gentle grade. The trail dead-ends at an overlook that is ringed by tall trees missing most of their lower limbs. From there you can gaze north toward Pacific Grove, and northwest to Spanish Bay, Asilomar, and Point Pinos.

When you have finished enjoying the view, return to the previous junction and turn left onto Summit Road. Just after making the turn, you pass a "Wildlife Guzzler," a shallow plastic pool that catches and stores rainwater for animals to drink during the dry season. On your right is the second of two water tanks. Now descending on a moderate grade, you pass a hillside with coffeeberry and blackberry vines, and soon reach a junction with Water Tank Road on the right. Turning right, you traverse the east side of Presidio Knoll, and arrive at a junction where Water Tank Road goes both left and right. Turning left, you pass a closed trail on the left, and then follow the road as it veers right, bringing you, after about 100 yards, to the junction with the Presidio View Trail you passed earlier. Now turn left and retrace your steps to the parking area.

15   Jacks Peak County Park
EARL MOSER LOOP

Length: 2.4 miles

Time: 1 to 2 hours

Rating: Easy

Regulations: Monterey County Parks; parking fee; dogs on leash, no bikes off paved roads. Park hours vary seasonally, generally opening at 10 A.M. in fall and winter, and at 11 A.M. in spring and summer; call for current hours.

Phone: (831) 372-8551

Web site: *www.co.monterey.ca.us/parks*

Highlights: Using the Earl Moser, Madrone, Rhus, Pine, and Sage trails, this varied loop explores a shaded pine forest and open hillsides of coastal scrub on its way through the east half of this 855-acre ridgetop park. You can enjoy the west half of the park by following the route descriptions for "Iris and Rhus Trails" and "Skyline Nature Trail," or you can combine various park trails to create an extended hike.

Directions: From the junction of Hwy. 1 and Hwy. 68 in Monterey, take Hwy. 68 east 1.6 miles to Olmsted Rd. Turn right, go 0.9 mile, and turn left onto Jacks Peak Dr. At 1.3 miles there is an entrance kiosk. (If the entrance kiosk is not staffed, pay fee at the self-registration station next to the kiosk.) Just past the kiosk is a **T**-junction. Turn left and go 0.3 mile to the east parking area.

Facilities: Rest rooms, water, picnic tables.

Trailhead: North side of parking area.

A beautiful view of Monterey Bay through the pines greets you as you set off on the Earl Moser Trail, built in 1981 and named to honor a local citizen for his two decades of community service. You follow a wide dirt path that skirts the picnic area, and soon a trail from the parking area joins from the right. Now you begin a moderate descent through coastal scrub, consisting here of California sagebrush, bush monkeyflower, coffeeberry, and coyote brush. Also here, in addition to the Monterey pines, are madrone and toyon.

Confronted by a five-way junction and two signs naming the various trails, you stay on the Earl Moser Trail, now a single track, as it climbs straight ahead into the pines on a moderate grade. The trail winds pleasingly through a dense forest of pine and coast live oak, with an understory of evergreen huckleberry, manzanita, honeysuckle, and poison oak. Gaining a ridge spiked with woodpecker-riddled snags, you cross a tree-ringed meadow and then begin to descend, passing a rest bench on an overlook that offers views of Carmel Valley and Point Lobos.

Heading south across a hillside, you have the ridgetop and a fence marking the park boundary uphill and left. A descent, aided by steps, brings you to a possibly wet area, and then the trail continues downhill to end at a **T**-junction with the Madrone Trail. (For a shorter version of this loop, turn right and follow the Madrone Trail to the five-way junction mentioned above.) Here, at about the 1-mile point, you turn left onto a dirt road and descend on a gentle, then moderate, grade. You may be startled by a noisy flock of band-tailed pigeons, scattering from their roost in the trees. The presence of this species—related to, but lovelier than our urban pigeon, or rock dove—explains a feature in the park's northeast corner called Band Tail Point.

The route levels, curves right, and then resumes its moderate descent. After reaching the bottom of a valley with towering pines, you begin a gentle climb that soon changes to moderate and brings you to a junction

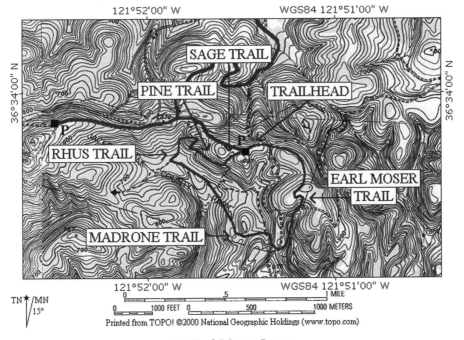

Printed from TOPO! ©2000 National Geographic Holdings (www.topo.com)

15. Earl Moser Loop

with the Ceanothus Trail joining from the right. Here you continue straight, perhaps noticed and scolded by a northern flicker. At a **T**-junction with the Rhus Trail, you turn right and begin a moderate climb that eventually levels. In fall, the coffeeberry bushes beside the trail are loaded with dark berries, inside each of which are two to three seeds resembling coffee beans, hence the name. Birds eat the berries, which have a laxative effect, and spread the seeds in their droppings.

When you reach a four-way junction with the Pine Trail, you turn right onto a single track and climb through a fern garden toward a ridgetop, gaining and then crossing it via a sharp switchback left. Now working your way up a south-facing slope, you pass through stands of manzanita, coast live oak, and young pines. Soon the Pine Trail ends at a junction (shown incorrectly on the park map) with the Sage Trail, which goes straight and also left.

Here you turn left, and on a sandy, rocky track cross a hillside of coastal scrub, mostly black sage. This plant, found on open slopes, is a member of the mint family. It has aromatic, lance-shaped leaves, and produces white to lavender flowers that bloom from April through July. Its genus, *Salvia*, marks it as a "true sage," as opposed to another member of the mint family, pitcher sage (genus *Lepechinia*) also found in this park. Pitcher sage, a member of the chaparral community, has broad leaves, clusters of pale lavender flowers, and, in fall, calyxes that resemble Japanese lanterns.

The view south from this open hillside takes in Carmel Valley and the Santa Lucia Range. Now the route curves left and reenters the shady forest on a level grade. Soon you reach trail's end at the west edge of the parking area, completing the loop.

16

Jacks Peak County Park
IRIS AND RHUS TRAILS

Length: 2 miles

Time: 1 hour or less

Rating: Easy

Regulations: Monterey County Parks; parking fee; dogs on leash, no bikes off paved roads. Park hours vary seasonally, generally opening at 10 A.M. in fall and winter, and at 11 A.M. in spring and summer; call for current hours.

Phone: (831) 372-8551

Web site: *www.co.monterey.ca.us/parks*

Highlights: This easy semi-loop, using the Iris and Rhus trails, is a great way to explore the west half of this 855-acre county park. The route winds through stands of Monterey pines, chaparral, and coastal scrub on its rolling, secluded, and shady course. You can enjoy the east half of the park by following the route description for Trip 15, the "Earl Moser Loop," or you can combine various park trails to create an extended hike.

Directions: Same as for "Earl Moser Loop" on p. 76, but when you reach the **T**-junction just past the entrance kiosk, turn right and go 0.7 mile to Jacks Peak parking area.

Facilities: Rest room, phone, picnic tables.

Trailhead: South side of parking area.

The Iris Trail, a sandy, pebbly track, leads south from the parking area on a gentle descent through coastal scrub, mostly coffeeberry, bush monkeyflower, poison oak, and berry vines. After several hundred feet, you reach a junction with the Rhus Trail, left, which is the return part of this loop. Now under beautiful, tall Monterey pines and scraggier coast live oaks, the trail crests a low rise and then descends to a junction with the Skyline Trail, right, closed to horses. Blue blossom, coyote brush, and pitcher sage decorate the ground beside the trail.

After reaching level ground, the route rises to a ridgetop via **S**-bends. Amid the pines and oaks are stands of manzanita—two of the common varieties found here are shaggy-barked manzanita (*Arctostaphylos tomentosa*) and Hooker's manzanita (*Arctostaphylos hookeri*). Manzanitas are members of the heath family, which also includes azalea, huckleberry, madrone, and rhododendron. Manzanitas are notoriously difficult to

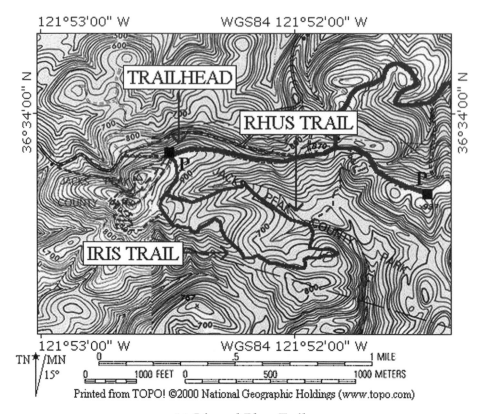

121°53'00" W   WGS84 121°52'00" W

TN ↑ /MN
  /15°

0   1000 FEET   0   500   1000 METERS

Printed from TOPO! ©2000 National Geographic Holdings (www.topo.com)

16. Iris and Rhus Trails

identify, in part because the criteria for separating types involves close examination with a hand lens, and in part because they sometimes hybridize. The name manzanita means "little apple" in Spanish, and refers to the plant's red berries.

After passing an unofficial trail, right, you soon find level ground atop a ridge that runs next to the park boundary, marked by a barbed-wire fence. Now leaving the ridgetop, you descend to a swale, passing trees draped with wispy strands of lace lichen. After traversing a possibly wet area, you climb again to a ridgetop, where uprooted pines show the power of the wind. Not long on this high ground, you work your way downhill through a wonderful area of chaparral, where chamise, toyon, and fuchsia-flowered gooseberry join the manzanitas.

Finally reaching the bottom of a deep, fern-filled jungle-like valley, you come to a **T**-junction with the Rhus Trail. Here you turn left and climb through an area of pines and coastal scrub, with thickets of poison oak that turn yellow and orange in fall. The trail takes its name from this colorful plant, which, alas, causes a severe rash in many people. (*Rhus diversiloba*, the former scientific name for poison oak, has been replaced by the more ominous-sounding *Toxicodendron diversilobum*.) A moderate ascent, with a ridge on your left, soon brings you to the junction with the Iris Trail you passed earlier at the start of this hike. From here, you bear right and retrace your steps to the parking area.

The Iris and Rhus trails route in western Jacks Peak County Park lead through coastal scrub, chaparral plant communities, and stands of Monterey pine.

Jacks Peak County Park
SKYLINE NATURE TRAIL

Length: 1 mile

Time: 1 hour or less

Rating: Easy

Regulations: Monterey County Parks; parking fee; dogs on leash, no bikes off paved roads. Park hours vary seasonally, generally opening at 10 A.M. in fall and winter, and at 11 A.M. in spring and summer; call for current hours.

Phone: (831) 372-8551

Web site: *www.co.monterey.ca.us/parks*

Highlights: This short and easy loop uses the Skyline, Jacks Peak, and Iris trails to circle and also climb the highest peak on the Monterey Peninsula. Views and nature study are the attractions here, appropriate any time of the year. You can enjoy the east half of the park by following the route description for Trip 15, the "Earl Moser Loop," or you can combine various park trails to create an extended hike. (**Boldface** numbers in the route description refer to numbered markers along the trail, which are keyed to "A Teacher's Guide to the Skyline Self-Guided Nature Trail," published by the Monterey County Parks Department. This pamphlet may be available at the trailhead, but if not, I have paraphrased some of its text below.)

Directions: Same as for "Earl Moser Loop" on p. 76, but when you reach the **T**-junction just past the entrance kiosk, turn right and go 0.7 mile to the Jacks Peak parking area.

Facilities: Rest room, phone, picnic tables.

Trailhead: West side of parking area.

At the trailhead for this short but delightful hike is an information board with a map and a holder for printed material about the park such as a guide to the Skyline Trail, a wildflower booklet, and a native plant list. You leave the parking area on a dirt trail that ascends moderately through tall Monterey pines. Joining the pines here are coast live oak, coffeeberry, gooseberry, bush monkeyflower, and poison oak. At marker **1**, to your right, look for the pear-sized female pine cones attached to tree limbs, and the "pine cobs" that lie discarded on the ground, stripped of their seeds by gray squirrels. The pines' male cones, which produce pollen in spring, are small and found on the ends of their branches.

Jacks Peak (1068') is the Monterey Peninsula's highest point, and an overlook on your right, marker **2**, gives you a fine view north of the Monterey waterfront, the sweeping curve of the Monterey Bay shoreline, and, in the distance, the Santa Cruz Mountains. Now you turn your back on this scenic vista as the route curves left and begins to descend. Marker **3**, right, refers to various types of lichens—actually two organisms, an alga and a fungus, growing together—found on nearby trees, rocks, and soil. Lace lichen, similar to the Spanish moss of the Southern United States, forms wispy strands that cling to tree branches.

Just ahead is a four-way junction with the Coffeeberry Trail, where you continue straight. In about 75 feet you reach marker **4**, left, a collection of marine fossils in a display case. Millions of years ago, the area from pre-

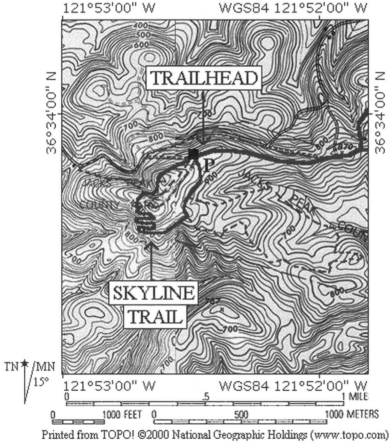

Printed from TOPO! ©2000 National Geographic Holdings (www.topo.com)

17. Skyline Nature Trail

A short, easy hike on the Skyline Nature Trail leads past this vantage point to views from the highest peak on the Monterey Peninsula.

sent-day Monterey inland to the San Joaquin Valley was under the ocean. Later, geologic forces lifted, folded, and fractured layers of the ocean floor, which can now be seen in road cuts and other places where the earth is exposed. Just behind the display case are exposed layers of rock, including Carmel Stone, a whitish rock used for paving and decoration.

Just past the display case, the route swerves right, then left, on an uphill course to marker **5**, left, indicating madrone. Although no large madrones are nearby, there are a few young trees established here, probably planted by birds. Madrone is a member of the heath family, which also includes manzanita, evergreen huckleberry, azalea, and rhododendron. Madrone is related to a similar tree found in the Mediterranean region, and its presence in California was noted by Friar Juan Crespí, a member of the 1769 Portolá expedition. Marker **6**, right, indicates soap plant, which had many uses for Native Americans.

To reach the summit of Jacks Peak, turn left at a signed junction onto the Jacks Peak Trail and walk several hundred feet to a clearing bordered by trees and low shrubs. Several rest benches await, and the views, although partially obstructed by vegetation, are nevertheless rewarding, especially those of Carmel Valley, Carmel River State Beach, Point Lobos, and the Pacific Ocean. When you are ready to depart this lofty spot, return to the previous junction and bear left, descending via steps and a switchback to marker **7**, indicating coastal scrub. This plant community, found mostly on open, south-facing slopes, consists of hearty plants such as California sagebrush, coyote brush, bush monkeyflower, and poison oak.

Traversing this open slope, you come to marker **8**, a vantage point for viewing the north end of the Santa Lucia Range, across Carmel Valley; several more rest benches entice you to stay awhile. Marker **9** refers to fog and fog drip, nature's irrigation system that operates during the rainless summer months. Now back in the trees, you pass marker **10**, for California sagebrush, left, and begin a series of switchbacks down a southwest-facing slope. Marker **11**, left, is for wildflowers found in the park, including bluedicks, blue-eyed grass, California poppy, yarrow, and morning glory. Marker **12**, right, refers to the variety of birds found here, both resident and migratory. Common residents include acorn woodpecker, California quail, scrub jay, and song sparrow.

Passing another rest bench and a viewpoint, the trail turns northeast and climbs on a gentle grade, passing marker **13**, for coyote brush. Now you walk through a corridor of coastal scrub to marker **14**, indicating mammals found in the park, most of which are nocturnal. Deer, squirrels, and rabbits may be abroad during the day. At marker **15**, notice that a coast live oak seems to embrace a Monterey pine with outstretched limbs. These two native species compete with each other: oaks predominate in open landscapes whereas pines prevail in dense forest. Soon the trail veers left and merges with the Iris Trail, which you follow on a rolling course past stands of coffeeberry and poison oak. About 100 yards past that junction is another, right, with the Rhus Trail. From here you climb on a sandy track to the parking area.

Manzanita County Park
CHAPARRAL LOOP

Length:	2.5 miles
Time:	1 to 2 hours
Rating:	Moderate
Regulations:	Monterey County Parks
Phone:	(831) 663-2699 (office at Royal Oaks County Park)
Web site:	*www.co.monterey.ca.us/parks*
Highlights:	Using a rolling dirt road to circle a fantastic sea of chaparral, this loop is ideal for hikers, joggers, bicyclists, and equestrians, and especially for anyone who enjoys native shrubs and wildflowers.
Directions:	From the junction of Hwy. 1 and Dolan Rd. in Moss Landing, take Dolan Rd. east 3.5 miles to its junction with Castroville Blvd. Continue straight, now on Castroville Blvd, another 2.5 miles to the Manzanita County Park entrance road, right, which is gated. If the gate is locked—

and it will be unless the park's sports fields are in use—use the parking area just outside. If the gate is open, follow the entrance road uphill 0.2 mile to a parking area for the sports fields.

From Hwy. 101 in Prunedale, take the San Miguel Canyon Rd. exit and go northwest 0.8 mile to Castroville Blvd. Turn left and go 0.7 mile to the Manzanita County Park entrance road, left, which is gated. If the gate is locked—and it will be unless the park's sports fields are in use—use the parking area just outside. If the gate is open, follow the entrance road uphill 0.2 mile to a parking area for the sports fields.

Facilities: None at the gate, but near the sports fields are rest rooms, water, and a phone.

Trailhead: Gate at the foot of the entrance road.

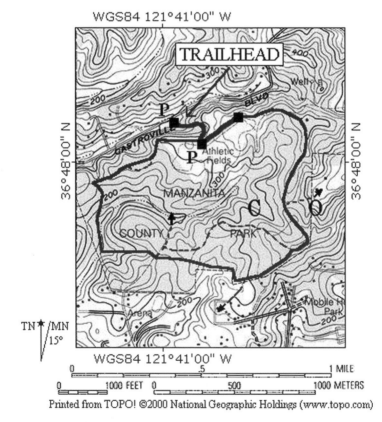

18. Chaparral Loop

The main attractions of this county park are its sports fields, which are leased to various organizations, and a batting-practice facility, which is run by a concessionaire. But hikers, bikers, joggers, and equestrians enjoy the park's trails, mostly dirt roads that penetrate its rolling hills densely cloaked with chaparral. Starting from the lower parking area, you walk uphill on the park's paved entrance road about 0.2 mile until you come to the sports fields (if the road is open

Coffeeberry, a native plant, belongs to the chaparral plant community.

you can drive this part). Ahead is a large parking area, and here the paved road swings left and uphill. Leaving it, you turn right and pass through a gap between a metal gate and a wood fence bordering a soccer field, gaining access to a wide dirt road.

This park is a paradise for native plant enthusiasts, and beside the road you will find several types of manzanita, along with bush monkeyflower, coffeeberry, black sage, chamise, and toyon. Also here are plantings of Monterey pine and coast live oak. Staying right where the road forks, you descend on a gentle grade through a spectacular sea of chaparral, soon joined by the left-hand branch of the road. You stick to the main road as it swings left, ignoring various side paths that split off from it. A riot of vegetation, including willows, blackberries, wild roses, thistles, and sedges, indicates a seasonal watercourse just left of the road.

Crossing a culvert that drains this watercourse in wet weather, the road swings left and begins to climb on a moderate grade via **S**-bends through a cool, shady forest dense with coast live oak and an understory of ferns. Now atop a ridge, the route levels and curves left, passing two fences, both right. Soon you are in a lovely corridor of shrubs and coast live oak, and at about the 1-mile point, you reach a junction with a trail heading left. Just past this junction, perhaps serenaded by a chorus of western scrub-jays, you crest a low hill with a view, left, across acres of chaparral to the distant sports fields. Hidden beneath the shrubs may be members of two bird species bearing our state's name, California towhee and California quail.

A level walk soon gives way to a moderate climb, and you pass a single-track trail taking off through a gap in a barbed-wire fence, right. Again atop a ridge, you enjoy a comfortable stroll amid Monterey pines and eucalyptus, with fine views east to Fremont Peak, the northern anchor of the Gabilan Range. A trail joins from the left, and now your route curves left and begins to descend. At the next junction, two trails converge and then join as one on the right. Ahead is a water tank with stands of pampas grass, a non-native species, to its left. Once past the tank, the route curves left and descends toward a parking area which is served by a circular road and used by equestrians.

At a four-way junction, you continue straight to a metal gate, which you pass on the left. Once past it, you merge with the two roads coming from the equestrian parking area, and then bear right at the next fork, near several trailers where park staff reside. Soon you reach a gravel turn-around and, just beyond, the park entrance road. You follow it past a baseball field, left, and, now on pavement, past the batting-practice facility, right, until you reach the parking area for the sports fields. If you did not park here, turn right and follow the paved entrance road downhill to the lower parking area.

Marina State Beach
DUNE BOARDWALK

Length: 1 mile

Time: 1 hour or less

Rating: Easy

Regulations: CSP; no dogs, no horses.

Phone: (831) 384-7695

Web site: *http://parks.ca.gov or www.mbay.net/~nbeaches*

Highlights: This short and delightful route through a restored area of coastal dunes can be done as an out-and-back hike using a boardwalk and then a sandy trail, or as a loop by walking back along the beach from the end of the trail. Spring and summer are the best times to enjoy the flowering dune shrubs and wildflowers, and don't forget binoculars for spotting birds, butterflies, and marine mammals.

Directions: From Hwy. 1 in Marina, take the Reservation Rd. exit and go west 0.1 mile to the parking area for Marina State Beach.

Facilities: Rest rooms, water, phone, picnic tables, snack shack, hang-glider school, surf shop.

Trailhead: Southeast corner of parking area.

The dunes that rise from the Monterey Bay shoreline between the Salinas River mouth and Monterey are among the highest on the California coast. Some of our state's rarest plants and animals live here, including Smith's blue butterfly, dune gilia, and Menzies wallflower, all endangered species. Development, increased human use, and the spread of invasive, non-native plants, such as European dune grass and iceplant, have taken their toll on this fragile environment. Fortunately, dune-restoration projects, like the one going on here, have begun to reverse decades of damage by removing non-native plants, rerouting trails, and sowing native-plant seeds.

From the southeast corner of the parking area, you follow a boardwalk south for about 30 feet to a **T**-junction where you turn left. At the next junction, about 75 feet ahead, you turn right and head south. In spring and summer, the dunes here are beautifully decorated with flowering shrubs and wildflowers, including a coastal variety of California poppy called beach poppy, lupine, paintbrush, beach evening primrose, beach bur, and beach sagewort, a plant that is often used for dune restoration.

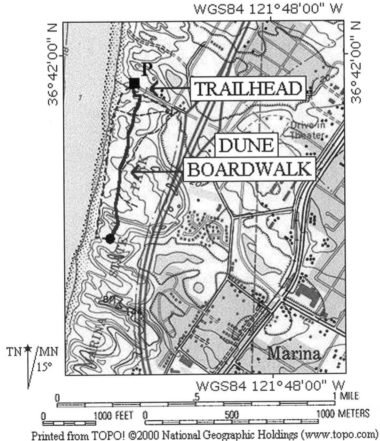

Printed from TOPO! ©2000 National Geographic Holdings (www.topo.com)

19. Dune Boardwalk

Signs along the way describe some of the native plants. Native dune plants adapt to harsh conditions—dry summers, wind, salt, and sand—by staying low, sending down long taproots, and producing thick, leathery leaves.

Also well-adapted to their environment are the various types of birds that spend time along our coast as residents or as migrants. One common shorebird is the killdeer, a member of the plover family. This robin-sized bird, brown above, white below, sports two dark neck bands, a long tail, and pinkish legs. Its call is a loud "kill-dee, kill-dee," often given in flight. Another plover found on the California coast is the snowy plover, a pale, sparrow-sized bird with dark marks on the sides of its neck. A dune nester, the snowy plover is listed federally as a threatened species: please obey all posted restrictions. You may see other members of the shorebird tribe—sandpipers, godwits, willets, and curlews—along the outer beach, feeding in the sand as the waves recede.

Strollers in spring and summer will enjoy wildflowers and flowering dune shrubs at Marina State Beach.

Two types of sand-verbena, yellow and pink, grow beside the boardwalk. Both are low-growing plants with thick, paddle-shaped leaves coated with a sticky film. The film traps blowing sand and creates a coating that protects the plant's leaves from further sandblasting. A waist-high shrub called lizard tail, a member of the sunflower family, grows in dense thickets. Its leaves, dull green above and white below, look like miniature fern fronds, and its daisy-like flowers are yellow. Also here is thrift, or sea pink, a member of the leadwort family, which sends up pink pom-poms on slender stalks that rise from clusters of dark green leaves. A seldom-seen creature of native-dune habitat is the black legless lizard, a pencil-sized reptile sporting a bright yellow belly and a shiny metallic back. The lizard lives among roots and travels below the sand at night, feeding on insect larvae.

If you tire of earthbound activities, you can take hang-gliding lessons at Marina State Beach. Or perhaps you prefer just to watch from the safety of the ground!

The boardwalk runs parallel to the shore, but your view of surf and sand is blocked by dunes on your right. Along the way, rest benches invite you to sit and enjoy the dune environment. Soon the boardwalk widens, and an overlook provides a fine view of the coastline. From here the route descends, and where the boardwalk ends, you continue your descent on a sandy slope, aided by a "sand ladder" of wires and wooden dowels. Now in a protected hollow, somewhat sheltered from the ocean breeze, you pass clumps of coast buckwheat, a small shrub with dark green, wrinkled leaves and pink-to-white spherical flower clusters that bloom from June through October. More than two dozen species of buckwheat grow in Monterey County. The endangered Smith's blue butterfly depends on coast buckwheat and its close relative, dune buckwheat, to survive.

Climbing out of the hollow, you come to an area devoid of vegetation, perhaps the result of wind blasting through the dunes from the ocean. The path now takes a rolling course through the dunes, and, at about the 0.5 mile point, turns right toward the shore. You can now walk back along the beach by following the path and then turning right when you reach the beach, or you can simply retrace your steps to the parking area.

Mission Trail Park
NATURE TRAIL AND NATIVE PLANT GARDEN

Length: 1.5 miles

Time: 1 to 2 hours

Rating: Easy

Regulations: City of Carmel-by-the-Sea; no dogs in the native plant garden.

Phone: (831) 624-3543

Web site: *www.carmelbythesea.com*

Highlights: This easy and delightful loop uses the Serra, Doolittle, Mesa, and Flanders trails to explore a small nature preserve in the southeast corner of Carmel-by-the-Sea. If a fine walk in the woods is not enough incentive, the loop also visits the wonderful Lester Rowntree Native Plant Garden, where you can learn about California's native plants. Carmel Mission, just across Rio Rd. from the trailhead, is an added attraction.

Directions: From the junction of Hwy. 1 and Rio Rd. just southeast of Carmel, take Rio Rd. northwest 0.5 mile and park along the right road shoulder, just opposite Carmel Mission.

Facilities: None

Trailhead: Gated dirt road on north side of Rio Rd.

Located just across Rio Rd. from historic Carmel Mission is this gem of a park, a 35-acre nature preserve nestled in a residential area, with about 5 miles of trails that wind through wonderful stands of native trees and shrubs. The Serra Trail, a dirt road, is the main route through the park, and the Doolittle and Flanders trails run parallel to it. There are also several other trails to explore. As you enter the preserve on the Serra Trail, you pass a rest bench and then veer right onto the Doolittle Trail. A line of willows indicates a creek, which you soon cross. During the rainy season this part of the park may be very muddy.

Once across the creek, you enter a forest of coast redwood, with an understory of French broom, berry vines, and lots of poison oak. The trail, a single track, climbs on a moderate grade, swings left, and comes to a clearing with a fine view of Carmel Mission. Crossing an open hillside, where native plants such as California sagebrush and blue-eyed grass share the stage with several huge century plants, the route soon levels and meanders amid stands of Monterey pine, which provide abundant shade and a carpet of pine needles. Downhill and left is the willow-lined creek you crossed earlier, and now the trail descends to it.

You cross the creek where it flows over a concrete spillway and then rejoin the Serra Trail, where you bear right. Near the creek look for wild onion, which has clusters of six-petaled white flowers drooping from atop long stems. Also nearby are non-natives such as wild radish, nasturtium, and calla lily. After about 100 yards, and across another spillway, you follow the Doolittle Trail as it branches right and uphill, past a rest bench. A moderate climb takes you past clumps of bush monkeyflower and black sage, and then into a forest of Monterey pine and coast live oak.

Traversing a hillside that falls away left, you pass an unsigned trail, left, and then climb on a gentle grade to a junction with the Mesa Trail, right, a semi-loop, also unsigned. Passing another rest bench, you soon reach a junction with the other end of the Mesa Trail, right. Turning right, you continue to climb, emerging on an open hillside that affords a great view of Carmel Mission and the Pacific Ocean. At a junction marked by a trail post, you turn right and descend into the forest, passing a

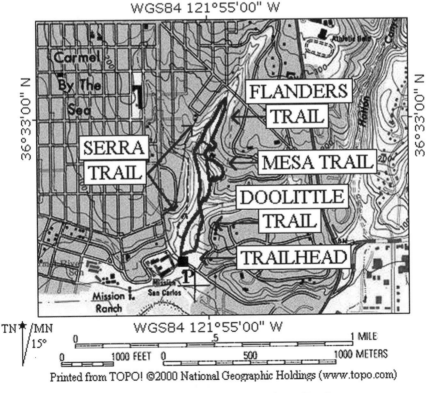

Printed from TOPO! ©2000 National Geographic Holdings (www.topo.com)

20. Nature Trail and Native Plant Garden

Monterey cypress along the way. A few switchbacks put you at a junction with the Doolittle Trail, where you turn right and retrace your steps to the start of the semi-loop Mesa Trail.

Now bearing left, you follow the Doolittle Trail to a junction just ahead with the Flanders Trail, where you turn right and work your way moderately uphill through a forest of pine, oak, and toyon. Crossing a plank bridge over a seasonal creek, you come to an unsigned fork, where you continue straight, now on a gentle uphill grade. At about the 1 mile point, you merge with a dirt road and bear right, crossing in several hundred feet a four-way junction, unsigned. In another 100 feet or so you come to a circular driveway and the Flanders Mansion. The mansion was built in 1924, and acquired by the City of Carmel-by-the-Sea in 1971. It has been on the National Registry of Historic Places since 1989.

To visit the Lester Rowntree Native Plant Garden, turn left and walk uphill on a paved road to the garden entrance, about 150 feet ahead. (Dogs are not allowed in the garden.) This 1-acre garden, well-tended by volunteers and with most plants labeled, is a wonderful resource for anyone interested in learning about California's native plants, specifically those that can be grown in home gardens. The garden honors Gertrude Ellen Lester Rowntree (1879–1979), a long-time Carmel resident who was the author of two books and more than 300 articles on horticulture, botany, and exploration.

Once you have finished enjoying this special place, return to the garden's entrance, cross the paved road, and follow a single-track trail to a T-junction with the Flanders Trail. Here you turn right and walk through a forest of tall Monterey pines, gaining elevation on a gentle grade. Soon the trail bends left and descends to a junction with the Serra Trail (signed SERA), a dirt road. Now turning left, you follow the Serra Trail, named for Father Junípero Serra, who explored Alta California with the 1769 Portolá expedition. The creek you crossed several times at the beginning of this hike is on your right. Soon you pass a trail, left, to the Flanders Mansion, and then reach a four-way junction with a trail, left, and a bridge across the creek, right.

Continuing straight, you descend through a dense forest of Monterey pine and coast live oak. A connector to the Doolittle Trail branches left and uphill, and then the Doolittle Trail itself departs left. Now you recross one of the two cement spillways you crossed earlier, and then, with the creek on your left, meet another junction with the Doolittle Trail. The woods are more open here, and you pass stands of young redwoods, acacias, and willows. Several rest benches are right, as is the Willow Trail, a dirt road. Look beside the road for Pacific silverweed, a prostrate plant, usually found on coastal beaches and in marshes. It has composite leaves with serrated leaflets and produces yellow, bowl-shaped flowers. Soon the Doolittle Trail joins from the left, and a few more paces return you to the park entrance.

Monterey State Beach
SHORELINE STROLL

Length: 1.2 miles

Time: 1 hour or less

Rating: Easy

Regulations: CSP

Phone: (831) 384-7695

Web site: *http://parks.ca.gov* or *www.mbay.net/~nbeaches*

Highlights: Combining a short stretch of the Monterey Bay Coastal Trail with a boardwalk over the dunes and a stroll along the shore, this easy semi-loop makes an ideal family outing or a relaxing break from sightseeing by car. This route is best from mid-to-low tide, when there is more exposed firm sand to walk on.

Directions: From Hwy. 1 in Monterey, take the Pacific Grove/Del Monte Ave. exit and go west 1 mile to a paved parking area on the north side of the road, opposite the Naval Postgraduate School gate.

Facilities: None

Trailhead: Northwest corner of parking area.

The Monterey Bay Coastal Trail, a proposed route for non-motorized travel between Castroville and Carmel, is already complete in many places, one of the most enjoyable stretches being the one from Roberts Lake to Lovers Point in Monterey. From the parking area's northwest corner, you bear left onto the trail, here a paved path built on a former Southern Pacific Railroad right-of-way. The path is lighted at night. Bicyclists, in-line skaters, and even joggers move at a good clip along this trail, which is marked with a yellow line down its center to separate traffic flow; you stay to the right.

You enter a grove of eucalyptus and Monterey cypress, with Monterey Bay hidden from view behind tall dunes. In about 100 yards, you reach a boardwalk on your right, opposite Sloat Avenue. The fragile dune environment is easily damaged by foot traffic, a problem that is somewhat alleviated by boardwalks. Turning right, you begin an easy uphill walk through the dunes, stopping to admire some of the wonderfully adapted plants that grow in this harsh environment, including pink sand-verbena, lupine, coast wallflower, mock heather, dune tansy, coast buckwheat, and sea lettuce. Towering over all are impressive stands of Monterey pine.

Dune restoration here, as elsewhere on the California coast, involves removing exotic species such as European beach grass and iceplant, and planting native vegetation.

The boardwalk, which goes up and then over the dunes, deposits you on a wide strand of sandy beach, some of it hard-packed by the twice-daily tidal influx. Turning left, you head toward Municipal Wharf, joined on a nice day by dozens, if not hundreds, of other beach walkers, joggers, kite fliers, picnickers, and dog owners. The curve of the Monterey Bay shoreline sweeps northward to Santa Cruz, and to the northwest lie the rocky shores of Pacific Grove, capped by Point Pinos. To your left, the dunes, diminishing in height as you go west, are backed by a line of Monterey cypress.

A residential complex, the Delmonte Beach Townhouses, left, soon gives way to a picnic area with volleyball courts and a large grassy lawn, and then to the Monterey Bay Kayak Company, which offers rentals, lessons, and tours. Here, about 100 yards from the wharf, you turn left and walk across the picnic area to rejoin the Monterey Bay Coastal Trail. Turn left again when you reach it, and enjoy the fragrance from the tall

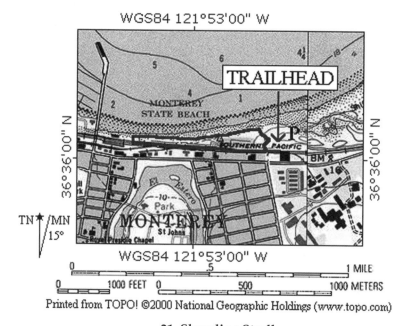

21. Shoreline Stroll

eucalyptus trees that border the trail. Adding color to the scene are plantings of ceanothus, sage, foxglove, and rock rose. When you reach the boardwalk where you began this loop, continue straight and retrace your steps to the parking area.

Children will love skipping along the Monterey State Beach boardwalk over the dunes to the shoreline.

Pebble Beach
BIRD ROCK TO INDIAN VILLAGE

Length: 1 mile

Time: 1 hour or less

Rating: Easy

Regulations: Pebble Beach Company; entrance fee for vehicles.

Phone: Pebble Beach Company, (800) 654-9300.

Web site: *www.pebblebeach.com*

Highlights: If you are touring 17-Mile Drive, take time out to explore this wonderful nature trail that leads from the Bird Rock parking area to a site that may have held a Native American village. Along the way you will encounter three habitats—shore, dune, and forest—each with its own plants and animals. (**Boldface** numbers in the route description refer to numbered markers along the trail, which are keyed to a brochure prepared by the Pebble Beach Company.)

Directions: From the junction of Hwy. 68 and 17-Mile Drive in Pacific Grove, go south 0.1 mile on the 17-Mile Drive to an entrance kiosk, where you pay a fee. Continue on 17-Mile Drive, which turns right at the 1-mile point. Continue on 17-Mile Drive another 2 miles to stop 10, the Bird Rock parking area.

From the junction in Carmel of Hwy. 1 and Ocean Ave., go west on Ocean Ave. 0.9 mile to N. San Antonio Ave. and turn right. Go 0.1 mile to a stop sign at 4th Ave., then stay on N. San Antonio Ave. as it jogs left, then right. Go another 0.1 mile to the 17-Mile Drive entrance kiosk, where you pay a fee. Continue on 17-Mile Drive 6 miles to stop 10, the Bird Rock parking area.

Facilities: Rest rooms, picnic tables, scopes to view marine mammals and birds on offshore rocks.

Trailhead: South side of parking area.

Before even hitting the trail, you will probably be captivated by the marine mammals and birds on Bird Rock just offshore, marker **1**, and you may be serenaded by the raucous bark of male sea lions—their mates prefer the warm waters of southern and Baja California—or the plaintive cries of gulls. Also present may be pelicans and cormorants, the latter nesting atop Bird Rock in great numbers. Your route, signed NATURE TRAIL, winds south through a picnic area perched on the edge of the coastal cliffs, past low-growing clumps of coyote bush, lizard tail, gum plant, buckwheat, and milk vetch.

Marker **2**, right, is for Seal Rock, a haul-out site for harbor seals. Compared with sea lions, harbor seals are shier, quieter, and much less agile on land. They also lack external ears. Now the trail turns east, away from the ocean, and you skirt Seal Rock Beach, marker **3**. A rest bench is left, and on the right are steps leading to this beautiful beach. Depending on seasonal storms and currents, the beach may have a thick covering of white sand or be scoured to bare rock. Search the scrubby areas beside the trail for western meadowlarks, white-crowned sparrows, and yellow-rumped warblers, which often pop up unannounced from their hiding places.

Reaching 17-Mile Drive, you cross it using a crosswalk that angles right, and, after about 100 feet on a sandy trail, come to a junction where you turn left onto a boardwalk. Climbing a low rise, you reach an observation deck, left, and marker **4**, which indicates a wetland near the mouth of Seal Rock Creek. The dense vegetation that cloaks the creek banks shelters land birds and black-tailed deer. Continuing uphill on the boardwalk to marker **5**, look in the sand nearby to find beach sagewort, mock heather, pink sand-verbena, paintbrush, and tiny asters. Also here,

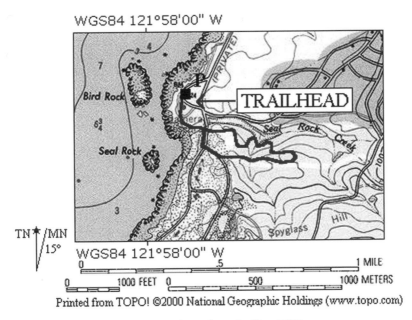

Printed from TOPO! ©2000 National Geographic Holdings (www.topo.com)

22. Bird Rock to Indian Village

Ocean meets coastal cliffs in dramatic scenes just off 17-Mile Drive in Pebble Beach.

according to the brochure, are Menzies wallflower and Tidestrom's lupine, both rare.

Now the boardwalk ends, and your climb on sand is aided by blocks of wood placed horizontally. Passing a rest bench, right, you enter a forest of Monterey pine and find marker **6**, right. The first line of trees forms a protective barrier to the wind and salt spray, allowing trees farther inland to flourish. Taking advantage of the shade, water (from fog drip), and soil enrichment the pines provide are understory plants such as blackberry, coffeeberry, hedge-nettle, and poison oak. At a **T**-junction in a clearing, you turn left and soon reach marker **7**, left, overlooking Seal Rock Creek, home to a fine stand of cattails. Marker **8**, right, is for a small pond formed by a spring, where forest wildlife such as deer, raccoons, rabbits, and squirrels come to drink.

At a junction with a trail going left, you continue straight to a large clearing with picnic tables and a log-cabin shelter. A rock, left, holds a metal plaque proclaiming this INDIAN VILLAGE, and dedicating it IN PERPETUITY TO OPEN SPACE. The text for marker **9** says Native Americans are thought to have had a village here and that they used water from the nearby spring for medicinal purposes. Bearing right across the clearing, you turn right onto a dirt road, signed NATURE TRAIL. Now enjoying a level walk through the pines, you come to marker **10**, right, indicating a Monterey pine forest. Some of the trees here are draped with lovely lace lichen, which resembles the Spanish moss found in the southern U.S.

At about the 1-mile point, you come to a wooden gate across the road, which you pass on the right. Ahead about 150 feet is a trail, right, but you continue straight, emerging from the pine forest. Just past the next gate is a junction with The Dunes Road, where you bear right. Just downhill is marker **11**, indicating sand dunes. Wind creates them, moving sand particles and forming ridges at right angles to the prevailing wind direction. Closest to shore are fore-dunes, where only the heartiest plants survive. Low-lying vegetation here traps wind-born sand particles and helps build the dune. Farther inland, shrubby plants that require some protection from the wind, salt, and sand take hold on stabilized dunes. Rear dunes and a transition zone, which may contain large shrubs and trees, complete the picture.

When you reach 17-Mile Drive, cross it and turn right, passing through a parking turnout for the Seal Rock Picnic Area. Ahead is the crosswalk where you first crossed 17-Mile Drive. When you reach it, turn left and retrace your steps to the parking area.

◆ Point Lobos State Reserve ◆

Point Lobos, a magnificent rocky headland several miles south of Carmel, has seen an astonishing variety of uses over the years. Native Americans gathered and prepared food here. Spanish mariners sailed by its rocky shores, naming it *Punta de los Lobos Marinos*, literally "Point of the Sea Wolves," for sea lions they saw and heard. Chinese fisherman built cabins near the shore. Granite rock was quarried from the coastal cliffs. Portuguese and Japanese whalers departed from Whalers Cove to brave the terrors of the open ocean and the fury of the creatures they pursued. Livestock grazed on the windswept grasses. Coal from a nearby mine was transported by rail to Coal Chute Point, where it was loaded aboard waiting ships.

In 1890, the Carmelo Land and Coal Company sold residential lots that would have filled the meadow facing Whalers Cove with dozens of homes. In 1898, a local businessman named A. M. Allan bought Point Lobos as an investment and began charging visitors a toll of 50 cents per vehicle to enter. Allan's purchase stopped the residential development, and over the next four decades the land was used for farming and dairy ranching. Allan, in partnership with a Japanese marine biologist, opened an abalone cannery, and also laid narrow-guage railroad tracks to carry sand from nearby San Jose Creek Beach to ships at Coal Chute Point.

In 1914, Hollywood discovered Point Lobos, and over the next 75 years, 46 movies, or parts of movies, were filmed in or near the area, including *Valley of the Moon, Foolish Wives, Treasure Island, Rebecca, Lassie Come Home,* and *The Graduate.* The state of California in 1933 purchased Point Lobos for $631,000, and it became part of the new state-park system, with a cypress grove named in honor of Allan and his wife. In 1960 the waters surrounding the point were added to create the nation's first underwater reserve. During World War II, the area was heavily used by the military for training and coastal defense.

The trails that crisscross this unique, magical place are generally level, although climbing Whalers Knoll involves an elevation gain of just under 200 feet. Hugging the shoreline are trails that give you spectacular views and the chance to see nesting and migratory birds, and marine mammals such as sea lions, harbor seals, sea otters, and whales. Vegetation here includes majestic Monterey pines and Monterey cypress trees, native to only a few locations on the California coast, as well as shrubs such as blue blossom, bush monkeyflower, California sagebrush, lizard tail, and poison oak. Spring wildflowers put on an impressive display, especially on the bluffs around Granite Point, whose name refers to Santa Lucia granite, the type of rock found along the north shore of Point Lobos.

The reserve's rangers have put together a list of rules and suggestions to protect the reserve and to enhance everyone's experience here. Respect the power of the ocean; keep a safe distance from it by remaining on designated trails and within wire guides. Stay away from rocky cliffs and the shoreline. Smoking is permitted only in picnic areas, parking lots, and in vehicles; no smoking on trails. Do not disturb or collect any natural objects. Fires, barbecues, and the use of stoves are prohibited. Pets are prohibited in the reserve, as are outdoor games, including Frisbee, football, and kite flying. Picnicking is allowed only in areas with tables—Whalers Cove, Piney Woods, and Bird Island parking areas. Bicycles are restricted to the reserve's paved roads and may not be ridden or walked on trails.

Views like this will delight you along the Point Lobos State Reserve "Grand Loop" route (Trip 24).

The reserve opens at 9 A.M. and closes at 5 P.M. during standard time (November to April); during daylight savings time (April through October) it closes at 7 P.M. On weekends and on holidays the reserve, which allows only a limited number of visitors at any one time, may be full, and those wishing to enter may have to wait in line. There is seasonal service by mass transit. Scuba and free diving, with access from a ramp at Whalers Cove, are by reservation only. Near the Whalers Cove parking area is the Whalers Cabin, a small museum devoted to the history of Point Lobos. At the Sea Lion Point parking area, there is often a helpful docent staffing an information station offering books, pamphlets, and posters about the reserve's plants and animals.

INFORMATION: (831) 624-4909

DIVING RESERVATIONS: (831) 624-8413

MONTEREY—SALINAS TRANSIT: (831) 899-2555

You can learn about the history of Point Lobos by visiting the Whalers Cabin museum.

Point Lobos State Reserve
CYPRESS GROVE

Length: 1 mile

Time: 1 hour or less

Rating: Easy

Regulations: CSP; parking fee; open 9 A.M. to 5 P.M. during standard time, and 9 A.M. to 7 P.M. during daylight savings time; no dogs, bikes on paved roads only.

Phone: (831) 624-4909

Web site: *http://pointlobos.org*

Highlights: This short and easy semi-loop excursion uses the Cypress Grove Trail to visit one of only two remaining native stands of Monterey cypress. Views of rocky coves and offshore islands from the trail are wonderful, and you can easily combine this route with a longer one elsewhere in the reserve. Point Lobos may be crowded on weekends and holidays.

Directions: From the junction of Hwy. 1 and Rio Rd. just southeast of Carmel, continue south 2.3 miles on Hwy. 1 to the reserve entrance, right. About 0.1 mile ahead is an entrance kiosk, where you pay a fee and can obtain a map and other park information. Continue another 0.6 mile to a parking area, right.

Facilities: Information kiosk, toilets.

Trailhead: North side of parking area.

If the information kiosk here is open, it has books, maps, and interpretive displays about the plants and animals of Point Lobos, all presided over by a helpful docent. As you leave the parking area on the Cypress Grove Trail, you can see a grove of Monterey cypress ahead, one of only two sites where these splendid trees grow naturally, the other being in Pebble Beach. The grove, on a stubby peninsula jutting northwest, honors Mr. and Mrs. A. M. Allan, who at one time owned most of Point Lobos. Beside the trail grow common plants that make up the coastal-scrub community, including California sagebrush, bush monkeyflower, coffeeberry, coyote brush, blackberry, and poison oak.

Staying left at a junction with the North Shore Trail, you follow a sandy, level trail with a fine view, left, to Sea Lion Point (from the Spanish *Punta de Los Lobos Marinos*. Many features of California's coast were named by Spanish mariners in the 17th and 18th centuries.) Scanning the low-growing shrubs for birds that pop up from the dense cover, you may spot a California thrasher—a brown bird, slightly larger than a robin, with a down-curved bill. Among the vegetation is blue blossom, else-where a tree-sized shrub, but here growing in stunted, woody clumps. The trail around the peninsula containing the cypress grove is a loop. At the fork ahead, you bear right, enjoying a dramatic view of wave-washed rocks in Cypress Cove, right. Several access paths along the way give you even better views from near the cliff's edge. Blue-green water, floating kelp beds, and crashing surf create spectacular scenes.

But the real attraction here is the wonderful cypress trees, their limbs twisted, their dense crowns flattened by gale-force winds. Each tree has its own personality, and some are garishly decorated with algae contain-ing orange-colored carotene pigment. Hedge-nettle, a member of the mint family, grows in their shade, and nearby coastal plants such as

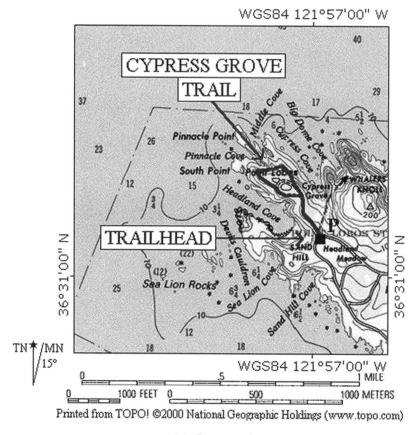

Printed from TOPO! ©2000 National Geographic Holdings (www.topo.com)

23. Cypress Grove

lizard tail and dudleya, or sea lettuce, cling to soil in rocky crevices. The trail soon veers left, climbs steps hewn in rock, and then rounds the peninsula's westernmost point, revealing dramatic views of the Pacific Ocean and the gorgeous coastline south to Point Sur. Each vantage point seems more spectacular than the one before. Turning east, you skirt Headland Cove and return to the junction at the start of this loop. From here, retrace your steps to the parking area.

24 Point Lobos State Reserve
GRAND LOOP

Length:	4.5 miles
Time:	3 to 4 hours
Rating:	Moderate
Regulations:	CSP; parking fee; open 9 A.M. to 5 P.M. during standard time, and 9 A.M. to 7 P.M. during daylight savings time; no dogs, bikes on paved roads only.
Phone:	(831) 624-4909
Web site:	*http://pointlobos.org*
Highlights:	Using the Bird Island, South Plateau, Carmelo Meadow, Granite Point, North Shore, Whalers Knoll, Sea Lion Point, Sand Hill, and South Shore trails, this loop explores most of the terrain accessible to hikers within Point Lobos State Reserve. Spring is the ideal time of year to visit here as the coastal wildflowers are in bloom, but this place is so wonderful that you should really visit it in every season. Be sure to bring binoculars for viewing birds and marine mammals.
Directions:	Same as for "Cypress Grove" on p. 105. When you reach the parking area 0.7 mile from Hwy. 1, follow the road another 0.9 mile to its end and park here.
Facilities:	Picnic tables, water, toilets.
Trailhead:	Southeast corner of parking area.

A steep climb on the Bird Island Trail, aided by steps carved in the dirt and reinforced with wooden blocks, starts you off on this wonderful loop, which circles the entire Point Lobos peninsula. Fantastic rock formations jutting out toward the ocean, birds circling overhead, and shoreline cliffs

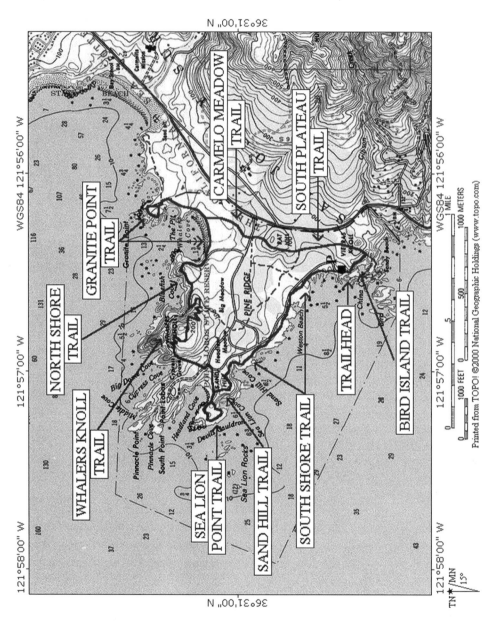

24. Grand Loop

covered with a colorful array of native plants—sights that will delight you along the way—are already present here at the start. Monterey pines rise beside the trail, which is also lined with blue blossom, California sagebrush, coffeeberry, bush monkeyflower, and poison oak.

The route soon levels and passes a short, steep trail that descends a wood stairway to the lovely sand beach in China Cove. You continue straight, following signs for Bird Island and Gibson Beach. At a **T**-junction ahead, the South Plateau Trail heads left, and the Bird Island Trail turns right toward Pelican Point, the vantage point for Bird Island. Here you turn left, and in about 50 feet pass the trail to Gibson Beach, one of the few large, sandy beaches on Point Lobos. Blackberry vines, growing in tangles, appear to thrive in the sandy soil, which also supports beach strawberry and wonderful displays of paintbrush and wild iris.

As you turn inland, you may notice the shrubs and trees here are taller, removed somewhat from the limiting effects of wind and salt spray. The South Plateau Trail has numbered markers keyed to a brochure available from a box at the trail's start near the entrance kiosk. Marker **10**, left, indicates coyote brush, a common shrub and a member of the coastal-scrub community. Now in a beautiful grove of Monterey pine, you walk on a carpet of pine needles, passing marker **9**, left, for blue blossom. This colorful shrub, also called wild lilac, produces fragrant flowers, attractive to bees and butterflies, from late winter to early spring.

A gentle descent past lichen-draped oaks brings you to marker **8**, left. Coast live oaks, represented here by some wonderful specimens, produce acorns that were an important source of food for Native Americans. Rushes bordering the trail indicate this to be a wet area during winter. Passing marker **7**, left, for coffeeberry, you make a moderate descent on a trail crossed by exposed pine roots. Several plank bridges help you across possible wet areas, and then you find marker **6**, beside a dead Monterey pine. Dead trees, called snags, are important sources of food and shelter for birds. The insects that attack trees are fed upon by many species of woodpeckers. Cavities within dead or dying trees become homes for small birds such as chickadees, nuthatches, and even pygmy owls.

After crossing another plank bridge, you begin a gentle climb and soon reach marker **5**, right, indicating Monterey pine. This species of pine, seemingly so common, has been widely planted throughout the world but is native to only three areas on the California coast, one of them right here. Check the ground under these tall, weathered trees for pine "cobs," the remains of cones stripped of their seeds by gray squirrels. Descending to a small stream bridged by a plank, you then come to a junction with the Pine Ridge Trail, left. You continue straight, and soon begin meandering through the forest on a course roughly parallel to Hwy. 1. A moderate climb and then a gentle descent brings you to the final cluster of markers, **3**, **2**, and **1**, indicating poison oak, wood mint, also called hedgenettle, and wild blackberry.

Now you reach the reserve's paved entrance road, with the entrance kiosk just to your right. After carefully crossing the road, you come to the Carmelo Meadow Trail. Previously this trail ran through an area that flooded in wet weather, but a project completed in 2000 set it farther east, on higher and drier ground. You follow its firm, sandy track downhill on a gentle grade through a forest of venerable Monterey pines, snags, and young trees springing up beside the trail. One of the woodpeckers found here is the northern flicker: listen for its sharp, clear cry, usually given after it lands on a perch. A sturdy bridge takes you across a creek flowing northwest into Carmelo Meadow and, eventually, into Whalers Cove.

Soon you arrive at a T-junction, just past the 1-mile point, with the Granite Point Trail. The scenic semicircle of water ahead is Whalers Cove, bounded by Cannery Point, left, and Coal Chute Point, right. Gentle surf laps at its shore, and great beds of kelp float just below its surface. Now turning right, you follow the Granite Point Trail as it hugs the cliffs near

As you hike Monterey Bay area trails, you may surprise a deer, like this one at Point Lobos.

the water's edge. After passing a bridge over a seasonal creek, you come to a **Y**-junction with the short loop trail to Coal Chute Point. This trail provides fine views of the cove just north of Coal Chute Point, called The Pit, and also of Carmel River State Beach.

Continuing on the Granite Point Trail, you pass through a corridor of coastal scrub—California sagebrush, coffeeberry, poison oak, and black-berry vines. You may hear the stuttering call of a wrentit in the distance, suggesting the sound of a stubborn car that refuses to start. Ahead in the distance is the Carmelite Monastery, which lends its name to Monastery Beach, which is also called San Jose Creek Beach. The beach borders Point Lobos State Reserve. Descending a set of dirt steps you arrive at a junction, signed, with the Moss Cove Trail, a dirt road. Also here is a short trail to The Pit, left.

Reaching the Moss Cove Trail, you turn sharply left toward The Pit, and then immediately right to ascend a set of dirt steps. Soon you reach a fork where a loop that circles Granite Point begins. Staying left, you enter a magical realm of wildflowers that, put on a dazzling spring display. Carpeting the crags and nestled in protected nooks are lupine, California poppy, nightshade, paintbrush, bluedicks, wild iris, sea pink, and seaside daisy—truly a botanist's paradise! Atop Granite Point, appropriately, is a large boulder, and from the tip of the point you have 360° views that encompass Carmel Bay and the Pacific Ocean. When you have finished enjoying this marvelous spot, retrace your steps to the junction of the Granite Point and Carmelo Meadow trails.

From here you continue straight on the Granite Point Trail, crossing a bridge over a creek that drains Carmelo Meadow, left, and splashes over a cliff into Whalers Cove. Soon you reach a paved road, across which is Whalers Cabin. The cabin and an adjacent building house excellent displays covering the history of Point Lobos, from Native American times to the present. Included are exhibits on whaling, Chinese fishing, World War II, and even Hollywood's use of the area as a location for films. To the right of the cabin, as you face it, is a trail post marking the Cabin Trail. This trail, which starts as an indistinct track, winds beneath huge Monterey cypress trees on its way up and across a hillside of coastal scrub. (To shorten the loop, take the Cabin Trail to its junction with the North Shore Trail, turn left, and then follow the route description below.)

Once you are done learning about this wonderful area and its varied history, follow the paved road downhill to a parking area at the foot of Cannery Point. Here you will find picnic tables, water, and rest rooms, along with an information board and display panels telling about marine life. This is a popular area for scuba divers, who come here to enjoy the cove's plentiful undersea plants and animals. At the north end of the parking area is a trailhead for the North Shore Trail, which climbs steeply on a set of dirt steps reinforced with rocks. Atop the steps, the trail divides: left is the North Shore Trail, and right is a short loop around

Cannery Point, where great vistas await. It is hard to find a spot with finer scenery in the Monterey Bay area.

Now you follow the North Shore Trail, signed here for Whalers Knoll and Cypress Grove. Climbing on a gentle grade, you skirt a rise topped with Monterey pines, right. Soon the trail swings left, and you pass Bluefish Cove on the right. At about the 3-mile point, you reach a junction with the Cabin Trail, left. An ascending traverse takes you across a hillside dotted with blue-flowing wild iris, lovely in spring. The route then levels and follows indentations in the shoreline, passing a trail to a viewpoint, right, and a rest bench, left. Downed trees here testify to the wind's fury. A junction, left, with the Whalers Knoll Trail, offers you a choice of routes. (To shorten the loop and avoid the climb over Whalers Knoll, continue straight to the junction of the Whalers and North Shore trails, and then follow the route description below.)

Climbing gently at first, the Whalers Knoll Trail swings sharply right and then passes a trail joining from the left. Now the grade alternates between gentle and moderate as you traverse a steep hillside falling away to the right. The many young pines here seem to offer hope for a rejuvenated forest. Switchbacking its way uphill, your trail is again joined by another from the left at an unsigned junction. Soon you crest a rise, descend a bit, and then enjoy a level walk to a rest bench and a vantage point with views northwest and northeast—the view north is blocked by a pine-covered rise. From this dramatic point you descend on a gentle grade, first over rocky ground, then through chaparral via **S**-bends.

At a **T**-junction with the North Shore Trail you turn left and follow a level course, continuing straight at a junction with the Old Veteran Trail. At the next junction, with the Cypress Grove Trail, you turn left and, in about 100 feet, come to a paved parking area with an information station. If the station is staffed, you can learn a lot about the natural history of Point Lobos from the helpful docent and the displays. On the west side of the parking area is the trailhead for the Sea Lion Point Trail, one of the park's most popular. (This trail is ADA-compliant and is excellent for people in wheelchairs.) The trail, bordered by low coastal scrub, runs west toward *Punta De Los Lobos Marinos*, or Sea Lion Point, a coastal peninsula noted and named by Spanish mariners for the sea lions they saw and heard here. As you make your way toward the point, Headland Cove is on your right, its beach a favorite haul-out spot for harbor seals.

Now you leave the pines and cypress behind, because the only plants growing beside the trail here are ones adapted to survive in this windy, salty environment. Among these are lizard tail, mock heather, and beach sagewort, all members of the sunflower family. Lizard tail is a woody shrub with tiny lobed leaves and yellow composite flowers, often rayless. Mock heather, also woody, has green leaves that resemble needles on a fir tree. Beach sagewort is a rangy plant with gray, deeply lobed leaves, resembling its cousin, California sagebrush.

Enjoying a level course through an increasingly rocky landscape, you pass the Sand Hill Trail, left, and then reach a vantage point for Sea Lion Rocks, separated from the peninsula's tip by a churning patch of water called Devil's Cauldron. Dramatic rock outcrops and a rocky beach combine with ocean views to make this a superbly scenic spot. For the first time on this route, you can see the wave-swept coastline south of Point Lobos, with its tall, often fog-shrouded hills receding toward Point Sur. Using binoculars, and staying safely back from the water's edge, you can study the birds—gulls, terns, and cormorants—and marine mammals that call this wild place home.

Returning now to the junction with the Sand Hill Trail, you turn right and skirt the edge of coastal cliffs that drop steeply to Sea Lion Cove. Soon you reach a junction with the South Shore Trail, where you turn right and walk down a set of dirt steps. A small meadow, left, holds California buttercup and checkerbloom. Crossing an area that may be soaked by water seeping across the trail, you reach a parking area beside the reserve's main road. Now the trail runs parallel to the road, which is just left, and you continue on a southeast course, reaching a second parking area at about the 5-mile point. Here you cross the pavement and find the continuation of the South Shore Trail about 30 feet past the parking area's southeast corner.

While hiking, take time for close-up examination of some of the native plants, like these seaside daisies and paintbrush.

At the third parking area, shown on the park map opposite Mound Meadow, the trail veers right and then curves back toward the road, passing the first of several short trails that lead to viewpoints, right. The coastline here is fractured into long fingers of water divided by rocky peninsulas. Ahead, in the distance, is Bird Island, a sure sign you are nearing the end of this wonderful loop. Passing Mound Meadow Trail, left, you skirt a fourth parking area, and then come to Hidden Beach, which has its own access trail. With a few more zigs and zags, the trail finally arrives at the parking area where the loop began.

Stop for a view (like this one northwest from Sand Hill Trail in the Point Lobos Grand Loop route).

25   Point Lobos State Reserve
SOUTH PLATEAU

Length: 1.3 miles

Time: 1 hour or less

Rating: Easy

Regulations: CSP; parking fee; open 9 A.M. to 5 P.M. during standard time, and 9 A.M. to 7 P.M. during daylight savings time; no dogs, bikes on paved roads only.

Phone: (831) 624-4909

Web site: *http://pointlobos.org*

Highlights: If you don't have time to hike the "Grand Loop" around the entire Point Lobos peninsula (Trip 24), consider this scenic loop, which uses the Bird Island, South Plateau, Pine Ridge, Mound Meadow, and South Shore trails. Along the way you will have fine views of Bird Island, a nesting site for sea birds, and enjoy a quiet stroll through a magnificent pine forest.

Directions: Same as for "Cypress Grove" on p. 105. When you reach the parking area at 0.7 mile from Hwy. 1, follow the road another 0.9 mile to its end, and park here.

Facilities: Picnic tables, water, toilets.

Trailhead: Southeast corner of parking area.

Follow the route description for "Grand Loop" on pages 107–108 to the **T**-junction with the South Plateau Trail, left, and the continuation of the Bird Island Trail to Pelican Point, right. Here you turn right and head toward a vantage point for Bird Island, the largest of about a dozen offshore rocks clustered around Pelican Point. A hillside, left, is draped with iceplant, an invasive, non-native plant that is being removed from many California coastal areas as part of a restoration effort. Native plants thriving here include redberry, lupine, coffeeberry, and mock heather. In spring and summer, gorgeous wildflowers abound.

Among the most common land birds found near the ocean are white-crowned sparrows, easily identified by their namesake head marking, and also by their call, a sharp "pink!" Like many other sparrows, members of this species usually feed in flocks, moving from bush to bush, and hoping for safety in numbers. Less common is Say's phoebe, a member of the flycatcher family. Look for this gray-breasted bird, which has a pale rufous belly, hovering low over the ground in search of insects. Also, keep your eye out for sea otters floating in kelp beds just offshore, and harbor seals hauled out on rocks near the waterline.

A fork in the trail indicates the start of a loop around Pelican Point, and here you turn right. China Cove is on your right, perhaps full of kelp and catching the light as it did in a famous Edward Weston photograph. Bird Island itself, easily studied with binoculars or a spotting scope from vantage points along the trail, is a nesting site for Brandt's cormorants during spring and summer. These seagoing birds—black, with snake-like necks—are often seen flying in formation low over the water. When you reach the end of the loop around Pelican Point, retrace your steps to the junction with the South Plateau Trail.

Here you continue straight, following the route description for "Grand Loop" on p. 109 to the junction with the Pine Ridge Trail, at about the 1-mile point. At the junction you turn left, and enjoy a level walk among tall Monterey pines, their branches draped with lace lichen, whose strands glimmer in the sunlight. Other than the sound of wind blowing through the tops of pines, and the chatter of birds, all is still. This is one of the most beautiful spots in the Monterey Bay area, and if you wish to linger, there is a handy rest bench ahead, just to the right of the trail.

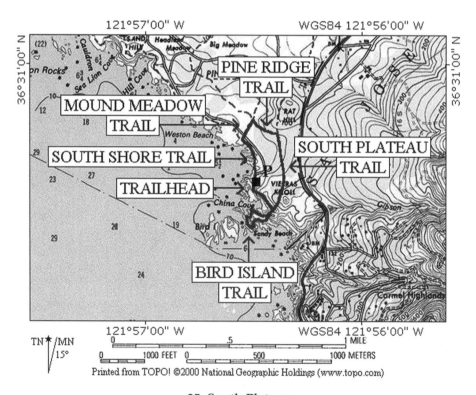

25. South Plateau

At a four-way junction with the Mound Meadow Trail, you turn left, and soon catch glimpses of the ocean through the trees. Emerging from the forest, you have the reserve's main road ahead. Crossing it carefully, you come to a T-junction with the South Shore Trail. Here you turn left again, and follow the trail as it zigzags beside the rocky shoreline. Observe the views of the wave-tossed Pacific, whose near-shore waters are studded with rocks and pierced by rocky promontories. Students of geology will enjoy examining the marine layers of rock and sediment—most lying horizontally, but some tipped vertically by forces too powerful to imagine—exposed beside the trail. Passing the trail to Hidden Beach, right, you soon reach the parking area where you began this loop.

26 Royal Oaks County Park
WOODLAND LOOP

Length: 1.5 miles

Time: 1 hour or less

Rating: Easy

Regulations: Monterey County Parks; parking fee.

Phone: (888) 588-2267

Web site: *www.co.monterey.ca.us/parks*

Highlights: This short, easy loop, using the Woodland Loop, Oak Ridge, Amolé, Pine Meadow, and Hermosa trails, lets you explore the wonderful variety of habitats found in this delightful county park—oak forest, chaparral, and open meadow—in about an hour.

Directions: From Hwy. 101 in Prunedale, take the San Miguel Canyon Rd. exit and go northwest 1.8 miles to Echo Valley Rd. Turn right, go 0.5 mile to Maher Rd., and turn left. Go 1 mile to the park entrance, right, which is not well marked. After passing an entrance kiosk, where you pay a parking fee, go 0.1 mile to a large parking area.

Facilities: Rest rooms, phone, picnic tables, fire grates, water, play area for children, tennis courts, basketball court, and a softball field.

Trailhead: From the east end of the parking area, walk southeast on a paved road, signed OVERNIGHT AREA and LIVE OAK. You will pass the Live Oak Group Area on your right. Several

hundred yards ahead, just before the pavement ends, you
veer right across a field to the Woodland Loop trailhead.

From the trailhead, you follow a single track into a densely wooded area,
where poison oak, whose leaves color our forests red, yellow, and gold in
fall, is plentiful beside the trail. Also here are other common coastal
shrubs and vines, such as coffeeberry, snowberry, wild rose, manroot, and
blackberry, and a lone Monterey pine towers above you. The trail switchbacks as it climbs among impressive coast live oaks, whose twisted
trunks and curving limbs give each tree its own personality. In the shade
under their canopy thrive several species of ferns.

The route soon nears the top of a ridge, which marks the park boundary. On the other side of the boundary, to the south, is the Monterey
Mushroom Plantation, which can emit an unpleasant odor. Now the trail
veers left and continues through an oak woodland to a T-junction. Here,
a short trail to Vista Point, where a fine view awaits, veers right, and the
Woodland Loop Trail continues left. Descending on a gentle grade, you
pass several species of manzanita, an important member of California's
chaparral community. There are more than a dozen species of manzanita
found in Monterey County, and telling them apart is tricky.

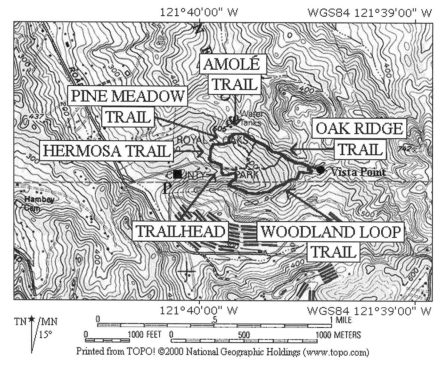

26. Woodland Loop

At a junction, you leave the Woodland Loop Trail where it turns left and downhill, and continue straight, now on the Oak Ridge Trail. Beautiful examples of manzanita line the trail, along with coffeeberry and black sage. At about the 1-mile point, an unsigned trail departs left, but you continue straight. Now making a moderate descent, you come to a **Y**-junction where the Amolé Trail goes left and the Oak Ridge Trail goes right. Here you turn left and descend gently through a lovely forest.

Soon the trail levels off and you come to a large meadow dotted with pines and other evergreens. Turning right, you follow the Pine Meadow Trail, a faint path along the meadow's north side, which is edged with black sage. Now the path curves right, and after about 100 feet comes to a **T**-junction with the Hermosa Trail, a dirt road. Ahead is an open field

Coast live oaks invite visitors to this shady picnic area in Royal Oaks County Park.

decorated with the yellow blossoms of telegraph weed. Turning left, you have the open field on your right, and a line of trees on your left. Margins between areas with different vegetation, like this one, are good places to look for birds. After a gentle descent, your route curves left and comes to the paved road opposite the Live Oak Group Area. Here you turn right and retrace your steps to the parking area.

27 Salinas River National Wildlife Refuge
BEACH TRAIL

Length:	1.6 miles
Time:	1 hour or less
Rating:	Easy
Regulations:	USFWS; no dogs; seasonal waterfowl hunting allowed only in posted area along the river; surf fishing allowed year round.
Phone:	(510) 792-0222
Web site:	*www.fws.org*
Highlights:	Explore a beautiful and undeveloped part of the Monterey Bay shoreline by following an easy trail, mostly a dirt road, that winds through open fields and then past a saline pond and a salt marsh south of the Salinas River. Bring binoculars or a spotting scope to view the many species of birds that inhabit this refuge. (The dirt road to the refuge's parking area may be impassible after heavy rain.)
Directions:	From Hwy. 1 between Monterey and Moss Landing, take the Marina/Del Monte Blvd. exit and go northwest on Neponset Rd. After 0.1 mile the pavement ends, and you continue on a dirt road between artichoke fields. At 0.6 mile, the road ends at a dirt parking area.
Facilities:	None
Trailhead:	North side of parking area.

A dirt road heading west, signed TO BEACH TRAIL, takes you over level ground between a weedy field, right, and a screen of Monterey pines, left. The field is full of coyote brush, wild radish, California asters, and bristly ox-tongue. This is perfect terrain for birds of prey, and you may see

American kestrels, northern harriers, and white-tailed kites patrolling the sky above or perched on shrubs or posts. Margins between woodlands and open fields are great places to look for songbirds. Among those found here are house finches, goldfinches, white-crowned sparrows, golden-crowned sparrows, and bushtits. Look here also for flycatchers such as the black phoebe. These aerial hunters dart from perches to catch insects on the wing.

The road curves right, then left, and soon you see a large saline pond bordered by sand dunes on its west shore and by a vast salt marsh elsewhere. These dunes are part of an extensive dune system that stretches from the Salinas River south to Monterey. The saline pond and its surrounding salt marsh are protected, and signs warn you not to enter this

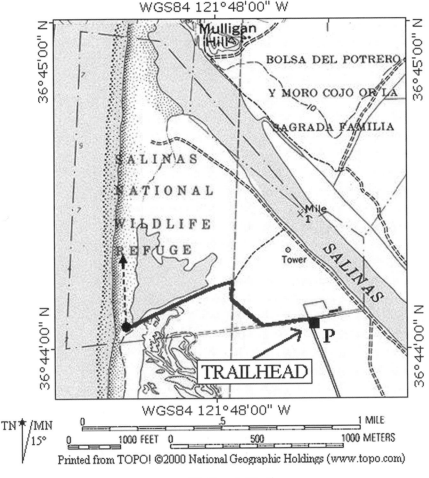

27. Beach Trail

sensitive wildlife habitat. The road skirts the pond, giving you a great opportunity to view its avian inhabitants with binoculars or a spotting scope. Depending on the season, you may find waterfowl, wading birds, and shorebirds, including long-billed curlews, black-bellied plovers, dunlin, killdeer, and small sandpipers. Watch the birds' behavior carefully—a sudden flight en masse may indicate the presence of a hawk or a falcon overhead.

At a junction, the road continues straight, but it is closed to public entry. You follow a single-track trail veering right and signed ACCESS TO BEACH ONLY, DUNES CLOSED TO THE PUBLIC. Now walking beside the saline pond, you can observe some common salt-marsh plants, including pickleweed, sea blite, alkali heath, salt grass, and gumplant. Soon you rejoin the road, which comes in sharply from the left, and then the road ends as you near the beach. Here a path through low dunes takes you to the edge of beautiful Monterey Bay. About 1 mile north from here is the mouth of the Salinas River, and you may see a huge congress of gulls feeding and resting there. Other denizens of the outer beach include brown pelicans and cormorants, which often fly in formation just above the waves. You may also see snowy plovers, a small shorebird listed federally as a threatened species.

If time, inclination, and weather permit, you can walk north along the outer beach to the mouth of the Salinas River for more birding and nature study. Otherwise, simply retrace your steps to the parking area.

Salinas River State Beach
DUNE TRAIL

Length: 2 miles

Time: 1 hour or less

Rating: Easy

Regulations: CSP; no dogs.

Phone: (831) 649-2836

Web site: *http://parks.ca.gov or www.mbay.net/~nbeaches*

Highlights: This short and easy out-and-back route follows a sandy trail through some of the loveliest dunes on the California coast. Along the way you will have stunning views of Monterey Bay, and the opportunity to study some of the specialized coastal plants that thrive in this salty, sandy, and often windy environment.

Directions: From Hwy. 1 just south of Moss Landing, take Potrero Rd. west 0.4 mile to a large dirt-and-gravel parking area.

Facilities: Toilets

Trailhead: Southwest corner of parking area.

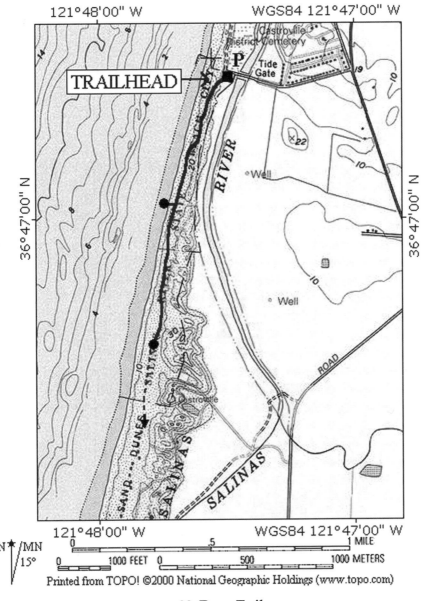

28. Dune Trail

This parking area is the middle of three access points to Salinas River State Beach, a 3-mile stretch of pristine beach and beautifully preserved dunes, bordered on the east by the old Salinas River channel and on the west by Monterey Bay. From here, a gated road goes north behind the dunes to Moss Landing. There are also two trails—a short one heading west to the beach, and your route, a longer one running south through the dunes. During spring and summer, this area may contain nests of snowy plovers, listed federally as a threatened species, so please stay on the trail and observe all posted restrictions.

Leaving the southwest corner of the parking area and climbing on a gentle grade, you have on your left an expanse of salt marsh divided by a slough, which before the early 1900s was the channel of the Salinas River, emptying into Monterey Bay at Moss Landing. Around 1910, the river overran the dunes at the spot where it now flows into the bay, about 3 miles south of here. That opening to the bay is maintained by the river's

A snail perches on sand-verbena at Salinas River State Beach.

own current in years of heavy rain, but in dry years, dredging keeps the river mouth open.

Bordering the sandy trail are some common marsh and dune plants, including gumplant, beach sagewort, sand-verbena, mock heather, buckwheat, and lizard tail. At this point, Monterey Bay is hidden from view, but as you climb higher into the dunes, you begin to feel the steady cooling breeze that usually blows inland from the west. Now near the crest of the dunes, you catch your first glimpse of Monterey Bay's shimmering blue water and roiling surf. On your left, between the slough and Hwy. 1, are agricultural fields used for growing artichokes. To the east are the mountains of the Gabilan Range, crowned by Fremont Peak, and stretching southeast is the Salinas Valley.

Among the birds to look for here are raptors such as northern harriers and white-tailed kites. These aerial hunters are within a few inches of each other in size, and the male harrier is similar in coloration to the kite. Fortunately for birders, their hunting styles easily tell them apart. Harriers skim low over the ground, often with their wings angled upwards, searching for small birds and mammals, whereas kites hover over open fields, dropping suddenly to snare rodents.

Just shy of the 0.5-mile point, a short path on your right climbs over a low dune and then descends to a lovely white-sand beach, strewn with seaweed and driftwood, and washed by foaming breakers. If you take this scenic detour, return to the main trail, where you enjoy a level walk and a feeling of isolation that belies the proximity of this area to the bustling Monterey Peninsula and busy Hwy. 1. The dunes here are almost completely covered with native vegetation, and, in spring and summer, colorfully decorated with lupine, paintbrush, and a coastal variety of California poppy called beach poppy.

At about the 1-mile point, the trail dips into a wind-sheltered gully where your progress is slowed by soft sand. From here the trail continues south to the state beach's southern access point at the end of Monterey Dunes Way, off Molera Rd. When you are finished exploring this wonderful area, turn and retrace your steps to the parking area. On the way back, you can turn left onto the beach-access path, and then, once on the beach, continue north to the trail leading back to the parking area.

29

Toro County Park
OLLASON PEAK

Length: 9 miles

Time: 5 to 6 hours

Rating: Difficult

Regulations: Monterey County Parks; parking fee; dogs must be leashed.

Phone: (831) 484-1108

Web site: *www.co.monterey.ca.us/parks*

Highlights: This rugged but supremely rewarding loop uses the Ollason, Toyon Ridge, Coyote Spring, Toyon Loop, East Toyon, and East Ridge trails to explore this wonderful park, which is removed from the hustle and bustle of busy Monterey. Along the way you climb remote Ollason Peak (1800′), and enjoy superb views from its summit. Spring is the best season to enjoy this park, when temperatures are mild, wildflowers are in bloom, and migratory songbirds are on the wing.

Directions: From Hwy. 68 between Monterey and Salinas, take the Portola Dr. exit. If you are coming from Monterey, turn right onto the park entrance road. If you are coming from Salinas, turn right, go under the highway, and then go straight into the park. At 0.1 mile there are an entrance kiosk and a self-registration station. Continue 0.5 mile past the kiosk to a road signed for the SYCAMORE GROUP AREA. Turn right, and then immediately left into a large parking area, signed for the QUAIL MEADOW GROUP AREA.

Facilities: Rest rooms, water, phone at Sycamore parking area, picnic tables, fire grates, softball fields, playgrounds, horseshoe pits, volleyball courts.

Trailhead: On the west side of the parking area, near its north end.

Immediately after leaving the parking area on the Ollason Trail, here a single track for hikers only, you cross a lovely creek on a wood bridge, and then merge with a trail joining sharply from the right. You veer left and walk parallel to the creek, with a hillside rising steeply on your right. Shade-providing coast live oaks are joined here by eucalyptus, California buckeye, and shrubs such as toyon, poison oak, and California sagebrush. Strewn beside the gently rising trail are colorful Chinesehouses,

California buttercups, Johnny jump-ups, shooting stars, and bluedicks. Early in the morning you may be serenaded by bird song, including the "Chi-ca-go" call of the California quail.

The route takes you generally south, past several trails that depart left across the creek. At one point, the trail runs through an open, grassy field that in spring may be carpeted with flowering lupine. Other wildflowers to look for include fiddleneck, with tiny yellow blossoms, and fiesta flower, which has dark blue, bowl-shaped blossoms. Soon a trail joins sharply from the left, and just ahead rises an old-fashioned metal windmill, a remnant of farming days. A set of steps helps you climb down to the creek, which is in a narrow ravine, left. You cross it on a wooden bridge, and then climb on tight switchbacks, aided by more steps. Just

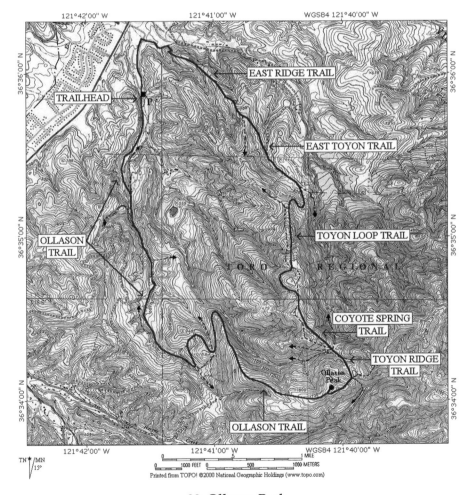

29. Ollason Peak

before the 1-mile point, you merge with a dirt road coming sharply from the left.

Now on a gentle uphill grade, you pass a metal gate and an unsigned junction with the Meyers Trail. In the area ahead, cows may be grazing. The creek is channeled back and forth under the road through culverts before ending up on your right. Deep purple larkspur and baby blue-eyes are among the springtime adornments you may encounter as the trail emerges in full sun. A beautiful oak savanna rises on your left, and from it you may hear the scolding chatter of western scrub-jays. Red-tailed hawks circling high above may add their piercing cries to the avian concerto. A trail, signed NO BIKES, joins sharply from the left, and several unofficial trails cut downhill through a meadow, right. Soon you pass a small stream that flows left to right under the road through a culvert on its way to join the creek.

Flowering lupine is just one of many wildflowers to delight the eye in Toro County Park.

A connector trail, left, leads to the Gilson Gap Trail, which equestrians must use on their return to the equestrian staging area near the park entrance. Behind you to the north is a high, rocky knob called Devil's Throne. Ignoring the unofficial trails, you continue on the road, passing a vast meadow that in spring is dotted with red maids, pansies, and suncups. The next junction is with the other end of the Meyers Trail (signed MEYERS LOOP), right, and now you walk through shady groves of coast live oak. Soon, at about the 2-mile point, the creek begins another series of passes under the road, and you begin a moderate ascent which leads to a T-junction (shown incorrectly on the park map as a four-way junction.)

Here the Ranch Trail goes right, but you stay on the Ollason Trail as it turns left and, after several hundred feet, begins a moderate climb through a scenic oak savanna. From this elevated perch, you have views north into the valley where the Ollason Trail began. One of the most common chaparral plants, chamise, thrives here on exposed slopes, along with bush monkeyflower. Now the route, still a dirt road, curves right and comes to a junction, left, with the Gilson Gap Trail, signed GILSON LOOP. Climbing moderately, the road swings left and rises across a hillside covered with an amazing profusion of bush lupine. Views from here take in the Monterey Bay coastline, often fog-shrouded, the agricultural lands of the Salinas Valley, and the Santa Cruz Mountains.

Angling sharply right, the road climbs just below the crest of a rounded, grassy ridge, with a steep drop down to a wooded canyon, left. In spring, the wildflower displays in Monterey County are superb, and here you may find blue-eyed grass, tiny blue-and-white lupine, and footsteps of spring, a curious, yellow-flowering plant whose leaves look like a flattened circle of lettuce. After a relentless ascent, the grade eases, and from the crest of a ridge you can now look south toward Carmel Valley, Tularcitos Ridge, and the Santa Lucia Range. In the distance to the northeast, the triangular summit of Fremont Peak rises through a gap in a nearby ridge. The open, treeless slopes up here are good places to look for songbirds such as western bluebirds and western meadowlarks.

Just past the 4-mile point, you reach a fork marked by a trail post. Here, the Ollason Trail, a dirt road, continues to the top of Ollason Peak, and the Ollason Loop, a single track closed to bikes (and not shown on the park map), veers right. Continuing straight, you reach the 1,800-foot-high summit after a few hundred yards. Fine views in all directions make this a rewarding place to stop for a while, besides the need to catch your breath. Especially impressive are the rugged, chaparral-clad peaks to the east. When you are ready to continue, retrace your steps to the previous junction, and then turn sharply left onto the Ollason Loop, following it around the south side of Ollason Peak. Soon you descend gently to a confusing junction marked by two trail posts.

To your left is Ollason Peak's very steep east face, on which the Ollason Trail cuts an eroded swath. To your right is a faint trail signed

SIMAS PEAK TRAIL and shown on the park map as the Black Mountain Trail. Ahead is the Toyon Ridge Trail, a faint, descending dirt road. There are also an unofficial trail veering left and an unimproved trail, shown on the park map as the Harper Canyon Trail, joining sharply from the right. Fortunately, all you need do is to continue straight and begin walking downhill on the Toyon Ridge Trail, heading northwest. Soon you come to a very eroded area where the road, for several hundred yards, has disappeared into a ravine. Unofficial trails across a hillside, right, allow you to bypass this area.

Descending moderately through a forest of coast live oak, you have a creek on your right, and some possibly muddy areas, trampled by cows, ahead. Now the creek is on your left, and, at about the 5-mile point, you reach another confusing junction, again marked by two trail posts, and shown incorrectly on the park map. To your right is the Marks Canyon Trail, unimproved, and to your left are two more unimproved trails—the Redtail Canyon Trail (Red Tail on the park map), closed to bikes, and the Whale Trail. Just a few feet ahead of this junction is a fork, marked by a trail post, where the Toyon Ridge Trail rises steeply up an eroded slope, and the Coyote Spring Trail takes a slightly gentler route to the right.

You bear right at the fork and, with a fissure in the ground to your left, begin a steep but short climb over rough terrain. Then, on a gentle grade that soon levels, you gain welcome shade from a grove of coast live oaks, before passing through an area of chaparral—chamise, redberry, silk-tassel—and other shrubs, including snowberry and fuchsia-flowered gooseberry. Your route, the Coyote Spring Trail, avoids the high ground, left, used by the Toyon Ridge Trail. At a trail post, left, you pass a short connector to the Toyon Ridge Trail. Following the Coyote Spring Trail as it curves right, you soon merge with the Toyon Ridge Trail, here a dirt road, coming sharply from the left.

A gentle descent over open ground brings you to a fork marked by a trail post. The single-track trail veering left is signed TOYON LOOP, and descends via **S**-bends. The unsigned road branching right, shown as the Toyon Ridge Trail on the park map, leads to a cattle gate. You stay left and follow the Toyon Loop Trail downhill through a corridor of chamise, manzanita, blue blossom, poison oak, and black sage. At the next junction, a fork, the Toyon Ridge Trail branches left, but you continue straight on the Toyon Loop Trail. About 30 feet ahead is another junction: here, the Toyon Ridge Trail, signed LOCKED GATE AHEAD, TAKE LOOP TRAIL, goes right, and your route, the Toyon Loop Trail, goes straight.

Alternating between a moderate and a gentle descent, the trail, rocky and eroded in places, stays between a ridgecrest, left, and a canyon, right. Soon you reach a junction marked by a trail post but not shown on the park map. Here, the Toyon Loop Trail veers left and rises to meet the nearby Toyon Ridge Trail. You continue straight, now on the East Toyon Trail, closed to bikes. After about 50 feet, the trail switchbacks right and begins to drop steeply through an area that, at least in late afternoon, is shaded from the sun's harsh glare. The steep downhill grade is broken by another switchback, this one left, and now you enjoy a gentle descent through beautiful green fields dotted with blue-eyed grass.

At about the 7-mile point, a trail post, right, marks a junction with a trail joining sharply from the right, signed here as the BLACK MOUNTAIN TRAIL but shown on the park map as the Marks Canyon Trail. Your route, now a level dirt road, continues straight but may be hard to follow because the road is overgrown with grass and weeds. A fence about 100 feet to your right helps you stay on course, and you soon resume a steep descent, aided by a couple of quick **S**-bends. An area that may be wet or even flooded indicates the presence of nearby Willow Spring. After unrelentingly regaining much of the elevation you recently lost, you finally reach a junction with the East Ridge Trail.

The Ollason Peak trail rises in elevation to afford distant views like this.

Here you turn right and follow a dirt road down the crest of a ridge bordered by chaparral. Sweeping views northwest take in the rolling hills and rugged canyons of Fort Ord Public Lands (Trips 6 and 7). The descent varies between gentle, moderate, and steep, but soon levels as you approach the parking and picnic areas near the park entrance. The trail ends at the equestrian staging area, which is adjacent to the Buckeye Group Area and the park office and maintenance center. When you reach pavement, turn right, go about 100 yards to a **T**-junction with another paved road, and turn left. After several hundred yards, you reach the park's main road. Here you cross the road, pass through an opening in a low fence, and then turn left onto a dirt path that runs parallel to the road. At about the 9-mile point, you pass the Sycamore Group Area. The path, now paved, turns right, and, after about 100 feet, swings left to cross the road leading to the Sycamore and Quail Meadow group areas. Your parking area is just several hundred feet ahead.

◆ Santa Cruz County ◆

◆ Big Basin Redwoods State Park ◆

Visitors to Big Basin enter a magical realm of coast redwoods (*Sequoia sempervirens*). These cone-bearing evergreens are found along the Pacific coast from central California to southernmost Oregon. Redwoods are the world's tallest trees, growing to more than 350 feet. The oldest known redwood lived for more than 2,000 years before it was cut. Redwoods depend on moisture gleaned from the atmosphere, or "fog drip," to survive. Instead of sending down deep taproots, redwoods anchor themselves with an intertwined system of shallow roots, most within the top 8 feet of soil. Seemingly invincible, these magnificent giants are thus susceptible to damage from wind, flooding, erosion, and soil compaction.

Before the mid-1800s, when logging began drastically to reduce their numbers, redwoods were found in extensive forests, growing together with other characteristic trees, shrubs, wildflowers, and ferns. Only remnants of such redwood forests survive today, and most are protected in parks such as Big Basin. These forests are called "old growth" or "ancient" because they have not been significantly altered by human intervention. Such forests are likely to contain trees at different points in their life cycles: mature trees, saplings sprouted around a fallen ancestor, standing dead trees, or "snags," and downed trees. All contribute to the health of the forest. Redwoods, with their thick, insulating bark, are well protected from the fires that sometimes roar through their midst.

The redwoods in Big Basin stand tall today thanks to the efforts of concerned citizens who banded together in 1900 to form the Sempervirens Club, an organization dedicated to the creation of a public redwood park. Big Basin was proposed as a site, and in 1902, following a successful lobbying effort in the halls of state government, California Redwood Park, encompassing 3,800 acres of mostly old-growth forest, was dedicated. In 1927, when the California legislature created the state-park system, the park was given its present name. Big Basin has the distinction of being California's oldest state park. In addition to the magnificent forests, the park hosts a wonderful array of plants and animals, including some rare and unusual species. One of these, the marbled murrelet, is a robin-sized sea bird that spends most daytime hours on the open ocean, diving for fish, but returning each night to its nest high in the redwoods.

Big Basin is located about 25 miles northwest of Santa Cruz via Hwy. 9 and Hwy. 236. The park's more than 18,000 acres contain about 80 miles of trails and dirt roads, covering terrain that ranges from easy to chal-

(previous page) During a difficult hike in Big Basin Redwoods State Park (Waterfall Loop, Trip 32), take a rest and watch Berry Creek Falls cascade into a pool.

lenging. The main hiking route through the park is the 38-mile Skyline-to-the-Sea Trail, which runs from Castle Rock State Park atop the Santa Cruz Mountains to Waddell Beach on the Pacific. There are eight different trail camps on the Skyline-to-the-Sea Trail, for which reservations are required. Camping is also available in campsites administered by the park and in tent cabins run by a private concessionaire. Interpretive programs are offered by park staff daily during summer and on some weekends during spring and fall.

From 1937 to 1942, workers from the Civilian Conservation Corps (CCC) and the Works Progress Administration (WPA) built trails, buildings, and other structures in the park. One of these buildings, shown on the park map as park headquarters, houses the park's ranger station and its visitor center. The visitor center, called the Sempervirens Room, provides books, maps, and displays of natural and human history related to the park, all presided over by helpful staff. In front of the visitor center is a cross-section from a redwood that sprouted in 554 AD. Marked on it are some historic events that took place during the tree's lifetime: the signing of the Magna Carta in 1215; Balboa's discovery of the Pacific in 1513; the Declaration of Independence in 1776; and the establishment, in 1902, of Big Basin as a park.

Across Hwy. 236 from park headquarters and just a short distance away are a gift shop, a snack bar, and a wonderful nature museum with exhibits about redwood forest ecology, geology, mammals, birds, and butterflies. Camping is permitted only in designated areas. Dogs are prohibited on all trails. Bicycles are permitted on roads but prohibited on trails. Horses are allowed on some trails and these are marked on the park map. Bus service to the park is seasonal and may be restricted to weekends only.

INFORMATION & TRAIL-CAMP RESERVATIONS: (831) 338-8860

CAMPING RESERVATIONS: (800) 444-7275

TENT-CABIN RESERVATIONS: (800) 874-8368

MOUNTAIN PARKS FOUNDATION: (831) 335-3174

SEMPERVIRENS FUND: (650) 968-4509

SANTA CRUZ METRO TRANSIT: (831) 425-8600

30   Big Basin Redwoods State Park
REDWOOD TRAIL

Length: 0.8 mile

Time: 1 hour or less

Rating: Easy

Regulations: CSP; fees for parking and camping; no bikes, no dogs, no horses.

Phone: (831) 338-8860

Web site: *www.bigbasin.org*

Highlights: This short and easy self-guiding nature trail is the perfect way to begin your visit to Big Basin. In a beautiful setting you will learn about the magnificent coast redwood trees this park was created to protect, and also about some of the other plants that make up a redwood forest. (**Boldface** numbers in the route description refer to numbered markers along the trail, which are keyed to "Redwood Trail Guide," a brochure available for a small fee from a trailside dispenser about 75 feet west of the trailhead.)

Directions: From the junction of Hwy. 9 and Hwy. 236 in Boulder Creek, take Hwy. 236 for 9.4 miles to the park headquarters, right, and an entrance road with a kiosk, left. Turn left, and then once past the kiosk, left again into a parking area.

Facilities: Campsites, tent cabins, rest rooms, water, phone, gift shop/snack bar, bike rentals, nature museum, and visitor center with maps, books, and helpful staff.

Trailhead: West side of parking area, near its entrance.

Walking west from the trailhead on a wide dirt trail bordered by a low redwood fence, you reach in about 75 feet a four-way junction. Here, a short trail to the Campfire Center goes right, and your loop, the Redwood Trail, goes both straight and left. The trail-guide dispenser is on a post to your right. You continue straight, and soon reach marker **1**, indicating a family circle of coast redwoods. These magnificent giants have two methods of propagation, seeding and cloning. The circle of redwoods here indicates the former presence of an ancestor tree, which sprouted new life from its root system. Just ahead is a five-way junction. Here, another trail to the Campfire Center goes sharply right, and also right is a trail to rest rooms. Straight ahead is a connector to the Skyline-to-the-Sea Trail, and left is your route, the Redwood Trail.

Turning left, you have Opal Creek, a major tributary in the Waddell Creek watershed, downhill and right, and a lovely meadow, left. Marker **2**, left, is for old redwoods that have fallen and decomposed, giving new life to other trees and shrubs. Marker **3**, right, indicates Opal Creek, which during floods brings nourishing silt to the valley floor. The creek's greenish color is caused by minerals and decaying plant matter. Soon the trail bends right, and you pass a huge fallen redwood. Although these majestic trees seem invincible, their shallow root systems makes them vulnerable to the elements, especially wind.

Marker **4**, left, is for tanbark oak, a tree commonly found in association with redwoods. Although not true oaks—these evergreens are more closely related to oaks of southeast Asia—tanbark oaks do produce acorns, which were an important food source for California's coastal Indians, including the Ohlone people who once lived here. Other redwood companions, such as evergreen huckleberry and western azalea, may be found nearby. Now the trail bends sharply left before curving right again to marker **5**, left. Redwood burls, the large lumps on a tree's trunk, are clusters of dormant buds that often assume fantastic and even grotesque shapes. Marker **6**, left, is for the Chimney Tree, a fire-hollowed

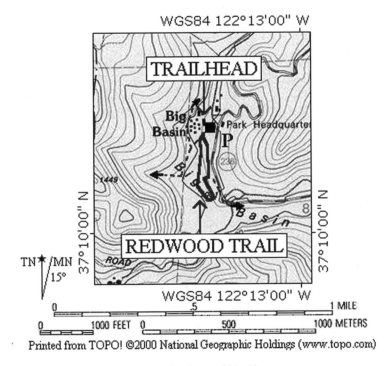

Printed from TOPO! ©2000 National Geographic Holdings (www.topo.com)

30. Redwood Trail

giant that is still alive. Step inside the open trunk, look up, and you can see the sky.

Marker **7**, right, is for another giant of the forest, Douglas-fir, a fast-growing evergreen commonly used for lumber. A water fountain, right, commemorates Andrew P. Hill (1853–1922), a photographer, painter, and conservationist who was instrumental in helping to protect Big Basin's redwoods. A rest bench, right, is a fine place to sit and view Mother of the Forest, at 329 feet the tallest tree in the park. Ahead is Father of the Forest, marker **8**, a tree 250 feet high and more than 66 feet around at its base. Beside the trail you may find California bayberry, also called wax myrtle, a shrub resembling western azalea but with fragrant, slightly serrated leaves and waxy berries.

Soon the route curves right and brings you to the 70-foot-circumferential base of Mother of the Forest, marker **9**. Just past the 0.5 mile point, a trail from Blooms Creek Campground joins sharply from the right. You continue straight, looking right to view a family circle of huge redwoods. Ahead is marker **10**, right, indicating a madrone tree that seems to be ailing. Now you come to the meadow you passed earlier on its opposite side; this is marker **11**. Formerly a wet bog, it was excavated in the 1940s and used as a swimming pool. Restored in 1952, the meadow is slowly recovering. Soon you reach the four-way junction where you began this loop. Here you turn right and retrace your steps to the parking area.

Coast redwoods towering above the forest floor impart both awe and serenity to hikers strolling beneath them in Big Basin Redwoods State Park.

31 Big Basin Redwoods State Park
SEMPERVIRENS FALLS

Length: 4 miles

Time: 2 to 3 hours

Rating: Moderate

Regulations: CSP; fees for parking and camping; no bikes, no dogs, no horses.

Phone: (831) 338-8860

Web site: *www.bigbasin.org*

Highlights: This wonderful loop uses the Sequoia and Skyline-to-the-Sea trails to explore the magnificent coast redwood forest near park headquarters. Among its many rewards are a visit to scenic Sempervirens Falls and a quiet stroll along Opal Creek.

Directions: Same as for "Redwood Trail" on p. 136.

Facilities: Campsites, tent cabins, rest rooms, water, phone, gift shop/snack bar, bike rentals, nature museum, and visitor center with maps, books, and helpful staff.

Trailhead: On the east side of Hwy. 236, at the south end of the parking area that is adjacent to park headquarters.

Amid giant coast redwoods that dwarf an understory of tanbark oak, coast live oak, evergreen huckleberry, and western azalea, you angle uphill and left on the Sequoia Trail, a wide dirt path. A fire-hollowed redwood, downhill and right, has three openings in its broad base that are large enough to walk through. The route levels and curves left, passing stands of tall and stately Douglas-fir, some specimens of which are almost as massive as Big Basin's famous redwoods. After crossing a seasonal creek on a plank bridge, you begin a rolling course that soon descends toward one of the park's paved campground roads. Here a connector to the Shadowbrook Trail goes right, across the road, but you continue straight.

Now on rocky and eroded ground, you continue over rolling terrain to the Wastahi Campground, at about the 1-mile point. Most of the shrubs beside the trail are evergreen huckleberry, but look here too for the long, slightly serrated, and fragrant leaves of California bayberry, or wax myrtle. In this densely wooded area, shafts of sunlight filtering through the trees make a dappled pattern on the ground. When you reach a parking area and rest rooms, a trail post with an arrow directs you onto pave-

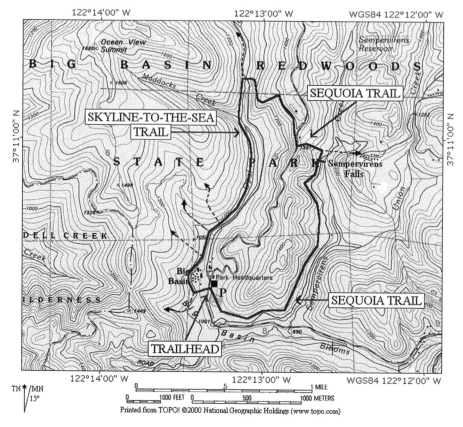

31. Sempervirens Falls

ment, skirting the parking area's west side. After about 100 feet, another sign—for campsites 98–102, the Sequoia Trail, and Sempervirens Falls— puts you back on the trail as it bears left at the north end of the parking area. (Water is available at campsite 99.)

Ahead is another huge redwood with an opening in its base big enough to walk through. Following the features of the landscape, the trail zigs and zags its way to the next junction, signed for Sempervirens Falls. Here you turn sharply right and descend to the paved campground road, which you cross. On the other side of the road, the trail, now fenced, turns sharply left and works its way down to an observation deck direct- ly across from Sempervirens Falls. A moss-covered rock cliff draped with ferns forms the backdrop for this lovely waterfall on Sempervirens Creek, which plunges into a deep pool. The stillness of the forest, combined with the effects of light and shade on the falling water, make this a place worth lingering.

When you are ready to continue, return to the previous junction and bear right. Soon the forest thins and you reach a clearing with a junction. Here the Shadowbrook Trail goes straight, but your route, the Sequoia Trail, turns left and meets a gently sloping hillside of exposed rock that soon steepens. You stay in the center of the rock slope, called Slippery Rock, navigating without the benefit of a trail or trail markers. It was at the base of this slope, on May 19, 1900, that the Sempervirens Club was formed to protect the redwoods. Note the dramatic change in terrain and vegetation: the forest has given way to a sunny zone of chaparral, with chamise, manzanita, and coffeeberry. At the top of the rock slope, the trail, marked by a trail post, resumes, and as you bear left you climb gently on a path that once was paved.

At about the 2-mile point, you come to Hwy. 236, which you carefully cross. There is water here, should you need to replenish your supply. On the other side of Hwy. 236, the Sequoia Trail angles right and follows a narrow ledge carved from a steep hillside that falls away left. Now descending past stands of massive redwoods, you enjoy the peace and quiet found in the depths of the forest. At a junction with a closed trail,

Singly or in clusters of colorful spring wildflowers, the Douglas iris flaunts its intricate beauty.

you turn sharply left, now beside Opal Creek, colored green by minerals and decaying plants. Beside the trail are trillium, redwood sorrel, wild rose, and sword fern, all members of the redwood forest community. A trail post, right, points you ahead to the Skyline-to-the-Sea Trail, and another post, left, signals North Escape Road.

About 30 feet past the second trail post, you reach North Escape Road. Here you turn right and cross Opal Creek on a wooden bridge. Once across the bridge, you leave the road by turning left onto the Skyline-to-the-Sea Trail. Now the creek is on your left and you are walking downstream. Soon you reach a circular clearing, once the site of a squatter's cabin on Opal Creek. Here the Maddock family lived and earned money stripping tanbark oak bark, used to tan cowhide, and making redwood products. The cabin, built in 1883, was demolished in the late 1930s when the crews from the Civilian Conservation Corps (CCC) built North Escape Road. At the clearing are two rest benches and a junction with a trail, left, to North Escape Road. There is also an unofficial trail, right.

On mostly level ground, you continue beside the creek, which here is bordered by ferns, elk clover, marsh grasses, and azalea. After walking through a large family circle of redwoods at about the 4-mile point, you come to a junction marked by a trail post. Here, the Creeping Forest Trail goes right, but you continue straight, passing a picnic table and fire grate, uphill and right. Soon you come to paved Gazos Creek Road, which you cross, keeping Opal Creek on your left. Just after crossing Redwood Creek, a tributary of Opal Creek, on a small wooden bridge, you have a junction with the Dool Trail, right, and a bridge across Opal Creek, left. Continuing straight, you cross Huckleberry Creek, another Opal Creek tributary. Now you reach a junction with a trail, left, to another bridge over Opal Creek. A sign here reads JAY TRAIL CAMPS.

You turn left and cross the long wooden bridge over Opal Creek. A five-way junction, where you continue straight, has the Redwood Trail, a loop, going right, and trails to rest rooms and the Campfire Center heading left. After several hundred feet, you pass a four-way junction with the other end of the Redwood Trail, right, and another trail to the Campfire Center, left. After about 75 feet you reach trail's end at the parking area.

32 Big Basin Redwoods State Park
WATERFALL LOOP

Length: 11 miles

Time: 5 to 6 hours

Rating: Difficult

Regulations: CSP; fees for parking and camping; no bikes, no dogs, no horses.

Phone: (831) 338-8860

Web site: *www.bigbasin.org*

Highlights: This rugged and adventurous loop uses the Skyline-to-the-Sea, Berry Creek Falls, Sunset, and Dool trails to explore the heartland of this wonderful state park, famous for its redwoods but also home to many other species of forest, streamside, and even chaparral plants. The park's stately forests are wonderful for birding, especially if you are adept at "birding by ear," or identifying species by their songs and calls. As for scenic rewards, the waterfalls on Berry Creek and its west tributary are sure to please, and you may even spy an ephemeral rainbow over one of them. You can make this an overnight trip by camping at Sunset Trail Camp, about the halfway point on the loop. Phone the park office, above, for reservations.

Directions: Same as for "Redwood Trail" on p. 136.

Facilities: Campsites, tent cabins, rest rooms, water, phone, gift shop/snack bar, bike rentals, nature museum, and visitor center with maps, books, and helpful staff.

Trailhead: West side of parking area, near its entrance.

You follow the Redwood Trail as it leaves the parking area amid towering coast redwoods, and continue straight through two junctions until you reach a bridge over Opal Creek. After crossing the bridge, you turn left at a signed **T**-junction onto the Skyline-to-the-Sea Trail. This trail, the main thoroughfare through the park, runs from Saratoga Gap, at the junction of Hwy. 9 and Hwy. 35, all the way to Waddell Beach on the Pacific coast.

Joining the massive redwoods here are other members of their forest community, including Douglas-fir, tanbark oak, coast live oak, western azalea, evergreen huckleberry, and sword fern. Acorn woodpeckers, one of the many species of birds that inhabit this park, are often seen and

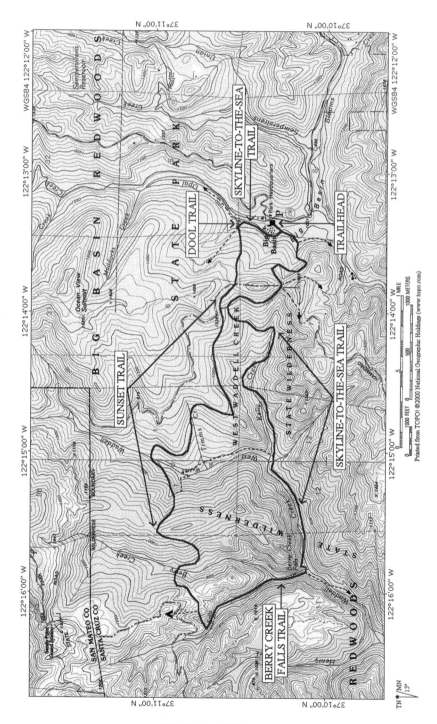

32. Waterfall Loop

heard here. You can identify an acorn woodpecker by its call, described in one book as "raucous laughing," and by the white wing-patches it flashes in flight. True to their name, acorn woodpeckers store their food supply, acorns, in holes gouged in trees and telephone poles.

At a junction with a connector to HIHN Hammond Road, left, you stay straight on the Skyline-to-the-Sea Trail, signed for BERRY CREEK FALLS. Beginning a gentle climb, you wander through an area of downed trees, some of them Douglas-fir, which are almost as massive as the redwoods. Surrounded by so many magnificent trees, you get a glimpse of what the Pacific coastal mountains were like before extensive logging began in the 19th Century. Seemingly indestructible, most of the old-growth redwoods are gone, and the ones that remain are clustered in a few state and federal parks.

The trail makes a curvy climb on a ledge cut in the side of a hill that falls away to the right. Along the way you may be scolded by a winter wren, a small, dark, short-tailed bird that lives in dense underbrush. Just past the 1-mile point, you reach a divide and a five-way junction. Running along the divide is Middle Ridge Road, a dirt fire-road. Across the road and angling left is the Howard King Trail to Mt. McAbee Overlook. Across the road and angling right is your route, the Skyline-to-the-Sea Trail.

Your trail is now perched on the edge of a steep hillside that drops left. An easy, gentle descent soon brings you to a junction with a connector to the Sunset Trail, right. After several hundred feet, you cross the first of several plank bridges over streams feeding Kelly Creek, whose waters eventually flow into the Pacific via West Waddell and Waddell creeks. When you descend to the creek itself, you enter a jungle-like area dense with ferns, including giant chain fern, and shrubs such as elk clover, hazelnut, and thimbleberry. At an unsigned junction just past a bridge, you continue straight, keeping Kelly Creek on your right and walking downstream. Nearby, there are many downed trees and also standing dead ones, called "snags." These may be riddled with woodpecker holes, and may also contain small cavities in which other forest birds build their nests.

Several trail posts mark the next junction, where a trail signed ALTERNATE TRAIL goes right. Again continuing straight, you follow the trail along a ledge above the creek, right. The sound of running water may be a lovely, welcome accompaniment here. Among the wildflowers that thrive in the dense shade and cool climate of a redwood forest are wild rose, hedge-nettle, trillium, red bead lily, also called clintonia, and redwood sorrel, all of which may be found beside the trail. Dropping to the level of the creek, beautiful with its shallow pools and riffles, you pass a junction with the Timms Creek Trail, right, just past the 3-mile point.

Now the waters from Kelly Creek merge with those of West Waddell Creek, which is also swelled by an unnamed tributary that you cross on a wooden bridge. Here the character of the creek changes—large boulders in it create many small waterfalls from the rushing water, making a dramatic scene. Adding to the visual beauty are stands of bigleaf maple, a tree often found beside creeks and rivers, whose leaves turn yellow and orange in the fall. A rolling course soon takes you to a rock promontory, right, where fine views of West Waddell Creek await—use caution near the promontory's edge!

Farther ahead on the trail, a set of dirt steps takes you down to two wooden bridges that span the creek's jumble of rocks and water. Overhanging maple branches frame this lovely creekside scene. Regaining the trail, you walk downstream with the creek on your left. A steep climb over rugged, rocky ground is rewarded by a view of Berry Creek Falls, the first waterfall you will encounter on this route. Soon you reach a rest bench where you may relax and savor the wonderful view. When you are ready to leave, turn sharply left and follow the trail down to Berry Creek, a tributary of West Waddell Creek.

Here the route curves right and crosses Berry Creek on a wood bridge, just upstream from where the two creeks merge. This area is rich with plant life, including the prehistoric-looking horsetail, and colt's-foot, a low-growing wildflower with large, circular, deeply lobed leaves. Once across Berry Creek, you come to a **T**-junction. Here the Skyline-to-the-Sea Trail swings left, but you turn right onto the Berry Creek Falls Trail and begin an upstream stroll. Now climbing, you soon reach an observation platform with a rest bench. From here you have a close-up view of Berry Creek Falls spilling over a rock face and cascading down to a pool. If you are lucky, a rainbow will frame the picturesque waterfall.

A steep climb, aided by switchbacks, brings you to the top of the falls, where another dramatic viewpoint awaits. Now on a rolling course beside Berry Creek, right, you pass the point where it and West Berry Creek merge. Just beyond, a bridge takes you across West Berry Creek, and you follow it upstream through a narrowing canyon whose floor is carpeted with a riot of ferns. The creek is on your left, and across it, around the 5-mile point, rises a steep rock cliff. Ahead is another waterfall, Silver Falls, spreading its lacy fingers over a rock face and tumbling into a pool. With the creek and its falls to your left, you begin a steep climb aided by steps, some cut in a rock cliff that presses in from your right. Assistance is also provided by cable strung between posts, left. Use caution: the cliff may be dripping with water and the steps may be wet.

A continuous series of falls and pools—white foaming water splashing over dark rock decorated with green moss and ferns—keeps distracting you from the task at hand, which is to climb safely. These falls are marked on the state-park map as Golden and Cascade, and climbing past them soon brings you to a trail post and junction with a closed trail. Here you turn sharply right onto the Sunset Trail, here unsigned, enjoying level ground and perhaps sunshine. After a little more than 100 yards, you reach a junction marked by a trail post. Here, a trail to Sunset Camp goes left, and the Sunset Trail continues straight. (Unless you are camping, there is no reason to visit Sunset Camp.)

Now in the realm of Douglas-fir, which here is joined by toyon, coffeeberry, and California nutmeg, you follow a rolling course that soon brings you to an open hillside that faces southeast. This sunny exposure favors such chaparral plants as chamise and manzanita. Also here are interior live oak and canyon live oak, growing side by side. The regenerative effects of fire are found, ahead, on a steep hillside. Despite a recent fire, the slope is covered with thick vegetation, out of which rise the charred trunks of trees. The trail drops moderately to a bridge over Berry Creek, which you cross. Turning away from the creek, you climb on a moderate grade, passing fire-scarred redwoods at about the 7-mile point.

In a dense forest, you work your way uphill to a divide between Berry and West Waddell creeks. Once across it, you descend steadily on a gentle grade to a junction. Here, the Timms Creek Trail goes right, but you stay on the Sunset Trail by following it sharply left. Your route crosses a steep hillside that falls away to the right, and then drops to a wet area that holds several small streams spanned by plank bridges. A moderate descent over rough ground brings you to West Waddell Creek, which you cross on a wooden bridge. The creek, spanned by many downed trees, flows through a lovely canyon colored in fall by bigleaf maple trees.

Climbing out of the canyon, you pass a rest bench, left, cross Timms Creek on a plank bridge, and then wind your way up to high ground north of Kelly Creek, around the 9-mile point. In a forest of mostly Douglas-fir, you traverse gently downhill across a southwest-facing hillside that may be brightened by the sun. This luminance doesn't last long, because soon you are amid giant redwoods that block out much of the light. After crossing more plank bridges, you begin a gentle climb that

In autumn, bigleaf maple trees display leaves of brilliant reds, yellows, and oranges.

brings you to a junction with a connector to the Skyline-to-the-Sea Trail, right.

Here you stay left on the Sunset Trail, cross a bridge over a gully, pass a rest bench, left, and soon arrive at Middle Ridge Road. Across it is your route, the continuation of the Sunset Trail, which descends via **S**-bends through a redwood forest with an understory of evergreen huckleberry. At a junction marked by a trail post, the Sunset Trail ends, and you turn right onto the Dool Trail, which descends parallel to Redwood Creek, which is left.

In an area with many downed trees, the Dool Trail ends at a junction with the Skyline-to-the-Sea Trail. Here you turn right and follow a level course through the redwoods, staying beside Opal Creek, which is left. Soon you pass a bridge over the creek, which you do not cross. Ahead is Huckleberry Creek, a tributary of Opal Creek, spanned by a wooden bridge. Once across it, you come to the junction where you began this loop. Here you turn left, cross Opal Creek on a bridge, and retrace your steps to the parking area.

33   Fall Creek State Park
LIME KILNS

Length:	3.2 miles
Time:	2 to 3 hours
Rating:	Moderate
Regulations:	CSP; no bikes, no dogs.
Phone:	(831) 335-4598 (Henry Cowell Redwoods State Park)
Web site:	*http://parks.ca.gov* (look under Henry Cowell Redwoods State Park).
Highlights:	Using the Bennett Creek, Fall Creek, South Fork, and Cape Horn trails, this enjoyable semi-loop helps you relive part of California's history—when in the late 19th and early 20th centuries this area was used to produce lime to make mortar for construction. The lime kilns are still standing, and there are interpretive displays that explain the entire lime-making process. Along the way, you pass through a lovely forest of coast redwood and Douglas-fir, never far from a creek's rushing waters. Fall is a perfect time to visit, because there are beautiful stands of bigleaf maple whose leaves turn vibrant shades of red, yellow, and orange.

Directions: From the junction of Hwy. 9 and Felton–Empire Rd. in Felton, take Felton–Empire Rd. east 0.6 mile to a partially hidden dirt parking area, right.

Facilities: None

Trailhead: North side of parking area.

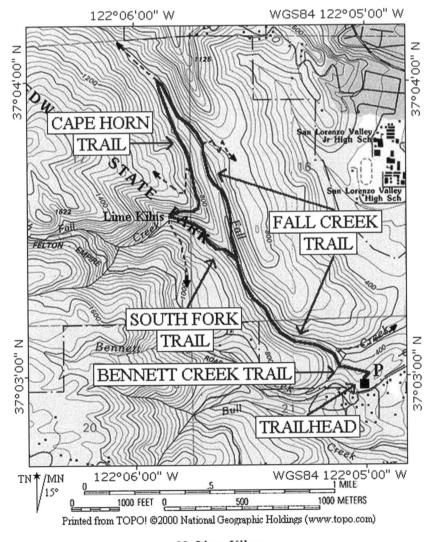

Printed from TOPO! ©2000 National Geographic Holdings (www.topo.com)

33. Lime Kilns

Heading north from the parking area, you follow the Bennett Creek Trail, a descending sandy track that in about 50 feet passes a large sign giving mileages to the park's other trails and points of interest. Here, you are in a lovely woodland of Douglas-fir, coast live oak, California bay, and tanbark oak, with an understory of manzanita, coffeeberry, hazelnut, and poison oak, which in fall adds color to the scene. After about 100 yards, you reach an information board, and then the trail swings left and descends via switchbacks toward Bennett Creek, a tributary of Fall Creek.

Now you enter the magic realm of coast redwoods and their companions, including blue elderberry, evergreen huckleberry, thimbleberry, redwood sorrel, wild ginger, and sword fern. With Fall Creek downhill and right, you follow the trail as it swings right and comes to Bennett Creek, which you cross on a plank bridge. Non-native plants brought here by early settlers, including English ivy, periwinkle, and forget-me-not, are found in various locations throughout the park and may be seen nearby.

At a junction beside Fall Creek, the Bennett Trail ends, and you join the Fall Creek Trail, which goes right and straight. Continuing straight, you follow Fall Creek upstream, now with bigleaf maple trees, colorful in fall, ranging overhead, competing with the tall redwoods for light. At an unsigned fork, one branch of the trail stays beside the creek, which is right, and the other takes a higher line to avoid possibly wet areas; the two branches soon rejoin. From a fallen bigleaf maple that spans the creek, four new trees have sprouted and are reaching skyward.

In a wet and jungle-like area, look beside the trail for wild rose, trillium, and various species of ferns. The trail runs along a ledge raised 10 or 15 feet above the creek. A trail post and then a sign mark an approaching junction, which is just on the other side of a bridge over South Fall Creek, another tributary of Fall Creek. Once across the bridge you are confronted by two trails: the Fall Creek Trail, right, and the South Fork Trail, left. You turn left and follow South Fall Creek upstream over rough ground littered with rocks and tree limbs. The creek is on your left, but ahead, in several places, the route crosses the creek, which you step across on logs or rocks.

With the creek again on your left, you climb gently uphill to an unsigned fork. Here you stay right and follow the trail through a little gully away from the creek. Soon, however, the route curves left and brings you to a junction, just past the 1-mile point, with the other branch of the fork. Now you turn right and enter the area that contains the lime kilns and remnants of other structures used in the processing of lime. Throughout are signs and interpretive displays explaining the history of the area and the process of quarrying limestone and converting it to lime.

From the 1870s until 1919, limestone from Blue Cliff, above South Fall Creek, was blasted from the hillside and sent downhill by a gravity tramway. The chunks of rock, originally part of the ocean floor, were burned in three wood-fired kilns to eliminate carbon dioxide and produce pure lime. After the lime cooled, it was loaded into barrels made in a nearby mill, hauled by horse-driven wagons to Felton, and sent via railway to Santa Cruz. Then the 250-pound barrels of lime went by ship to San Francisco for distribution throughout California to make mortar for construction.

You can wander over to the kilns themselves, made from giant blocks of granite with arch-shaped openings for limestone and wood. Each firing, tended round-the-clock by men on 12-hour shifts, took three to four days and consumed about 70 cords of redwood. Most of the workers, including quarrymen, kiln operators, loggers, mill operators, coopers, and teamsters, lived in cabins along the creek. The first company to operate here, IXL Lime Company, bought the land, built the kilns, and produced lime until 1896.

In 1900, after four years of disuse, the operation was bought by Henry Cowell, owner of the Cowell Lime and Cement Company, which operated it until 1919, when oil replaced wood as a more efficient fuel. Cowell became one of the wealthiest men in Santa Cruz County and the owner of much forest and ranch land. It was 1,600 acres of Cowell's land in nearby Felton that helped create Henry Cowell Redwoods State Park. In 1972, a foundation established by Cowell's son gave more than 2,000 acres of land to the state of California, which created the Fall Creek unit of Henry Cowell Redwoods State Park. The park is now officially called Fall Creek State Park. When you finish exploring the kiln area, continue walking upstream on the South Fork Trail.

Falls tumble exuberantly down the South Fork of Fall Creek.

Several hundred feet past the kiln area is a **T**-junction. To the left and going across South Fall Creek is the Kiln Trail, which passes an information board that explains the process of quarrying limestone. Your route, going right, is the Cape Horn Trail, an old wagon road that climbs on a gentle grade and makes a sweeping right-hand bend. The creek and kiln area are now downhill and right. Madrone and toyon rise beside the trail, joining Douglas-fir and second-growth redwoods encircling the massive stumps of their ancestors. As the trail curves left, "around the horn," you begin to hear the rushing waters of Fall Creek, which is downhill and right.

Soon you reach a junction with the Lost Empire Trail, climbing steeply left. You continue straight over easy ground to a fork, where you bear right and join the Fall Creek Trail, signed here as the NORTH FORK TRAIL. Now you turn right and begin walking downstream on a single-track trail beside Fall Creek, which is left. A log that has been split lengthwise and notched for traction helps you across the creek. Just ahead is a junction, left, with the S-Cape Trail. After crossing the creek a second time, again aided by split logs, you go uphill for a short distance and then resume walking downstream on level ground.

After several hundred yards, a third crossing puts you in a jungle-like area thick with red alder, elk clover, thimbleberry, and an amazing collection of ferns, including five-finger fern and giant chain fern. The trail now takes a rolling course over obstacles as it tries to stay close to the creek. A fourth crossing puts the creek on your left, and soon the route curves right and brings you to the junction with the South Fork Trail and the bridge over South Fall Creek. Here you turn left, cross the bridge, and retrace your steps to the parking area.

34 Fall Creek State Park
WEST RIDGE

Length:	8.3 miles
Time:	5 to 6 hours
Rating:	Difficult
Regulations:	CSP; no bikes, no dogs.
Phone:	(831) 335-4598 (Henry Cowell Redwoods State Park)
Web site:	*http://parks.ca.gov* (look under Henry Cowell Redwoods State Park).
Highlights:	This rugged and adventurous hike uses the Bennett Creek, Fall Creek, and South Fork trails to explore the Lime Kiln area on South Fork Creek, and then negotiates the park's steep west ridge using the Lost Empire and Big Ben trails. Along the way you pass the Big Ben Tree, a massive coast redwood, and also the Barrel Mill, where blocks of redwood were milled into staves and barrel heads, and then fashioned into barrels used to transport lime throughout California during the late 19th and early 20th centuries.
Directions:	Same as for "Lime Kilns" on p. 148.
Facilities:	None
Trailhead:	North side of parking area.

Follow the route description for "Lime Kilns" on pages 148–52 until you reach the junction of the Cape Horn and Lost Empire trails, at about the 1.7-mile point. Here you turn left on the Lost Empire Trail and climb a short, steep pitch that relents after a single switchback. Now a long, rising traverse on a gentle grade eventually gains the ridge separating Fall Creek and South Fall Creek, atop which you turn sharply right. After passing a closed trail, left, you resume climbing steeply, just below the ridgecrest, in a severely eroded gully.

The ascent, alternating between moderate and steep, continues over rough ground and soon brings you to a possibly wet and muddy area, where a stream flows across the trail. Rising tall beside the trail are coast redwoods and Douglas-firs, some scarred by fire. Also here are tanbark oaks and a few madrones. The sound of rushing water and the appearance of bigleaf maple trees indicate your approach to a tributary of Fall Creek called Barrel Mill Creek, which is downhill and right in a deep ravine.

Your route curves to the left and crosses a steep hillside littered with fallen logs. At about the 3-mile point, you reach Lost Camp, beside Barrel Mill Creek. Here you turn right and cross the creek on logs, then follow the trail as it veers right and begins to climb on a moderate grade. The trail is on a narrow ledge, and the creek, right, is at the bottom of a near-vertical drop. Soon the trail swings left, away from the creek, and then angles sharply left as it heads for the top of a ridge.

Once on top, the route turns right, and you follow the ridgecrest as it stair-steps uphill, alternating between almost-level and moderate grades. The forest canopy up here is less dense, allowing bright sunlight to filter through the trees and illuminate your surroundings. At a **Y**-junction marked by a trail post, you come to the Big Ben Tree, a redwood about 30

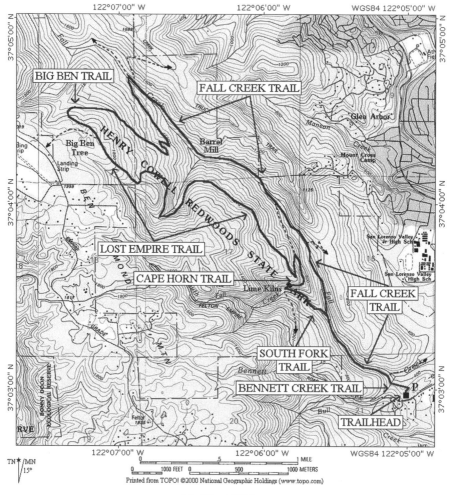

34. West Ridge

Sit for a moment and enjoy the light filtering through the forest in Fall Creek State Park.

feet in circumference and fire-hollowed on one side. Here the Lost Empire Trail veers left, but you bear right onto the Big Ben Trail, a descending track with a grade varying between gentle and moderate.

The trail bends right and makes a long traverse down a northeast-facing hillside. A switchback left steers you toward another possibly wet and muddy area, and once past it you descend via more switchbacks (not shown on the park map) toward Fall Creek. A plank bridge takes you over a tributary stream, and then you cross Fall Creek itself, using fallen logs. Once across, you climb an embankment and come to a trail post and a **T**-junction, at about the 5-mile point, with the Fall Creek Trail. (To the right, the Big Ben Trail overlaps the Fall Creek trail for about 0.1 mile before going its separate way.)

Here you turn right, and walk downstream beside Fall Creek, which is on your right. The massive redwoods and Douglas-firs here are accompanied by other members of a coastal forest, such as elk clover, wild ginger, redwood sorrel, and sword fern. Soon the Big Ben Trail departs left, and you come to an area where fallen trees force you to duck under or climb over them. If you choose the latter method, use caution, as the drop to the creek is severe.

The seclusion here is remarkable, and as you stand amid the tall trees, serenaded by the sound of splashing water, try to imagine what this area was like in the late 19th and early 20th centuries, when the limestone quarry on South Fall Creek was in its heyday. Ahead is the Barrel Mill area, where the old water-powered milling equipment used for manufacturing barrels still remains. You can examine the antique machinery by following a path that branches right from the trail. An information board explains the barrel-making process—how the staves and barrel heads were milled from redwood blocks, and then hauled to the cooperage near the lime kilns to be fashioned into barrels.

Leaving the Barrel Mill area, you work your way through an eroded stretch where more trees have collapsed across the trail. The creek's foaming waters are here and there interrupted by beautiful waterfalls flowing into crystal-clear pools. Thimbleberry, horsetail, and colt's-foot line the trail, above which arch the graceful limbs of bigleaf maple trees. Now you descend the trail toward the creek, which you cross on a split log that has been notched for traction. With the creek on your left, you continue a downstream stroll, soon reaching a fork and a junction with the Cape Horn Trail. Here you veer left, toward Fall Creek, and follow the route description for "Lime Kilns" on page 151 back to the parking area.

Barrels to ship lime were once produced in present-day Fall Creek State Park, where you can still see lime kilns and learn about the processing of limestone into lime.

◆ The Forest of Nisene Marks State Park ◆

Unlike other state parks in the Santa Cruz Mountains where old-growth forests have been preserved, the Forest of Nisene Marks State Park shows visitors an ecosystem recovering wonderfully from the intensive logging that occurred here during the late 19th and early 20th centuries. During the Spanish and Mexican periods, the ruggedness of the area kept it mostly pristine. But in 1883 the Loma Prieta Lumber Company, in combination with the Southern Pacific Railroad, began an era of exploitation that lasted 40 years and removed all but a few old-growth redwoods, a total of 140 million board feet of lumber.

Today, the results of this logging frenzy can be seen throughout the park in the form of huge redwood stumps, often surrounded by family circles of second-growth trees. In fact, the forest is well on its way to recovery, and there are only a few indications that the area once contained Santa Cruz County's largest sawmill, as well as a thriving town, Loma Prieta, complete with a railroad station, a post office, a saloon, a company store, and houses for company directors and employees.

The park honors Nisene Marks, the matriarch of a Salinas Valley farming family. In the 1950s, the Marks family purchased approximately 9,000 acres of lumber-company holdings and adjacent land. In 1963, with help from The Nature Conservancy, the Marks children donated the land to the state of California in memory of their mother. New properties have since been added, bringing the park's size to slightly more than 10,000 acres. The landscape is rugged, and the park's convoluted canyons and ridges are evidence of seismic activity along the San Andreas fault, which runs just north of the park, and along lesser faults that run through it.

The main route through the park is Aptos Creek Fire Road, open to hikers and bicyclists. A 40-mile network of hiking trails, some easy, some challenging, follow canyons or climb to ridgetops. Some of the trails follow old railroad beds. You may see ties poking up from the ground. Aptos and Hinckley creeks, the park's two watersheds, originate high atop Santa Rosalia Ridge, and they, with their tributaries, form lovely riparian corridors that complement the park's other terrain—redwood canyons, hillsides of mixed evergreen forest, and open chaparral slopes.

Although the land is protected from human alteration, Mother Nature is under no such restriction. Floods during the 1980s washed away trails and trestles, and in 1989, the Loma Prieta earthquake, centered in the park and about 12 miles beneath the earth's surface, further altered some of the landscape, although there are no dramatic, visible signs at the epicenter itself.

The park is open from dawn to dusk every day, but winter rains may make some roads and trails impassable. Dogs are allowed only along the park's entrance road south of the steel bridge, and must be on a leash no longer than six feet at all times. Horses are permitted only south of the steel bridge, which is 1.2 miles past the park's entrance kiosk. Bicycles are restricted to the fire roads and only those trails south of the steel bridge. South of the steel bridge, joggers, hikers, horseback riders, and bicycles all use the trail system. Please use courtesy and obey the trail restrictions.

There is a small day-use parking fee collected only when the entrance kiosk is staffed. Overnight camping at the West Ridge Trail Camp requires an advance reservation and payment of a small fee. There is a pit toilet at the trail campsite. Fires are prohibited, there is no water, and you must pack out your trash. Parking for overnight visitors is allowed at either the West Ridge trailhead or at George's Picnic Area, about 0.3 mile south of the trailhead, depending on the time of year.

INFORMATION AND CAMPING RESERVATIONS: (831) 763-7063 (Sunset State Beach entrance kiosk)

CALIFORNIA STATE PARKS, SANTA CRUZ DISTRICT, SOUTH SECTOR HEADQUARTERS: (831) 763-7064 (Sunset State Beach)

ADVOCATES FOR NISENE MARKS STATE PARK: (831) 688-9615

A spider web glistens in the Forest of Nisene Marks State Park.

35

The Forest of Nisene Marks State Park
APTOS CREEK

Length: 11 miles

Time: 5 to 6 hours

Rating: Difficult

Regulations: CSP; day-use parking fee when entrance kiosk is staffed; no bikes, no dogs, no horses.

Phone: (831) 763-7063

Web site: *http://parks.ca.gov*

Highlights: A long, athletic, and rewarding hike is provided by this semi-loop route, which uses Aptos Creek Fire Road and the Aptos Creek and Big Slide trails to explore beautiful Aptos Creek and rugged China Ridge. Along the way, you will experience the solitude of a coast redwood forest, and learn something of the history of this area—about how the solitude was broken by men and machines intent on harvesting as many trees as possible. Along the way, the trail passes the epicenter of the 1989 Loma Prieta earthquake, although no evidence of that event can be seen.

Directions: From Hwy. 1 in Aptos, take the State Park Dr. exit and go northeast to a traffic signal at Soquel Dr. Turn right, go 0.5 mile to Aptos Creek Rd., and turn left. At 0.5 mile there is a turnout, right, and an information board. At 0.8 mile there is an entrance kiosk, a self-registration station, and toilets. At 2 miles you cross a steel bridge, and at 3 miles you come to the parking area for the Porter Family Picnic Area. Use caution when driving in the park, because the road is heavily used by hikers, joggers, and bicyclists.

Facilities: Toilet adjacent to parking area; picnic tables downhill beside Aptos Creek.

Trailhead: At the locked gate across Aptos Creek Rd., just north of the parking area.

The driveable part of Aptos Creek Road ends just beyond the parking area at a locked gate. From here, it changes its name to Aptos Creek Fire Road and becomes the main thoroughfare for hikers, joggers, and bicyclists exploring this wonderful, densely wooded park. The road continues for 14.5 miles to a junction with Buzzard Lagoon Road high atop Santa Rosalia Ridge, gaining more than 2,000 feet on the way. For some of the distance, the road follows Aptos Creek, which collects water from a number of creeks in the park and then flows south to empty into Monterey Bay at Seacliff State Beach.

Walking through a gap beside the gate, you head north on Aptos Creek Fire Road through a forest of coast redwoods and their common companions, such as tanbark oak, coast live oak, coffeeberry, hazelnut, and thimbleberry. Although these redwoods are second growth, they are nevertheless impressive in stature, as befits the species that lays claim to being the world's tallest tree. After about 100 yards, Aptos Creek, which

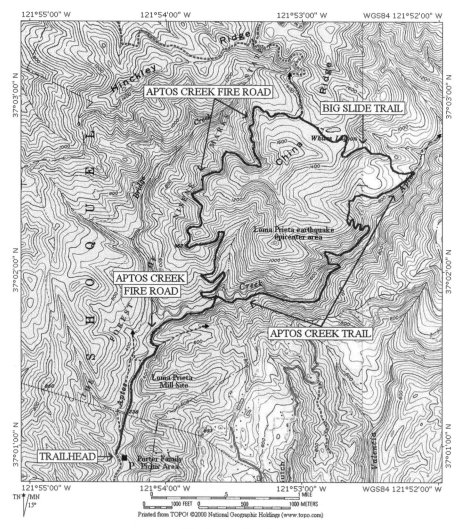

35. Aptos Creek

was hidden behind an embankment, is revealed on your right, perhaps illuminated by shafts of sunlight filtering through foliage.

Passing a junction, left, with Loma Prieta Grade, a dirt track that follows an old railway bed, you descend to the creek and cross it on a wooden bridge. The creek is now on your left, and once again it is hidden by the terrain and a thick screen of trees and shrubs, among them red alder and bigleaf maple, whose leaves turn gorgeous colors in autumn. Soon you reach a clearing, right, crossed by a dirt road. A sign here describes a forest-restoration project designed to remove non-native species such as acacia, French broom, pampas grass, and English ivy, all of which are considered invasive pests.

To your left, beside Aptos Creek, is the Loma Prieta Mill Site, with a rest bench and an interpretive display with photographs and a description of the sawmill constructed here in the 1880s. Logging activities took place from 1883 to 1923, and the mill was destroyed in 1942 by a suspicious fire. Little remains of the mill but a handful of fire-scarred timbers. Continuing on, the road curves right and passes Mill Pond Trail, left. You follow a meandering course along Aptos Creek, walking beside a steep hillside that rises right. At about the 1-mile point, the road divides to circle a few redwood trees, and then passes Trout Gulch Trail, right.

Now the creek is just left of the road, about 30 feet downhill in a ravine overgrown with evergreen huckleberry, elk clover, and giant chain fern. After crossing the creek on a metal bridge with wood planks, you climb on a gentle grade to a rest bench and a junction with the Aptos Creek Trail, where you turn right. Descending the single-track trail, you soon reach lovely Aptos Creek, which here flows through a narrow, high-walled canyon shaded by tall redwoods and Douglas-firs. Finding your way across the creek on rocks, you follow the trail as it veers right, heading uphill and away from the creek via several switchbacks.

Leveling and then bending right, the trail heads through a narrow, jungle-like ravine choked with snowberry, wild rose, honeysuckle, and poison oak. Now beside the creek again, you cross it on rocks or fallen logs. Once across, you turn left, walk briefly downstream, and then climb a narrow track etched in the hillside. The trail switchbacks to the right to find level ground above the creek, which is on your right. Soon you come to a sign marking the epicenter of the 1989 Loma Prieta earthquake, although the nearby terrain reveals no visible evidence of the massive jolt that destroyed lives and property in the Monterey Bay and San Francisco Bay areas.

Now the route climbs moderately via switchbacks and then finds a rolling course high above the creek, which is hidden from view. In the thick duff of redwood twigs and needles beside the trail, look for starflower and colt's-foot, two low-growing forest plants that hold their flowers aloft on single stems. At about the 3-mile point, the route drops briefly into a narrow ravine to cross a tributary of Aptos Creek, flowing from left to right. When you reach the crossing, which is aided by a fallen tree, look upstream to view several small waterfalls—narrow bands of water cascading over rock and perhaps glinting in the sun.

After winding into and out of several more ravines, the trail turns away from Aptos Creek and switchbacks up a steep hillside over rough and eroded ground. An overlook, right, gives you a dramatic view of exposed, chalky cliffs looming high above Aptos Creek. Now losing some hard-won elevation, you reach a flat, marshy area thick with elk clover and giant chain fern. Ahead and to your left is a pond covered with a green mat of algae. The trail here is indistinct, but you bear

The five-finger fern, this one in the Forest of Nisene Marks State Park, seems aptly named.

northeast, keeping the pond on your left, and begin a steep ascent that soon eases. Continuing northeast on a rolling course, you reach in about 0.5 mile a junction with the Big Slide Trail, left, at about the 4.5-mile point.

Here you turn left and climb gently amid huge redwood stumps and their associated family circles of second-growth trees. Joining the towering redwoods here and competing for light are tanbark oaks, whose bark was used in the tanning industry and whose acorns were an important food source for Native Americans. Unlike true oaks (genus *Quercus*), tanbark oaks have bristly acorn caps and belong in a different genus (*Lithocarpus*), although both are members of the beech family. The climb grade alternates between level, gentle, and moderate as you ascend China Ridge, the divide between Aptos and Bridge creeks.

Now a rolling course brings you to a **T**-junction with Whites Lagoon Road. Whites Lagoon, about 0.2 mile to your right, is a sag-pond, a body of water found in depressions caused by subsidence. Sag-ponds are associated with active earthquake areas, and the water that fills them comes from springs upwelling along fault zones, or, as is the case with Whites Lagoon, from winter rains. Surrounded by cattails and other freshwater marsh plants, the pond is a haven for wildlife. If you want to visit the pond, turn right at the junction; otherwise, turn left and follow the road uphill on a gentle grade. At an unsigned junction, a road merges sharply from the right, and now you begin to descend toward Aptos Creek Fire Road.

At about the 7-mile point you reach a **T**-junction with Aptos Creek Fire Road, where you turn left and continue to descend. Where the roadside embankment has eroded, you can see the typical root system that supports a coast redwood forest. Instead of growing a single taproot, each redwood sends out shallow but widespread roots that interlock and provide mutual support. Redwood roots are usually within the top 8 feet of soil. Besides redwoods in shadier drainages, you may find pockets of chaparral plants such as manzanita, toyon, yerba santa, and bush monkeyflower on sun-warmed hillsides.

Just below the 1,000-foot elevation line is a sign on the right that reads TOP OF INCLINE. This refers to the upper terminus of a narrow-gauge railway that ran between here and Aptos Creek, some 650 feet below. Built by the Molino Timber Company, the railway operated from 1910 to 1918 and was used to haul wood split from giant redwood logs. At about the 9-mile point, the road begins a series of swooping **S**-bends to quickly lose elevation. After descending more than 500 feet in a mile, you arrive at the junction with the Aptos Creek Trail where you began this loop. Now simply retrace your steps to the parking area.

36 The Forest of Nisene Marks State Park
WEST RIDGE

Length:	8 miles
Time:	4 to 5 hours
Rating:	Difficult
Regulations:	CSP; day-use parking fee when entrance kiosk is staffed; no bikes, no dogs, no horses.
Phone:	(831) 763-7063
Web site:	*http://parks.ca.gov*
Highlights:	On this adventurous loop in a former logging area, you climb the West Ridge Trail through a rejuvenated forest of coast redwood and Douglas-fir, and then descend via the Ridge Connection, Big Stump Gap Trail, and Loma Prieta Grade to Aptos Creek Fire Road and the Porter Family Picnic Area. From there the route follows Aptos Creek Rd. back to the trailhead. Along the way you pass Hoffman's Historic Site, where you will see remnants of a logging camp, and the Porter House Site, where historical photographs are on display.
Directions:	Same as for "Aptos Creek" on p. 159, but when you reach the steel bridge at 2 miles, go only another 0.3 mile to the trail-camp parking area, left. If that small parking area is

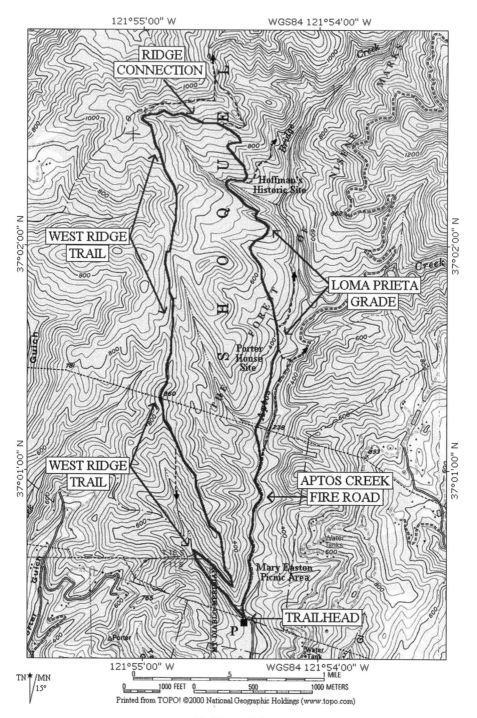

36. West Ridge

> full, continue another 0.2 mile to the Mary Easton Picnic
> Area, which has several parking areas.

Facilities: None

Trailhead: Just uphill from the trail-camp parking area, on the west
                  side of Aptos Creek Rd.

Leaving Aptos Creek Road, which is shared by motorists, hikers, joggers, and bicyclists, you set off on the hikers-only West Ridge Trail, which climbs through a dense forest of coast redwood, Douglas-fir, bigleaf maple, coast live oak, tanbark oak, and red alder. From the trailhead to the West Ridge Trail Camp atop Hinckley Ridge, the trail gains about 1,000 feet in 6 miles. Beside the single-track trail grow common members of the redwood forest community, including thimbleberry, coffeeberry, hazelnut, trillium, redwood sorrel, and sword fern. A deep ravine, left, holds a tributary of Aptos Creek, and soon you cross it on a wooden bridge.

Although the redwoods in this area were heavily logged in the late 19th and early 20th centuries, the second-growth trees that replaced their ancestors—many in family circles gathered around huge stumps—are impressive in their own right, inspiring a sense of awe and wonder. After following the tributary for a short distance, a trail post with an arrow pointing right directs you to cross it, which you do on rocks. Now the trail swings right and climbs away from the tributary into an area where the trees are thinner and more light reaches the ground. Here you may find madrone, manzanita, toyon, gooseberry, and snowberry.

The trail bends left and finds the northward course it will hold for the next 3 miles or so as it climbs a ridgecrest. In fall, poison oak adorns the hillsides with colorful hues. At about the 1-mile point, the trail becomes steep and eroded, with many roots crossing your path. Soon, however, the grade moderates, and as you ascend, if you are lucky enough to have a sunny day, you may see the beautiful dappled effect of light filtering through foliage. Steller's jays and chestnut-backed chickadees are among the forest birds to look for here.

With the ridgeline slightly above and left, you merge with a dirt road coming sharply from the left. A trail post with an arrow keeps you on course heading north. Now the trail, a wide dirt path, climbs to a clearing crossed by powerlines. Once again on the ridgecrest, the trail begins to descend on a grade that alternates between gentle and moderate. When you reach level ground, look around at the giant redwoods towering overhead, some of them fire scarred, and at the massive stumps remaining from the logging activities. Nearby you may find some berry-producing plants of the redwood forest, including Oregon grape, honeysuckle, and Hooker's fairybell.

Somewhat below the ridgecrest, you traverse a hillside that slopes gently down to another tributary of Aptos Creek. Soon the hillside steepens until the trail is merely a narrow ledge. At a junction marked by a trail post, a trail joins sharply from the left, and here your route swings briefly right to negotiate the head of a draw. Back on course, you head north across a narrow divide between two redwood-filled canyons, and then, around the 3-mile point, begin a moderate climb over eroded ground. Now you arrive atop the ridge you have been flirting with for several miles, which divides Grover Gulch, the large valley on your left, from the Bridge Creek drainage on your right.

A trail post standing in a clearing marks a junction with the Ridge Connection, a single-track trail that departs right. Here you turn right and begin to descend on a gentle grade. The lovely ravine on your right holds a tributary of Bridge Creek. Soon you reach the end of the Ridge Connection and merge with the Big Stump Gap Trail, which joins from the left. Several switchbacks help you lose elevation as you wind downhill into the midst of a redwood forest. The trail is very eroded and crossed by roots, so use caution. Now you begin to see remains of old wooden structures, collapsed and slowly being covered by redwood duff—an example of the forest recycling its own products.

This is Hoffman's Historic Site, a logging camp that was active between 1918 and 1921. The buildings here included several bunkhouses, a cookhouse and mess hall, a warehouse, a blacksmith shop, and animal stables. Running through the camp was a railway line used for transporting logs to the mill. Mr. Hoffman was camp superintendent, and his wife nicknamed the place "Camp Comfort," whether in jest or earnest we do not know. Here you merge with the Loma Prieta Grade, a trail which follows much of the former railway bed. Some of the ties are still visible, but most lie buried beneath the ground.

Descending through the redwoods, you soon cross the tributary of Bridge Creek you followed earlier, and now find yourself on a very narrow track cut from a nearly vertical hillside that falls away to the left. Ferns and mosses give this area a rain-forest feel, especially where the trail wanders several times into narrow, picturesque ravines that hold seasonal streams. At about the 5-mile point, the Loma Prieta Grade descends on a southward course, following the curves of the landscape, to a junction with the Bridge Creek Trail, left.

Here you continue on the Loma Prieta Grade by angling slightly right, and then curving right into a ravine where a wooden bridge takes you across a seasonal stream. Across the bridge looms a giant fire-scarred redwood, whose partially exposed root system overhangs the embankment above the trail. From its massive stump sprout a fistful of trunks, making the entire tree look like a creature from a Walt Disney movie, about to become animated. Contrasting with this almost grotesque vision are the lacy, hand-shaped patterns formed by clusters of five-finger ferns.

A trail post, left, marks a junction with the Mill Pond Trail, and here you also find the Porter House Site, with a rest bench and an information board. Photographs from 1890 show a beautiful house in the logging town of Loma Prieta, established here in the mid-1880s. At its peak, the town had a population of about 300. The site is named for Warren Porter, secretary of the lumber company who lived here with his wife, Mary Easton, and his son John. Porter went on to become California's lieutenant governor in 1907. Today nothing remains of this human habitation except a few eucalyptus trees and tangles of periwinkle, a non-native plant with blue flowers that blooms year-round.

With Aptos Creek now on your left, you follow a level track that soon curves right and descends to cross one of the creek's tributaries on a long wooden bridge. On a rolling course, you pass an unsigned trail, right, and then descend to meet Aptos Creek Fire Road, where you bear right. This wide dirt road is shared by hikers, joggers, and bicyclists. After several hundred yards, you come to a metal gate and the Porter Family Picnic Area. Another 0.5 mile of level walking brings you to the Mary Easton Picnic Area, and about 0.2 mile beyond is the parking area for the West Ridge Trail.

◆ Henry Cowell Redwoods State Park ◆

Located along the San Lorenzo River about 6 miles north of Santa Cruz via Hwy. 9, this wonderful state park, though small, has a surprising variety of terrain. Most visitors come to enjoy the short nature trail that winds amid magnificent, pristine redwoods, many of which are more than 200 feet tall and hundreds of years old. But there are about 20 miles of other trails and fire roads waiting to take hikers, bicyclists, and equestrians through 1,750 acres of wooded canyons, lush meadows, and sunny, chaparral-covered hillsides. The park has a visitor center, a nature center with displays on natural and human history, a picnic area with fire grates, and a year-round campground with sites suitable for tents and RVs (although there are no hook-ups).

The park honors Henry Cowell, a famous figure in Santa Cruz history. Like many others who came to California during the gold rush, Cowell found his fortune not in mining but in helping others pursue their often elusive dreams of golden wealth. Cowell and his brother, both originally from Massachusetts, arrived in California in 1849 and began hauling supplies and equipment from the San Francisco Bay Area to the Sierra foothills. The Cowells prospered, and in 1865 Henry Cowell settled in Santa Cruz on land that later became the University of California campus. Cowell founded a lime and cement business and bought existing limestone quarries in the Santa Cruz Mountains. Within a few decades, Cowell had amassed great wealth and thousands of acres of land.

During the same time, a railway line was built from San Jose to Santa Cruz, and an 8-mile spur was added north to Felton. Soon, in addition to lumber and freight, the railway began bringing tourists to enjoy Santa Cruz's lovely beaches and magnificent forests. Visitors, including two U.S. presidents, flocked to the new Welch's Big Trees Resort, located in a pristine redwood grove near the railway. The Welch family in 1930 sold the 120-acre redwood grove to the county, which used it to create Santa Cruz County Big Trees Park. Surrounding the park was land owned by the Cowell family. In 1953, Cowell's son Samuel, his sole surviving heir, gifted more than 1,600 acres of land to the state of California, provided the county did likewise with its Big Trees park. This plan was approved, and the next year saw the dedication of Henry Cowell Redwoods State Park.

The park is open year-round from sunrise to sunset. Camping is permitted only in designated areas. Bicycles are allowed only on Pipeline Road, Rincon Fire Road, Ridge Fire Road, and Powder Mill Fire Road. Bicyclists under 18 must wear a helmet. Horses are not allowed on the following trails: Redwood Grove Trail, Meadow Trail, Ox Trail, and

Pipeline Road south of Rincon Fire Road. Dogs must be leashed at all times and kept in cars or tents at night. They may not be left unattended. Dogs are allowed in the picnic area, in the campground, and on Pipeline Road, Graham Hill Trail, and Meadow Trail. They are not allowed on any other trails or interior roads.

Roaring Camp & Big Trees Railroad, a tourist attraction, is just east of the day-use parking area. A brochure with information about the railroad, which has year-round sightseeing trips through the redwoods and seasonal service between Felton and Santa Cruz, is available at the park's entrance kiosk. Visitors who pay the park's entrance fee and park in the day-use parking area may also visit Roaring Camp.

RANGER STATION: (831) 335-4598

CAMPGROUND: (831) 438-2396

NATURE CENTER: (831) 335-7077

MOUNTAIN PARKS: FOUNDATION (831) 335-3174

ROARING CAMP & BIG TREES RAILROAD: (831) 335-4484

A cross section of a coast redwood, its rings signed with dates of contemporaneous historic events, puts human history in perspective. Henry Cowell Redwoods State Park.

37 Henry Cowell Redwoods State Park
REDWOOD GROVE

Length: 0.8 mile

Time: 1 hour or less

Rating: Easy

Regulations: CSP; entrance fee; no bikes, no dogs, no horses.

Phone: (831) 335-4598

Web site: *http://parks.ca.gov*

Highlights: This self-guiding loop through a magical redwood grove is the perfect way to begin an exploration of this wonderful state park, which has about 20 miles of varied trails, enough to keep an avid hiker happy for several days. The nature trail leads you past a 300-foot-tall redwood tree and a campsite used by John C. Frémont, a controversial figure in California history. (**Boldface** numbers in the route description refer to numbered markers along the trail, which are keyed to "Redwood Grove Nature Trail," a pamphlet available at the visitor center.)

Directions: From the junction of Hwy. 1 and River St./Hwy. 9 in Santa Cruz, take Hwy. 9 northwest 6 miles to the state park entrance, right. At 0.5 mile there is an entrance kiosk, and at 0.6 mile there is a large day-use parking area.

Facilities: Visitor center/gift shop and nature center with helpful staff; rest rooms, water, telephone; camping on east side of park off Graham Hill Rd.

Trailhead: Southwest corner of parking area.

From the southwest corner of the parking area, adjacent to the visitor center/gift shop, you walk on a paved path southeast about 75 feet to a four-way junction with a paved road. Across the road, you have on your left a cross-section of a giant coast redwood from Humboldt County, estimated to have been nearly 2,200 years old when it was felled in 1934. The rings of this cross-section, measuring about 9 feet across, have been marked to indicate important dates in world history, starting with the birth of Christ somewhere near the tree's center, and passing outward through Drake's landing in California (1579) and the Declaration of Independence (1776) to the establishment in 1902 of Big Basin Redwoods State Park.

About 50 feet past this awe-inspiring history lesson is a wonderful nature center, right, with displays about redwood forest ecology, including a diorama with stuffed animals—mammals, birds, and reptiles—and a butterfly collection. The center, open from 10 A.M. to 4 P.M. Memorial Day through Labor Day, and from 11 A.M. to 3 P.M. during the rest of the year, is definitely worth a visit. Just past the nature center is a junction where the Redwood Grove Trail, a loop, goes straight and left. Here you continue straight on a dirt path bordered on both sides by a low fence.

Just ahead is marker **1**, right, indicating the trees towering above you, old-growth coast redwoods. This species of tree, the world's tallest, grows only in a narrow band along the Pacific coast from central California to southern Oregon. Associated with redwoods are other plants you may see beside the trail, including California bay, tanbark oak, hazelnut, wild ginger, redwood sorrel, and sword fern. Trees that try to compete with redwoods often surpass the limit of their stability and topple over. Sometimes new trees sprout vertically from the trunks of fallen ones.

Redwood trees are red because they contain tannic acid, which, together with their thick bark, helps defend them against insects, fire, and disease, as indicated by Marker **2**, left. Marker **3**, also left, is for fire, an important component of redwood forest ecology. Most forest fires cannot burn through redwood bark, but if the fire is hot enough, it may hollow out part of the trunk, leaving an opening that is sometimes big enough to

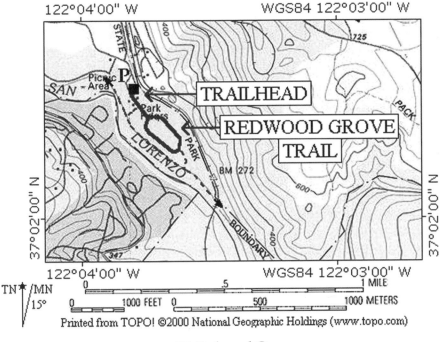

37. Redwood Grove

Almost unimaginably huge, coast redwoods awe and inspire mere human hikers.

stand in or even walk through. Soon the trail swings left, passing marker **4**, Douglas-fir, on the right. Massive in its own right, Douglas-fir is among the world's most important timber species, growing in many areas of the Western U.S. and Canada.

Marker **5**, right, is for circular groups of redwoods that cluster around the stumps of a fallen ancestors. Sprouting from buried roots, these groups are known commonly as family circles, fairy rings, or cathedral groups. A rest bench on the left allows you to sit and stare upwards at these giants, an amazing spectacle. Even more astonishing—and disturbing—however, is that logging over the past 150 years has destroyed most of the world's old-growth redwoods and that only a handful of parks protect those that remain.

Marker **6**, left, is for fallen trees that enrich the forest by providing homes for insects, which in turn are eaten by birds and small mammals. The decaying trees also supply the soil with nutrients. The park's tallest tree, nearly 300 feet high and 17 feet in diameter, is indicated by marker 7. This tree is so tall that its crown just begins at a height where other trees reach their apexes. Several benches are nearby, and the trail splits to circle the tree's massive base.

The trail now swings right to reach Marker **8** and the Fremont Tree, named for John C. Frémont, who camped here during his explorations of California in the 1840s. In a clearing by the Fremont Tree are benches carved from logs, a picnic table, and rest rooms. Nearby is a junction with a connector to the River Trail. After visiting the Fremont Tree, you walk back through the clearing with the rest rooms on your right, and then continue straight.

In about 100 yards, you come to marker **9**, for California bay and tanbark oak, two trees often associated with redwoods. On certain days, bay trees provide a rich aroma that permeates the forest. Marker **10**, left, is for some of the animal members of the redwood forest, including acorn woodpeckers, Steller's jays, deer, gray squirrels, and fox squirrels, a nonnative species. Redwood trees are often covered with odd-shaped growths called burls, as indicated by marker **11**, left. Burls are actually masses of dormant buds, that sprout new growth if the tree is damaged.

Passing several rest benches, you come to marker **12**, for redwood sorrel, a ground cover that thrives in cool, moist conditions. Marker **13** is for a group of at least 10 redwoods sprouting from a single base. Unlike other conifers, or cone-bearing trees, redwoods can reproduce either from seeds contained in their cones or from their roots. An albino redwood, with a few branches of white needles, is indicated by marker **14**, left.

As you finish your walk through this wonderful redwood grove, you may hear a train whistle, country and Western music, and even yodeling—all coming from Roaring Camp, a tourist attraction just east of the parking area. Now, with the nature center ahead, you reach pavement and the junction where you began this loop. Here you turn right and retrace your steps to the parking area.

38 Henry Cowell Redwoods State Park
RIVER AND RIDGE LOOP

Length: 4.5 miles

Time: 3 to 4 hours

Rating: Moderate

Regulations: CSP; entrance fee; no bikes, no dogs; equestrians can refer to the park map to create a similar loop that avoids trails closed to horses.

Phone: (831) 335-4598

Web site: *http://parks.ca.gov*

Highlights: Using Pipeline Road, Ridge Fire Road, and the Eagle Creek Trail, this wonderfully varied semi-loop leaves the redwood groves next to the San Lorenzo River and climbs to an observation deck surrounded by chaparral and ponderosa pines. Then you descend to the park's campground and complete the trek by enjoying a stroll along lovely Eagle Creek. (If you are staying in the campground, you can easily tailor this route to start and end there.)

Directions: Same as for "Redwood Grove" on p. 170.

Facilities: Visitor center/gift shop and nature center with helpful staff; rest rooms, water, telephone; camping on east side of park off Graham Hill Rd.

Trailhead: Southwest corner of parking area.

From the southwest corner of the parking area, adjacent to the visitor center/gift shop, follow a paved path southeast about 75 feet to a four-way junction with a paved road. Here you turn right and walk several hundred feet to a junction with Pipeline Road, left. This paved road runs alongside the San Lorenzo River, which is tranquil for much of the year but sometimes rages after winter storms. Between the river and the road is the River Trail, a dirt track used by equestrians. Pipeline Road is shared by hikers and bicyclists, and it is wise to stay alert, especially where your visibility may be obscured.

After about 0.3 mile, you pass a trail, left, that leads into the park's famous redwood grove and connects with the Redwood Grove Trail. Ahead is a trestle for tracks of the Santa Cruz, Big Trees & Pacific Railway, which offers seasonal service between Roaring Camp in Felton and Santa Cruz. The road descends to pass beneath the trestle, which also spans the San Lorenzo River. An information board, left, has a map of the park.

Beside the road are stands of coast redwood, coast live oak, tanbark oak, California bay, box elder, white alder, and hazelnut. Adding color in fall are bigleaf maples and tangles of poison oak.

The road climbs gently to a four-way junction with the Eagle Creek Trail, which you will use later on this route. Just past the junction, at about the 1-mile point, the road crosses a culvert holding Eagle Creek, a tributary of the San Lorenzo River. Now rising on a moderate grade, you soon pass a junction with Rincon Fire Road, a dirt road open to bikes and horses. (The park map adds the word "Fire" to all of the park's dirt roads, as in "Rincon Fire Road," but park signs omit this word.) As you gain elevation, there are fewer tall trees, and this allows more light to reach the forest floor, encouraging plants such as bracken, one of the types of fern that enjoys open, dry areas. A creek bed, right, holds a riot of jungle-like vegetation, including giant chain fern, a species commonly found near water.

Winding uphill and briefly becoming steep, the road finally levels at a four-way junction with Ridge Fire Road, where you turn left. Now on a sandy trail, you are soon climbing steeply over rough ground into a marvelous sunbaked garden of chaparral, where manzanita, chinquapin,

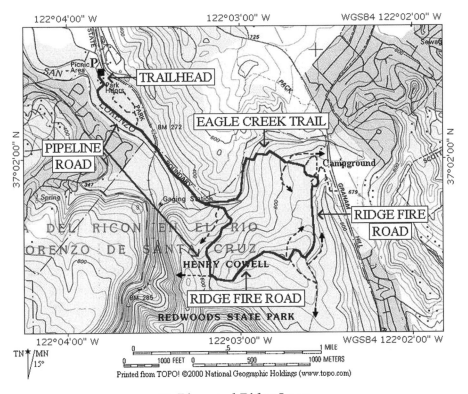

38. River and Ridge Loop

chamise, and yerba santa thrive. The redwoods for which this park is famous grow in the San Lorenzo River valley, but up here you find other wonderful trees, such as Douglas-fir, madrone, tanbark oak, interior live oak, and knobcone pine. In places where the sand is deep, the going is slow—it's like climbing a sand dune.

About 0.5 mile from Pipeline Road, you reach an observation deck with a picnic table and a water fountain. Surrounding the deck, and partially blocking the views from it, are another of the park's specialty trees, ponderosa pines. These tall trees, identified by their irregularly shaped plates of yellowish bark, are most commonly found in Western mountains between 4,000 and 8,000 feet, so seeing them this low and this close to the ocean is a real treat. After resting for a while, or perhaps enjoying a picnic, you continue east on Ridge Fire Road.

Just past the observation deck, one branch of the Pine Trail departs left toward the campground, and several hundred feet ahead, another branch of the Pine Trail goes right toward Powder Mill Fire Road. Now Ridge Fire Road makes a swooping descent to a **T**-junction, shown incorrectly on the park map. Here a connector to Powder Mill Fire Road goes right, but you turn left, still on Ridge Fire Road. The road curves right and descends on a gentle grade to the campground, where water and rest rooms are available.

When you reach a paved road in the campground, you turn right and follow it several hundred yards to a **T**-junction with another paved road, just past campsite 4. Here you turn right, and in about 100 feet come to another **T**-junction, again with a paved road, here signed for campsites 52–113. Now you turn left, and in about 150 feet reach a fork, where you bear left. Continuing straight, and ignoring a road on the right, you soon come to campsite 84, left, at about the 3-mile point. Just beyond the campsite is your route, the Eagle Creek Trail, left. The trail, a single track, passes through a gate and then, after several hundred feet, comes to a four-way junction with the Pine Trail.

Continuing straight on a sandy, dusty track, you pass through several areas of chaparral and then reach a spot where the trail has been rerouted abruptly to the left and then to the right. Now you have regained a dense redwood forest, cool and shady. After a moderate downhill, you are next to Eagle Creek, which is in a gully on your right. Turning sharply right, you cross the creek on a bridge, and then follow a rolling course that soon changes to a moderate descent. Along the way, look beside the trail for such redwood companions as trillium, starflower, sword fern, and horsetail. At a **T**-junction with Pipeline Road, turn right and retrace your steps to the parking area.

Natural Bridges State Beach
Nature Trail

Length: 1.2 miles

Time: 1 hour or less

Rating: Easy

Regulations: CSP; entrance fee; no bikes, no dogs, no horses.

Phone: (831) 423-4609

Web site: *http://parks.ca.gov*

Highlights: This easy and enjoyable loop uses the Monarch and Moore Creek trails to explore the Monarch Butterfly Nature Preserve, a grove of eucalyptus trees where thousands of monarch butterflies spend fall and winter. The route also visits a beach that offers tide pools and vantage points to view sea birds and shorebirds, migrating whales, seals, and sea lions. Bring binoculars to see the butterflies, birds, and other wildlife. The park is heavily used on weekends during fall and winter. The trail through the wetland bordering Moore Creek may be impassible in wet weather.

Visitor-center hours are 10 A.M. to 4 P.M. The center is open Friday through Monday from July through mid-October, and then daily from mid-October through February. From March through June, the center is open only on weekends and on days with especially low tides. (**Boldface** numbers in the route description refer to numbered markers along the trail, which are keyed to "Natural Bridges Nature Trail," a brochure available at the visitor center.)

Directions: From the junction of Hwy. 1 and River St./Hwy. 9 in Santa Cruz, take Hwy. 1 west 2.1 miles to a traffic signal at Swift St. and turn left. Go 0.3 mile, turn right onto Delaware St., and after 0.4 mile turn left onto Swanton Blvd. Go 0.3 mile to a **T**-junction with West Cliff Dr. Turn right into the state beach entrance where there are an entrance kiosk and a short-term parking area. Continue past the kiosk 0.3 mile to a visitor center and a large parking area.

Facilities: Visitor center with helpful staff, butterfly garden, picnic tables, fire grates, water, phone, rest rooms.

Trailhead: East side of visitor center.

A blue sign picturing a monarch butterfly marks the start of the Monarch Trail, your gateway to a magical grove of eucalyptus trees where each winter 10,000 to perhaps 150,000 of these orange-and-black migratory marvels gather to rest and escape extreme cold. In spring and summer, monarchs leave their resting places in California and Mexico and disperse throughout the Western U.S. and Canada, but the onset of autumn brings them back to frost-free areas. Unlike the case with birds, several generations of monarchs are born during northward migration, so the individuals that winter here do not return. Flying hundreds and perhaps several thousands of miles, and at altitudes that may reach 10,000 feet, monarchs are the only insects known to undertake such long round-trip migrations.

Adjacent to the sign is a garden of milkweed, the only type of plant eaten by monarch caterpillars. During northward migration, female monarch butterflies lay their eggs on milkweed plants, usually on the underside of the leaves. In 2 to 12 days, depending on temperature, the caterpillars hatch and begin to feed on the milkweed leaves, increasing in weight several thousandfold. After two to three weeks, the caterpillars form chrysalises, and 10 to 15 days later they emerge as monarch butterflies. These adults now resume the journey and the cycle begins again.

The butterfly garden is next to a paved road, the continuation of the park's entrance road. Across the road is a boardwalk, which you follow downhill through a forest of eucalyptus trees growing above tangles of

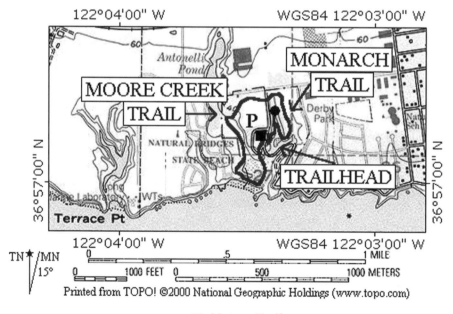

Printed from TOPO! ©2000 National Geographic Holdings (www.topo.com)

39. Nature Trail

poison oak and blackberry vines. Besides butterflies, this is a great spot to look for birds, especially during spring migration, when warblers and other songbirds flying south along the coast are often forced by storms or fog to seek shelter in wooded areas. A Steller's jay, one of the resident species here, may complain loudly at your intrusion into its territory.

Monarch butterflies cannot fly at air temperatures less than 55° F.

Soon the boardwalk swings sharply left, passes a duckweed-covered pond, and then comes to a junction with the Monarch Trail, a paved path on the right that changes to dirt after about 50 feet. You continue straight. A sign here reads MONARCH RESTING AREA. If you are visiting anytime from mid-October through February and the temperature is above 55°—monarchs cannot fly at lower temperatures—you may see a few dozen butterflies flitting about. If you have never visited a monarch resting area before, you may be tempted to say, "What's the big deal?"

Before doing so, use your binoculars to look up at the eucalyptus leaves and branches. What you probably mistook for leaves are in fact thousands upon thousands of monarchs with their wings folded, a stunning sight! An observation platform at the end of the boardwalk is just ahead. When you have finished enjoying one of nature's great spectacles, return to the junction with the Monarch Trail, now on your left. You leave the boardwalk and join the Monarch Trail, which, after about 50 feet of pavement, changes to dirt. Marker **1**, left, is for two species of eucalyptus found here, red gum and blue gum.

After several hundred feet the trail veers left and begins to climb on a gentle grade, but soon it descends to the cattail-fringed pond, where marker **2**, for the pond's residents and neighbors—mallards, kingfishers, American coots, Pacific treefrogs, and red-legged frogs—stands on the shore. Now turning away from the pond, you climb over rocky ground and follow the trail as it curves left and then finds a level course beside a weedy field punctuated with Monterey pines and dotted with clumps of coyote brush. The eucalyptus forest is left, and Marker **3**, indicates non-native plants that arrived with the Spanish missionaries and their cattle. Among these are wild oats, wild radish, and mustard, is on your right. At a junction with an unofficial trail, right, you find marker **4**, for coyote brush and poison hemlock.

The margin here between forest and field is a great place to look for birds—the trees may hold warblers, chickadees, and bushtits, and the brushy areas may conceal flocks of sparrows. Passing marker **5**, right, for Monterey pine, a species threatened by a disease called pine pitch canker, the route swings left and descends into a thicket of willows, berry vines, English ivy, and poison oak. Now the route crosses a plank bridge over a seasonal stream, beside which grows a stand of curiously twisted eucalyptus trees. Marker **6**, right, is for Monterey cypress. The Monarch Trail soon ends at a junction with a paved road, the continuation of the park entrance road.

Across the road is your route, the Moore Creek Trail, and after about 75 feet, you come to marker **7**, left. Here was the site of a proposed luxury hotel, the brainchild of Fred W. Swanton, who built the Santa Cruz casino and boardwalk. The hotel never materialized, and in 1933 the state bought the land and created the state beach we enjoy today. A grove of Monterey cypress trees is on your right, and an open, brushy field is left. Also left is marker **8**, for the natural bridge that gives this state park its name. Prior to the early 1900s, there were three bridges at the beach, but erosion and storms took their toll on the soft Santa Cruz mudstone, and by 1980 only one was left. With a grove of eucalyptus on your right, the trail turns left and passes a rest bench, right. Now you can see the shore and the beautiful mudstone bridge, a roosting place for brown pelicans, cormorants, and other sea birds. Among the land birds to look for here are northern mockingbirds, black phoebes, and mourning doves.

Marker **9**, left, is for Moore Creek, which originates in the Santa Cruz Mountains and carries runoff from there and from U.C. Santa Cruz. Increasing flows over the years have deepened the creek channel and altered the landscape. Moore Creek is on your right, and the wetlands bordering it are thick with cattails, sedges, rushes, and spring wildflowers. Now descending into a thicket of willows, coyote brush, and blackberry vines, you reach a boardwalk and marker **10**, right, indicating the transition from coastal scrub to dune and salt-marsh plants. Marker **11**, for iceplant and pickleweed, is on your left. Now the boardwalk alternates with stretches of dirt trail through a flat expanse of low-lying marsh. Soon you cross Moore Creek on a plank bridge, and as you near the beach, you pass mats of iceplant, a non-native formerly planted along California's beaches to control erosion but now considered an invasive pest. Iceplant is being removed from the dunes at the park entrance to restore them to a more natural state.

At about the 1-mile point, you come to a lagoon behind the wide, sandy beach. Swinging to the right, the trail finds its way along a ledge beside the lagoon. Across the wide beach to your left is a path leading uphill through the picnic area to the parking area and the visitor center. On the right are low rock terraces you can climb to get a better view of the shore and of Monterey Bay. Tide pools, accessible only during extreme low tides, are located farther to your right as you face the bay.

Among the shorebirds you may see are black-bellied plovers, willets, marbled godwits, black oystercatchers, black turnstones, and sanderlings. Common gull species here include western gull, which is large and has a dark mantle; ring-billed gull, which is medium sized and has a black ring around its bill; and Heermann's gull, which is all gray and has a reddish bill. When it is time to return, simply walk northeast across the beach and climb the path through the picnic area to the parking area.

Stop in at Natural Bridges visitor center, where a knowledgeable staff will provide information and a Nature Trail guide.

Pogonip
LOOKOUT LOOP

Length: 3 miles

Time: 1 to 2 hours

Rating: Moderate

Regulations: City of Santa Cruz Parks & Recreation; no bikes, no dogs, no horses.

Phone: (831) 420-6207, ranger station; (831) 420-5270, park administration.

Web site: *www.santacruzparksandrec.com*

Highlights: This splendid semi-loop uses the Lookout, Spring, Brayshaw, and Pogonip Creek Nature trails, and paved Golf Club Dr., to explore a gem of a park located only a few minutes from downtown Santa Cruz. Despite its proximity to a bustling town and to busy Hwy. 1, Pogonip has much to offer, including lush redwood groves, open grasslands, secluded ravines, and wonderful views.

Directions: From the junction of Hwy. 1 and River St./Hwy. 9 in Santa Cruz, take River St. northeast 0.3 mile to Golf Club Dr. Turn left, go 0.1 mile, and park along Golf Club Dr. There is no legal parking west of the railroad overpass. Walk west along Golf Club Dr. to the trailhead.

Facilities: None

Trailhead: On Golf Club Dr. about 0.2 mile west of the railroad overpass.

This curiously named park—*pogonip* is a Native American word believed to mean "icy fog"—has an equally interesting history. In the 1930s and 1940s, polo enthusiasts from around the world gathered at the Pogonip Social and Polo Club, and before that, the park's grounds were the site of the Casa Del Rey Club and Golf Links. In 1989, the City of Santa Cruz bought Pogonip from a philanthropic foundation set up by Harry Cowell, son of cement magnate Henry Cowell, who once owned thousands of acres of timber and ranch lands in Santa Cruz County. Gifts of land from the Cowell Foundation created Henry Cowell Redwoods State Park, adjacent to Pogonip, in the 1950s, and Fall Creek State Park in the early 1970s.

Golf Club Drive, a paved road whose name harks back to the past, is bordered by Monterey pines, acacias, coast live oaks, willows, and coffeeberry. After about 0.25 mile, you come to an information board and a four-way junction. Here, the Pogonip Creek Nature Trail, a loop, goes left and also straight, parallel to the road. Across the road to the right is an unnamed trail that cuts through a weedy field and then joins the Lower Meadow Trail. You turn left, and set off through a grassy clearing that soon gives way to a lovely forest. The trail, a single track, descends on a gentle grade into a dense understory with berry vines, hazelnut, and poison oak.

Now beside beautiful Pogonip Creek, a sandy-bottomed stream, you find yourself amid second-growth coast redwoods, the virgin stands having been logged in the mid-to-late 1800s for lumber and for fuel to feed limestone kilns. Also here are California bay trees, lending their pungent

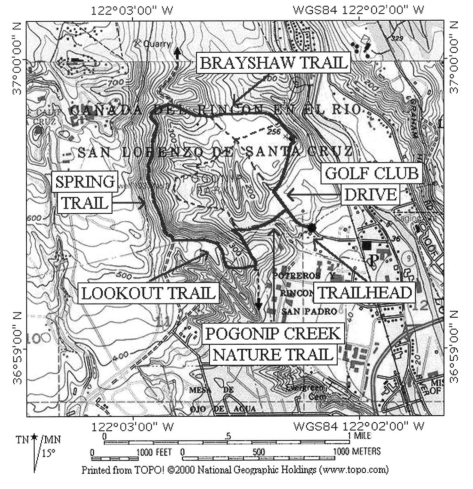

40. Lookout Loop

fragrance to the cool, moist air. Crossing the creek on rocks, you then climb away from the creek to a junction with the Lookout Trail (shown incorrectly on the park map). Here the Pogonip Creek Nature Trail veers right, but you stay straight, now on the Lookout Trail. Climbing on a gentle grade, you soon switchback left, emerging from the forest at a clearing dotted with coyote brush.

From here you have a fine view toward Santa Cruz and one of its landmarks, the white steeple of the Holy Cross Church, built atop a commanding hill on the site of the town's original Spanish mission. At a junction ahead, you follow the Lookout Trail as it turns sharply right and begins a steep climb. After several hundred feet the trail turns left and the grade eases. You may be watched from above by a circling red-tailed hawk—these aerial hunters are equally at home in wilderness or near urban areas. Nicknamed "chicken hawks" and sometimes hunted by farmers, red-tailed hawks feed mostly on rodents, thereby controlling rodent populations.

Continuing uphill, and now in the shade, the route curves right and passes under a set of powerlines. At about the 1-mile point, you pass through a gap in a ramshackle fence and then stroll through a lovely meadow bordered by trees. Soon you arrive at a four-way junction with a dirt road. The road is called the Spring Trail, and it is open to hikers and to leashed dogs. Across the road is a closed trail. Here you turn right onto the Spring Trail and enjoy a level walk through a forest of redwood and bigleaf maple.

A semicircle of excavated cliffs, left, was the site of a quarry that may have supplied limestone rocks for kilns located a little more than 0.5 mile north, on the Rincon Trail. The wood-fired kilns reduced the limestone to lime, which was used to make mortar for construction. Continuing on a level grade, you cross a seasonal creek and then come to a wet area that in spring and summer may be decorated with a white variety of nightshade. Here a stream flows under the road through a culvert, and just ahead is a junction with the Brayshaw Trail, right, open to hikers and leashed dogs.

You turn right and descend moderately on a dirt road scattered with loose gravel. The grade eases, and soon you pass a small concrete reservoir located near where a house, later destroyed by fire, once stood. Among the non-native plants found nearby are eucalyptus, acacia, periwinkle, and even a palm tree. At a junction with the Prairie Trail, right, you continue straight, still on the Brayshaw Trail, a dirt road that eventually finds level ground beside a ravine on your left. The Fern Trail departs left, and now you cross a creek that flows seasonally beneath the road through a culvert. The dense woodland beside the road may be alive with birdsong, including the chirping of chestnut-backed chickadees.

The Brayshaw Trail leads to the park's ranger station, where you will find a picnic table and a toilet. Just past the ranger station is a junction with the Prairie Trail, right, and ahead is the Pogonip clubhouse, a remnant of earlier days. The rustic style of the clubhouse was common among resorts built in the Santa Cruz Mountains in the early 1900s. The building, designed by architect L. D. Esty, features wood-shingle siding, wide overhanging eaves, and unstripped redwood log pillars on the porch. Today, the Pogonip clubhouse stands as the last of its kind from the period to be found in Santa Cruz County. The City of Santa Cruz in 1998 approved a plan to renovate the clubhouse, which is currently closed.

Just past the clubhouse, the Brayshaw Trail ends at Golf Club Drive, here a paved road with an uneven surface. The road curves right and comes to a trail junction with the Lower Meadow Trail, left. Staying on the road, you descend on a gentle grade and then curve left to the four-way junction where you began this loop. From here, continue straight and retrace your steps to the parking area.

Carry binoculars for viewing birds and other wildlife at Pogonip and other Monterey Bay area parks.

41   Pogonip
POGONIP CREEK NATURE TRAIL

Length: 1.8 miles

Time: 1 hour or less

Rating: Easy

Regulations: City of Santa Cruz Parks & Recreation; no bikes, no dogs, no horses.

Phone: (831) 420-6207

Web site: *www.santacruzparksandrec.com*

Highlights: Using Golf Club Dr. and the Pogonip Creek Nature Trail, this pleasant loop visits a redwood grove along Pogonip Creek, and then climbs through grassy meadows for fine views of Santa Cruz and Monterey Bay.

Directions: Same as for "Lookout Loop" on p. 182.

Facilities: None

Trailhead: On Golf Club Dr. about 0.2 mile west of the railroad overpass.

Follow the route description for "Lookout Loop" on pages 183–84 to the junction of the Pogonip Creek Nature Trail and Lookout trails (shown incorrectly on the park map). Here you bear right on the Pogonip Creek Nature Trail, a level single track carpeted with redwood twigs and needles, and follow Pogonip Creek upstream. After several hundred feet, you come upon a huge family circle of redwood trees—their ancestor was logged perhaps more than 100 years ago, but its descendants sprouted skyward from concealed roots and now reign as lords of the forest. Kneeling before them are their vassals, clusters of sword fern.

Now climbing away from the creek, you glimpse open fields and meadows on your right, in contrast with the dense wooded area to your left. Among the plants to look for here are snowberry, wild rose, telegraph weed, and pennyroyal, a low-growing herb with blue flowers clustered in spheres. The rolling course alternates between grassy meadows and wooded areas, and at one point passes the remnants of an orchard whose trees are riddled with woodpecker holes. At about the 1-mile point you pass through a gated barbed-wire fence, and then climb past stands of coast live oak and madrone, enjoying ever-improving views as you gain elevation.

At a four-way junction with the Prairie Trail, you continue on the Pogonip Creek Nature Trail by turning right. Far to the southeast, on the skyline, are several peaks at the north end of the Gabilan Range, including Fremont Peak. A wide expanse of grassland ahead, lush green in spring, provides a sweeping foreground that leads your gaze toward Santa Cruz, marked by the white tower of Holy Cross Church, and across Monterey Bay. Ahead is another gated barbed-wire fence, and once past it you soon reach the junction where you began this loop. From here, retrace your steps along Golf Club Drive.

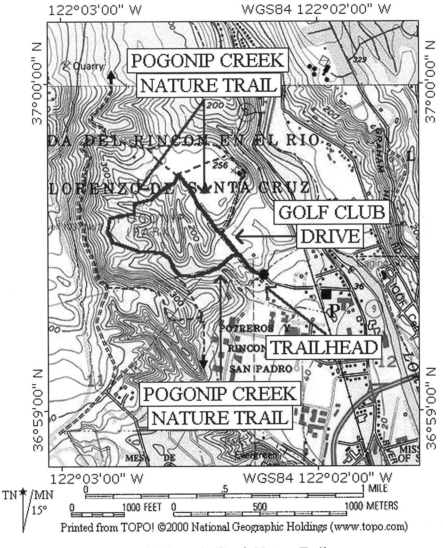

41. Pogonip Creek Nature Trail

42

Wilder Ranch State Park
BACKCOUNTRY LOOP

Length: 7 miles

Time: 3 to 4 hours

Rating: Moderate

Regulations: CSP; parking fee; no dogs.

Phone: (831) 423-9703, ranger station; (831) 426-0505, visitor center.

Web site: *http://parks.ca.gov*

Highlights: This loop uses the Engelsman Loop, Wild Boar, Old Cabin, Eucalyptus Loop, Twin Oaks, and Wilder Ridge Loop trails to explore part of this wonderful, sprawling state park on the outskirts of Santa Cruz. All the park's trails on the north side of Hwy. 1 are multi-use trails shared by hikers, bicyclists, and equestrians. South of the highway, horses are prohibited. Despite its proximity to a busy town and a highway streaming with cars, you may come upon coyotes, bobcats, wild pigs, and even mountain lions here. Some of the park's trails are subject to seasonal closures; call the ranger station or the visitor center for more information. The park also contains a cultural preserve, centered around the Wilder Ranch buildings. Park docents lead tours of the ranch, or you can follow a self-guiding walking tour described in a brochure available from the visitor center.

Directions: From the junction of Hwy. 1 and River St./Hwy. 9 in Santa Cruz, take Hwy. 1 west 4.4 miles to the Wilder Ranch State Park entrance, left. After 0.1 mile you reach an entrance kiosk. Just past the kiosk is a large parking area on the right.

Facilities: Visitor center with helpful staff, rest rooms, water; telephone beside the ranger's house (near entrance kiosk).

Trailhead: East side of parking area.

A paved pathway, signed TO CULTURAL PRESERVE, heads south from the parking area and then forks beside an information board. You stay right, and after about 40 feet come to a junction with the Old Cove Landing Trail, a dirt track heading right. Continuing straight on the paved path, you descend through a weedy field overgrown with fennel, mustard, and wild radish. Ahead is a organic garden growing mostly Swiss chard. Other agricultural fields nearby, leased by the state park to local farmers, are planted in brussels sprouts. These fields alone yield approximately 12% of the total U.S. production of brussels sprouts.

Now you reach the continuation of the park's paved entrance road, where you bear right. After several hundred feet, you turn left into the Wilder Ranch Cultural Preserve, an area containing Native American vil-

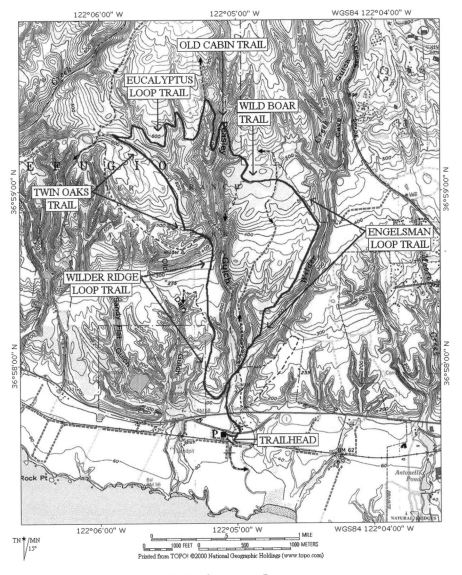

42. Backcountry Loop

lage sites, a Mexican-era adobe, and 19th and 20th century ranch buildings, all in the process of being restored. The state of California acquired
the lands for this state park in 1974 from the Wilder family, who had operated a dairy here for nearly 100 years. Many of the ranch buildings are
open to the public, and there are antique farm equipment and a few farm
animals on the property.

Passing the visitor center and the main ranch buildings on a paved
path bordered with lovely flowers, you soon reach a tunnel under Hwy.
1. Once on the north side of the highway, you come to a gated fence and
an information board showing the park's 33 miles of multiple-use trails
on a color-coded map. Dogs are prohibited beyond this point. Now on a
dirt road lined with California buckeyes, willows, California bay trees,
and blackberry vines, you pass an equestrian area, right, and then reach
two forks, staying right at each. Soon you merge with a dirt road joining
sharply from the left.

At a junction with the Cowboy Loop Trail, right, you continue straight,
and almost immediately come to two branches of the Engelsman Loop
Trail, one going left and uphill, the other going straight. You stay straight,
following the dirt road on a level course past shrubby willows and majestic coast live oaks. The park's backcountry consists of several marine terraces that form a giant staircase leading inland and uphill from Monterey
Bay. You begin a moderate climb over sandy, eroded ground, ascending
to the next terrace via **S**-bends in the road. As you gain elevation, be sure
to stop from time to time and admire the ever-improving view, but keep
a sharp eye out for descending bicyclists.

At an unsigned junction with a road curving left, you continue
straight, climbing steadily on a gentle grade. In a densely wooded area
around the 1-mile point, Douglas-fir, madrone, white alder, and even a
few coast redwoods occupy level ground. Soon, however, you resume
climbing, first gently, and then, as the trail swings left, on a moderate
grade. Open areas on your left offer sweeping vistas, but as the route
again levels, you find yourself hemmed in by coast scrub and chaparral
vegetation, including manzanita. Now descending for the first time in a
while, you come to a four-way junction.

Here the Engelsman Loop Trail bears left, the Long Meadow Trail
heads right, and your route, the Wild Boar Trail goes straight. A short,
steep pitch soon gives way to level ground as the trail approaches a **Y**-
junction with the Old Cabin Trail, where you bear right. Now on a single-
track trail, you descend into a magical, fern-filled forest of redwood, coast
live oak, Douglas-fir, and fragrant California bay. The trail bends left and
crosses a culvert at the head of a ravine that holds a seasonal stream. The
stream is now on your left, and soon you cross it on a plank bridge, then
climb on a curvy course amid tanbark oak, hazelnut, wild grape, gooseberry, and thimbleberry. Sharing the ground with a riot of ferns are two
redwood companions, wild ginger and redwood sorrel.

Emerging from the forest at about the 3-mile point, you reach a **T**-junction with the Eucalyptus Loop Trail, a dirt road. Here you turn left and stroll between a meadow, right, and a line of trees, left. Winding downhill on a gentle grade and entering the forest again, you soon switchback left and then cross a seasonal stream on a plank bridge. Now on a narrow trail, and with a ravine on your left, you drop to cross a gully and a culvert that runs under the trail. Around you rise massive coast redwoods, some fire-scarred. Still paralleling a ravine, left, you return to lighter, more open terrain. Swinging sharply left, the trail takes you across a creek on a plank bridge, and then brings you to a junction with the Twin Oaks Trail, left (shown incorrectly on the park map).

The Twin Oaks Trail may be closed because of flooding. If so, stay on the Eucalyptus Loop Trail for a few hundred yards until you merge with a dirt road coming sharply from the right—this is the other end of the Eucalyptus Loop Trail. You veer left, and in about 125 feet come to a confusing junction. Here you meet two branches of the Enchanted Loop Trail, right, and a paved road, straight. Follow the paved road 0.1 mile to the Wilder Ridge Loop Trail and then bear left at a fork. Follow the Wilder Ridge Loop Trail southeast about 1 mile until you meet the Twin Oaks Trail joining sharply from the left. Then follow the route description below.

If the Twin Oaks Trail is open, you turn left onto it. Crossing a gully with a culvert, the trail, a single track, bends sharply left and enters a forest of mostly Douglas-fir. Not staying long amid the towering trees, your route soon sets off across a vast expanse of grassland dotted with trees and shrubs. Passing an unsigned trail, right, the level course soon changes to a winding descent that alternates between gentle and moderate. Reaching a creek, which you cross on a plank bridge, you now climb to a junction with the Wilder Ridge Loop Trail, a dirt road. This junction, at about the 5-mile point, marks the end of the Twin Oaks Trail.

Here you veer left onto the Wilder Ridge Loop Trail and begin descending through a shady, fragrant forest. In places you have views through the trees toward Monterey Bay. At the next junction, you meet the other end of the Wilder Ridge Loop Trail, a single track joining sharply from the right. (This junction is shown incorrectly on the park map.) As you pass a pond surrounded by marsh vegetation, right, your view takes in the park's entrance kiosk, its parking area, and the adjacent agricultural fields. As you descend the last marine terrace above Hwy. 1, the trail makes a sweeping bend to the left and then merges with a dirt road coming in sharply from the right. After a few feet you take a switchback to the right, and then after about 200 feet, join the dirt road you used at the start of this loop. Ahead is the tunnel under Hwy. 1, and from here you retrace your steps to the parking area.

43 Wilder Ranch State Park
OLD COVE LANDING TRAIL

Length: 3 miles

Time: 1 to 2 hours

Rating: Easy

Regulations: CSP; parking fee; no dogs.

Phone: (831) 423-9703, ranger station; (831) 426-0505, visitor center.

Web site: *http://parks.ca.gov*

Highlights: This out-and-back route uses the Old Cove Landing Trail to traverse the seaward edge of a marine terrace between Wilder and Sand Plant beaches. Besides enjoying the wonderful views of Monterey Bay, you may encounter coastal birds and marine mammals, and you will also have opportunities to examine some of the hearty native plants that cling to these windswept lands. (**Boldface** numbers in the route description refer to numbered markers along the trail, which are keyed to "Old Cove Landing Trail," a pamphlet available at the visitor center.) The park also contains a cultural preserve, centered around the Wilder Ranch buildings. Park docents lead tours of the ranch, or you can follow a self-guiding walking tour described in a brochure available from the visitor center.

Directions: Same as for "Backcountry Loop" on p. 188.

Facilities: Visitor center with helpful staff, rest rooms, water; telephone beside the ranger's house (near entrance kiosk).

Trailhead: East side of parking area.

You follow a paved pathway, signed TO CULTURAL PRESERVE, that heads south from the parking area to an information board. Here the path forks, and you follow the right branch about 40 feet to a junction with the Old Cove Landing Trail, a dirt track heading right. You turn right, and after about 100 feet, merge with a dirt road coming sharply from the right. Marker **1**, left, indicates an overview of the cultural preserve, which contains Native American village sites, a Mexican-era adobe, and 19th and 20th century ranch buildings, all in the process of being restored. The rocky, eroded track descends through an open weedy area full of coyote brush, wild radish, curly dock, and bristly ox-tongue. A marshy area nearby holds rushes and beautiful, tall sedges.

Carefully crossing a set of railroad tracks, you traverse a marine terrace cut by a ravine, left, that holds Wilder Creek. Among the plants growing here are two common non-natives, poison hemlock and mustard. Also beside the trail you may spot California aster, a daisy-like flower with lavender rays that blooms from summer into fall. Marker **2** is for the park's agricultural fields, which are leased to commercial growers of brussels sprouts. Approximately 60% of the U.S. sprout crop is grown between Half Moon Bay and Santa Cruz.

Now your trail curves south, and you begin to see coastal cliffs and a large, sandy beach fronting Monterey Bay. Marker **3** indicates an estuary formed by Wilder Creek near where it empties into the bay. Estuaries are fragile ecosystems where freshwater and saltwater mix. Ahead are a rest bench, an observation deck overlooking the sandy beach, an information board, and, about 30 feet beyond, marker **4**, for snowy plovers, small shorebirds that nest on coastal beaches. The beach below is closed to protect the plovers, which are listed federally as a threatened species.

The route, now near the edge of steep cliffs that drop abruptly to Monterey Bay, winds beside brussels sprout fields, passing marker **5**, left, for pigeon guillemot, a small, dark sea bird with white wing-patches and red feet. Guillemots nest in burrows dug in coastal cliffs, but spend most of their time on the water, where they dive for fish, crustaceans, and mollusks. The low-growing, woody shrub forming the predominate ground

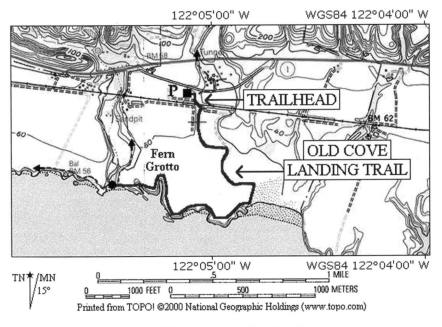

43. Old Cove Landing Trail

Cyclists pause along the Old Cove Landing Trail at Wilder Ranch State Park.

cover here is coast buckwheat, which, with its cousin, dune buckwheat, is the food source for larvae of the endangered Smith's blue butterfly.

Soon the route turns right and begins a level but winding course that follows the promontories and indentations of the coastline. Marker **6**, above a cove with a lovely beach at about the 1-mile point, is for cormorants and their nests. Like guillemots, these slender black birds dive for fish and make their nests on coastal cliffs, often in large colonies. The dramatic view west takes in a line of cliffs splashed by white foam launched from breaking waves. To your left, on rock shelves near the waterline, you may see groups of harbor seals relaxing and looking as if they had not a care in the world. You may also spy sea otters floating just offshore. The harbor seal haul-out rocks are indicated by marker **7**.

Now the trail curves right and follows a narrow indentation, at the head of which is a large cave, called Fern Grotto. Just before reaching a dirt road beside a sprout field, you turn left onto a trail that descends toward the grotto. Bear left at a fork and continue downhill until you reach sandy Fern Grotto Beach, then turn right to find the grotto itself, which drips year-round with water and contains an amazing display of ferns, mostly deer fern and giant chain fern. Also growing here, on the cave floor, is New Zealand spinach, and just outside the cave you may find blackberry and willows.

Retracing your steps uphill to the fork, you turn sharply left and in several hundred feet reach a **T**-junction with the dirt road mentioned above. Here you turn left and again follow the coastline, heading generally west. Marker **9**, left, is for coastal geology, including some of the features near Fern Grotto Beach. If you scan the wave-washed rocks near shore, you may be lucky enough to spot a black oystercatcher, a member of the shorebird tribe. Oystercatchers are chunky black birds with pink legs and a long, red, chisel-shaped bill. As their name implies, they feed on mollusks, using their bills to sever the muscle that holds shut the shell of their prey.

Just before angling right, the trail reaches a spot overlooking a sandy beach, called Sand Plant Beach, behind which are a lagoon and a wetland. A sprout field is on your right, marked by an AREA CLOSED sign. Here you follow an unsigned trail left onto a promontory above Sand Plant Beach, and then descend over rough ground to the beach itself. This marks the end of the Old Cove Landing Trail. Across the beach, to the west, is the

Experience a view of the wave-washed shoreline along the Old Cove Landing Trail in Wilder Ranch State Park.

Ohlone Bluff Trail, which begins by rising diagonally across a coastal cliff and then continues generally west for several more miles along the coast. From here you can do more exploring, or return to the parking area by retracing your steps. When you reach the trail coming up from Fern Grotto, stay on the dirt road. Then, just past the head of Fern Grotto Beach, angle right at a junction.

◆ San Benito County ◆

44

Fremont Peak State Park
FREMONT PEAK

Length: 1.5 miles

Time: 1 hour or less

Rating: Moderate

Regulations: CSP

Phone: (831) 623-4255

Web site: *http://parks.ca.gov*

Highlights: This short out-and-back route uses the Fremont Peak Trail to circle and ascend Fremont Peak, the northern anchor of the Gabilan Range and the place where the first American flag was raised over California. The best time to visit this dry, inland park is when temperatures are mild and visibility is excellent. The long drive up to the park is made interesting by the wide variety of trees and shrubs that border the road. Camping is available; for information, call the park office, above. There is an observatory that presents public astronomy programs; for information, call the Fremont Peak Observatory Association, (831) 623-2465.

Directions: From Hwy. 101 south of Gilroy, take the Hwy. 156 East/San Juan Bautista/Hollister exit, go southeast 3.1 miles to a traffic signal at The Alameda, and turn right. Now reset your odometer to 0. At 0.1 mile, The Alameda becomes Salinas Rd. At 0.2 mile you bear left onto Mission Vineyard Rd., and then immediately right onto San Juan Canyon Rd., following signs for Fremont Peak State Park. At 10.8 miles, you pass the Fremont Peak Observatory. At 11 miles you come to a parking area for the Madrone Picnic Area. From here, take the road signed SCENIC OVER-LOOK 0.1 mile to the upper parking area.

Facilities: Near the lower parking area are campsites, picnic tables, water, telephone, and rest rooms. There are toilets at the upper parking area but no other facilities.

Trailhead: Southeast corner of upper parking area.

(previous page) Rock formations reach skyward at Pinnacles National Monument.

The rocky peak ahead, with a flagpole atop its 3,169-foot summit, is named for one of California's most controversial figures, John Charles Frémont. Born in 1813, Frémont was an explorer and mountain man who became a captain with the U.S. Topographical Engineers. In 1846, he made his third expedition to the West, charged with mapping trails and charting the shortest route to the Pacific. In March of that year, Frémont and his party of armed men camped on what was then known as Gabilan, or Hawk, Peak (*gabilan* is Spanish for hawk).

At that time California was still part of Mexico, and the capital of the province was in nearby Monterey. Frémont's presence, coinciding with pressures to make California (and indeed much of the Southwest) part of the U.S., rankled the Mexicans, who assembled troops at San Juan Bautista under General José Castro. Though armed conflict was avoided for the moment, Frémont had raised an American flag, the first to fly over California. The flag was raised not on Gabilan Peak, but from a lower hill at the head of Steinbach Canyon, about 2 miles away. Some historians say

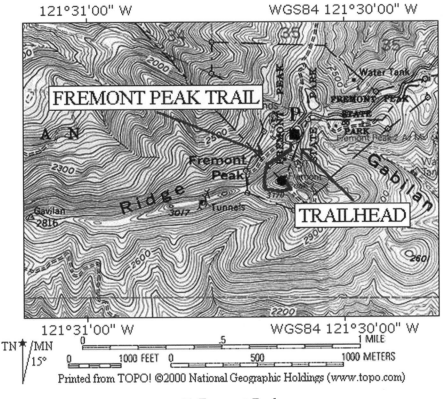

44. Fremont Peak

A short, moderate hike takes you to the top of Fremont Peak. Along the way, you see this lovely view to the west.

Frémont helped incite the Bear Flag uprising in Sonoma later in 1846, an event that all but precluded a peaceful settlement of California's status.

Frémont went on to lead American troops in the Mexican War, and served for 50 days as military governor of California. A dispute with General Stephen W. Kearny, commander of the U.S. Army of the West, led to Frémont's court-martial, but he was later pardoned by President Polk. Seemingly unstoppable, Frémont continued his political career, first in the U.S. Senate, and then as the Republican nominee for president in 1856. Returning to the army, he became a general during the Civil War. Afterwards, Frémont became territorial governor of Arizona from 1878 to 1883, returned to California's gold-mining country, and eventually died in New York City in 1890. Although Frémont's name was attached to several features of the new state of California—a county, a canyon, and a pass—as his reputation declined, some names were changed. Fremont Peak endures, as does one of the names Frémont himself bestowed, the "Golden Gate."

From the southeast corner of the upper parking area, you walk uphill on a paved road signed AUTHORIZED VEHICLES ONLY. After about 75 feet, you turn right onto the Fremont Peak Trail, a single track. Walking through a corridor of shrubs, you have a spectacular view over their tops of the rolling hills and rugged canyons that border Fremont Peak. Downhill and right are Coulter pines, a big-cone species similar to gray pine but with denser, darker foliage and stouter limbs. Joining the pines are coast live oaks, madrones, and blue elderberry. Uphill and left are the summit's rocky ramparts, where you will stand in a few minutes.

A mostly level traverse takes you across a steep hillside falling away to the right. As the trail curves left, your view southwest to the distant Santa Lucia Range is framed by several intervening ridges and, much closer, by an adjacent peak, also rocky. Now circling to the south side of Fremont Peak, you cross a gully on a wooden bridge. In the gully, just uphill, are sculpted rock formations punctured by caves and caverns. On the dry, south-facing slope, thrive California buckeye and hollyleaf cherry. Ahead, on a neighboring peak, are communication towers, seeming also to thrive as they sprout skyward. Soon the trail, lined with telegraph weed and vinegar weed, begins to climb on a moderate grade, and you can see the flagpole atop the summit of Fremont Peak, uphill and left.

The trail makes several switchbacks and then leads to a saddle between your summit, left, and the summit holding the communication towers, right. Please ignore the unofficial trails and shortcuts that beckon: despite its rugged appearance, this area is fragile and subject to erosion. After about 0.75 mile, you come to a **T**-junction with a dirt-and-gravel road. A sign on a trail post directs you to turn left and walk uphill to a flat spot where the road ends and a rest bench awaits. From here, the trail, again a single track, heads moderately uphill over very rough and rocky ground to the summit, a pyramid of rock. The plants with large seedpods beside the trail are milkweed, the exclusive food source of the monarch caterpillar.

Now the trail swings around the peak's east face, gaining elevation via concrete-and-rock steps. Where the trail soon degenerates to a rocky track, you are forced to scramble uphill on slippery slabs and loose out-croppings. (Unless you are surefooted and have proper footwear, omit this final ascent.) From the summit, the 360° views on a clear day are superb. The often fog-covered waters of Monterey Bay are west, and south lie the fertile agricultural lands of the Salinas Valley. Almost due north rise the peaks of Henry W. Coe State Park, and northeast is San Luis Reservoir, which is just east of Pacheco Pass on Hwy. 152. When you have finished enjoying this wonderful spot, simply retrace your steps to the parking area.

◆ Pinnacles National Monument ◆

Located just east of the Salinas Valley in the heart of the Gabilan Range, Pinnacles National Monument is a favorite destination for hikers of all abilities, and it is easy to see why. Set aside as a national monument in 1908 and administered by the National Park Service, Pinnacles features an impressive array of jagged peaks, fractured crags, and colorful cliffs, surrounded by rolling hills covered with pine, oak, and chaparral. In the center of the monument are the Pinnacle Rocks, crowned by the High Peaks, where a hiking trail built in the 1930s by the Civilian Conservation Corps (CCC) clings to a cliff face. Other trails wander through shady canyons, traverse steep hillsides, and ascend scenic ridgetops.

Pinnacles has two entrance points, east and west. The east entrance, reached from Hollister via Hwy. 25 and then Hwy. 146, contains park headquarters and the Bear Gulch Visitor Center. The west entrance, at the Chaparral Ranger Station, is reached from Soledad via Hwy. 101 and then steep and narrow Hwy. 146 (not recommended for motor homes and trailers). There is no through road connecting the east and west sides of the monument. The monument is open year-round, but the best times to visit are during spring and fall. In summer, daytime temperatures may exceed 100° F. Most of the annual rainfall occurs from December to February. Weekdays are the quietest times to visit. Parking areas at popular trailheads often fill up early on spring and fall weekends.

In addition to attracting hikers, Pinnacles is a magnet for rock climbers, who come to test their skills on the vertical cliffs and spires. The monument has two talus caves, formed when huge boulders fell from nearby cliffs into slot canyons, forming roofs over them. Balconies Caves can be visited via the Balconies Trail from the monument's west entrance, or via the Old Pinnacles Trail from Chalone Creek Picnic Area on the east side. A flashlight is required. Bear Gulch Cave, located near the Bear Gulch Visitor Center, is closed to protect a colony of Townsend's big-eared bats. The park is home to a wonderful variety of plants and animals, including nesting prairie falcons and golden eagles. In spring, beautiful wildflowers abound.

When you look at the Pinnacle Rocks today, you are seeing the eroded remnants of an ancient volcano that was formed more than 20 million years ago. At that time, the location of this 8,000-foot-high, 15-mile-long volcano was 195 miles south of here, near present-day Lancaster, California. When the San Andreas fault formed between the North American and Pacific plates, it split the volcano in two. The volcano's east flank, today called the Neenach Formation, remained attached to the North American plate, but the volcano's other half rode northwest with the Pacific plate to its present position at Pinnacle Rocks. The monument was created to protect the unique geological features found here. President Clinton added nearly 8,000 acres to the monument, increasing its size from 16,000 to 24,000 acres.

The monument's more than 30 miles of hiking trails are for day use only. Overnight parking and camping are prohibited within Pinnacles National Monument. A private campground, Pinnacles Campground, is close to the monument's east entrance (see below). There are several public campgrounds within driving distance from the west entrance. Motels and other lodging may be found in Hollister, Soledad, and King City. Campfire programs are presented at Pinnacles Campground on Friday and Saturday evenings from March through May. Ranger-led walks and talks are sometimes offered on the east side during spring and fall weekends.

Bicycles and dogs are not allowed on the monument's trails. There is no potable water once you leave the developed areas, so carry plenty to drink, especially on longer hikes during warm weather.

INFORMATION: (831) 389-4485

PINNACLES CAMPGROUND: (831) 389-4462

Hikers on High Peak Trail, Pinnacles National Monument.

Pinnacles National Monument
BALCONIES CAVES

Length: 6 miles

Time: 3 to 4 hours

Rating: Moderate

Regulations: NPS; entrance fee; no bikes, no dogs.

Phone: (831) 389-4485

Web site: *www.nps.gov/pinn*

Highlights: This route, mostly a level out-and-back, but with a short, athletic loop at the far end, follows the Old Pinnacles Trail beside botanically rich Chalone Creek and its West Fork, and then uses the Balconies Caves and Balconies Cliffs trails to explore several caves and the high ground above them. A flashlight is required to explore the caves: do not attempt to enter them without one. You should also have shoes with good traction, because the rocks inside the caves can be wet and slippery. (**Boldface** numbers in the route description refer to numbered markers along the trail, which are keyed to "The Balconies Self-Guiding Trail," a brochure available for a small fee from the Bear Gulch Visitor Center and the Chaparral Ranger Station. This self-guiding trail starts just east of the Chaparral Ranger Station on the west side of Pinnacles National Monument, and thus only 11 of the trail's 20 markers are encountered on this route.)

Directions: From Hwy. 101 in Gilroy, take the Hwy. 25 exit, signed for Hollister and Pinnacles National Monument, and go southeast to Hollister. Once in Hollister, follow Hwy. 25 on city streets: at 13 miles from Hwy. 101, turn left on Nash Rd., and at 13.7 miles, angle right onto Airline Hwy. Still on Hwy. 25, go southeast another 28.5 miles to a junction with Hwy. 146, and turn right.

At 2 miles, you pass the privately owned Pinnacles Campground. At 2.5 miles there is an entrance kiosk, where you pay the entrance fee, good for seven continuous days. (If the kiosk is not staffed, proceed ahead another 2.5 miles to the Bear Gulch Visitor Center and pay the entrance fee there.) At 3.8 miles, turn right onto a paved road signed for the CHALONE CREEK PICNIC AREA. Go 0.2

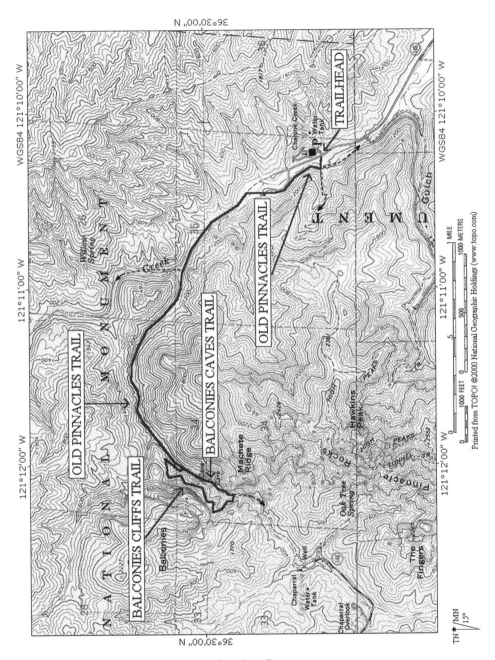

45. Balconies Caves

mile to a gate blocking your way, turn right, and then almost immediately turn left into the picnic area. Parking is along the west side of the picnic area.

Facilities: Picnic tables, fire grates, water, phone, rest rooms.

Trailhead: Southwest corner of parking area.

From the parking area, cross the paved road just south of the gate blocking vehicle access. On the road's west side is the start of your route, a dirt track marked by a sign that says: STAY ON TRAIL. Just downhill is a wayside exhibit and a map showing the picnic area and your route, the Old Pinnacles Trail to Balconies Caves. Bordered by gray pine and coast live oak, the trail leads gently downhill to a sandy wash holding Chalone Creek. Growing in the sand are shrubby clumps of California buckwheat, bush lupine, and California poppies. Spanning the creek and its adjacent flood channel are two wooden bridges, which you cross.

For safety, explore the fascinating Balconies Caves only if you have a flashlight and sturdy footwear.

About 25 feet past the second bridge is a four-way junction. Here the High Peaks Trail goes straight, the Bench Trail goes left, and the Old Pinnacles Trail, your route, goes right. Notice the huge pinecones beside the trail—in the area covered by this book, only Coulter pines make bigger cones than the gray pine. Along with the gray pines and oaks, look for willows and blue elderberry beside the creek. This area is a botanical wonderland, and within a few hundred feet you may find shrubs such as chamise, hollyleaf cherry, redberry, gooseberry, and mountain mahogany. In spring, the air may be filled with the fragrant scent of buckbrush, a tall shrub that produces gorgeous sprays of white flowers.

Chalone Creek occupies a wide valley, with a rugged wall rising left, and rolling, chaparral-cloaked hills in the distance to your right. The trail, a sandy track, parallels the creek, and crosses it many times. Some of these crossings are bridged, but higher up, where the creek is narrow, you merely step across it on rocks. Water in arid country acts like a magnet for birds, and you may be accompanied on your stroll by the repetitive trill of a wrentit, or the insistent separate notes of an oak titmouse.

With tall manzanitas on either side of the trail, and the creek to your right, you enjoy a level walk that soon brings you to a wood bridge spanning the creek. Once across it, you follow the trail as it bends left, now walking between the creek and an abandoned dirt road, right, which soon ends. Impressive rock formations are beginning to show themselves on the other side of the creek, uphill and left. Even the creek bed is getting rockier, and when the creek is full, the water flowing over rock ledges makes many small waterfalls that splash into beautiful little pools.

You may notice beside the trail a tall, rangy shrub with large, light-gray, wrinkled leaves. This is wooly yerba santa, sharing the same genus (*Eriodictyon*) with yerba santa, a common member of the coastal-scrub community. Yerba santa (Spanish for "saintly herb") was used as medicine by Native Americans and early settlers. At about the 1-mile point you cross the creek on a wood bridge, enjoying ever improving views of the wonderful rock pinnacles that dominate this national monument and give it its name. As the route curves left, the valley holding Chalone Creek narrows and becomes more canyonlike.

Among the common birds to look for in this lovely wooded area are black phoebes, spotted towhees, dark-eyed juncos, and, in wintertime, golden-crowned sparrows. Toyon, a common component of the chaparral community, makes an appearance here, as do the vines of blackberry, poison oak, and clematis, or virgin's bower. There are also stands of California buckeye beside the trail. Soon you come to a junction with the North Wilderness Trail, which angles right. Here, Chalone Creek divides into two tributaries, the West and North forks.

You stay on the Old Pinnacles Trail and follow West Fork Chalone Creek, at times walking in its sandy bed and twice stepping across its narrow channel, aided by conveniently placed rocks. Now on a gentle uphill grade, the trail wanders through stands of blue oak and an occasional California juniper, which provide foreground for the dramatic cliffs and terraces above. You cross the creek several more times, and then reach an unsigned junction, where you continue straight. After about 100 yards, the trail that departed right from the previous junction rejoins sharply from the right.

California blue oak.

Where it reaches a gravelly flood channel, the trail becomes indistinct, so you bear right toward the creek and then cross it on rocks. Now in view are the Balconies, a large and complex rock wall looming impressively ahead. The tall pines and the even taller cliffs direct your gaze skyward. In fact, so much of your time on this route is spent looking up that you may get a stiff neck! Soon you reach the end of the Old Pinnacles Trail at a junction marked by a trail post, right. Here, the Balconies Cliffs Trail, which you will explore later, joins from the right, but you swing left onto the Balconies Caves Trail.

The trail climbs gently beside West Fork Chalone Creek in a beautiful wooded canyon. The Balconies, a sheer face of rock broken by ledges and terraces, rises abruptly on your right. After passing a sign urging you to use caution and to carry a flashlight, follow the trail now squeezed between the creek and the cliffs at the base of the Balconies. In places you actually walk in the creek bed, hopping from rock to rock and negotiating a passage between huge boulders. Marker **16**, left, refers to the rocks framing the opening to Balconies Caves, and to the legend that the notorious Mexican bandit Tiburcio Vasquez hid out here in the mid-1800s.

A metal gate with a door marks the entrance to Balconies Caves, and it is here, if you are without a flashlight or otherwise unprepared to make a steep climb on wet rock, that you should turn back. Once inside the cave, you have the creek on your right, and a low boulder ahead that you must duck under. Gaps in the roof overhead provide a bit of daylight, but soon you will be in the realm of absolute darkness. When you lose the last of the natural light, use your flashlight to pick out white arrows painted on the rocks: these mark the route, which is steep and may be wet.

After a short but exhilarating passage, you emerge in an area filled with a fantastic jumble of rocks and boulders. Now you descend into the next cave, aided by steps cut in the rock and a metal railing on your left. The vaulted ceiling above, and the rocky floor below, under which the creek flows, are indicated by marker **17**. Temporarily on level, dry ground, you follow a narrow dirt track between vertical rock walls, crouching several times to pass beneath wedged boulders.

At about the 3-mile point, you have another gate, and marker **18**, right. The Balconies Caves are "talus caves," formed when boulders loosened by erosion, faulting, and earthquakes fell and were caught between the narrow walls of a canyon, leaving a passage below. Just past the gate, you angle left through a narrow, gravelly passage, and then climb along a rock ledge out of the caves and into more-open terrain. Machete Ridge, an impressive 700-foot-high cliff, looms just left, and the trail, now dirt, angles right and uphill. Marker **19** indicates fracturing and faulting in rock layers, and the process water plays in creating many of the unusual formations found in Pinnacles National Monument.

Soon the route bends right and crosses a streambed, which may be dry. Marker **20**, right, is for coast live oak, a tree which supplied California's coastal Indians with acorns, an important food source. If you hear voices from above, don't be alarmed: rock climbers practice their sport on nearby cliffs and they communicate by shouting. A beautiful rock formation, Elephant Rock, pierces the sky ahead as you reach a **T**-junction at the end of the Balconies Caves Trail. Here the Balconies Trail, which originates at the Chaparral Ranger Station, joins from the left, but you turn right onto the Balconies Cliffs Trail.

The route zigs and zags to gain elevation, passing marker **10**, indicating the Balconies and Machete Ridge, and then marker **11**, for an exposed outcrop of rhyolite breccia, a volcanic rock. Spring bloomers such as shooting stars, paintbrush, fiesta flower, larkspur, bluedicks, and wallflower may have the hillsides ablaze with color. A trail post, left, with a sign showing a carabiner, marks an access point for climbers heading for a route called Tilting Terrace. A level walk gives you a chance to stop and look south to the High Peaks, the jagged crown of Pinnacles National Monument.

Cresting a divide, you begin to descend on a gentle grade, accompanied perhaps by a noisy chorus of Pacific treefrogs. These small frogs, found throughout the Pacific states and in parts of Idaho and Nevada, live near water in dense underbrush, from sea level to the mountains. Marker **12** indicates chaparral, a plant community adapted to hot, dry conditions. Marker **13**, right, is for the white-faced cliffs on a mountain to the northeast. A landslide exposed soft sandstone at the mountain's core, revealing a geologic composition very different from the volcanic Pinnacles.

Just before you reach the junction with the Old Pinnacles and Balconies Caves trails, you pass marker **14**, right, indicating a fine view of Machete Ridge, and then marker **15**, left, for two common chaparral plants, chamise and buckbrush. At the junction, you make a sharp left and retrace your steps to the parking area.

Pinnacles National Monument
BEAR GULCH RESERVOIR

Length: 2.4 miles

Time: 1 to 2 hours

Rating: Easy

Regulations: NPS; entrance fee; no bikes, no dogs.

Phone: (831) 389-4485

Web site: *www.nps.gov/pinn*

Highlights: This popular loop, using the Moses Spring, Rim, and High Peaks trails, has as its destination Bear Gulch Reservoir, a lovely body of water whose shores are perfect for picnicking and relaxing. Along the way, you wander beside Bear Creek as it enters a deep and narrow ravine, where rock formations tower above and climbers practice their craft on the vertical cliffs. A former attraction, Bear Gulch Cave, is currently closed to protect roosting Townsend's big-eared bats, a species of special concern in California. (**Boldface** numbers in the route description refer to numbered markers along the trail, which are keyed to "Moses Spring Self-Guiding Trail," a brochure available for a small fee from the Bear Gulch Visitor Center.)

Directions: Same as for "Balconies Caves" on pages 204–06, but when you reach the junction with the paved road signed for the CHALONE CREEK PICNIC AREA, curve left over a bridge and go another 1.2 miles to the Bear Gulch Visitor Center and a parking area on the left. Weekends, especially in spring, are very crowded here. Plan to arrive early in the day or visit midweek.

Facilities: Picnic tables, fire grates, rest rooms, water, phone, and visitor center with displays, maps, books, brochures, and helpful staff.

Trailhead: Southwest end of parking area.

From the southwest end of the parking area, you cross a paved road and then find a dirt track that winds through a picnic area on the south side of Bear Creek. This is a lovely wooded area, with stands of blue oak, coast live oak, California buckeye, blue elderberry, and gray pines, some of whose trunks are riddled with woodpecker holes. A short stroll brings you again to the paved road, which enters a parking area, right. There are rest rooms and water here, along with an information board giving details about hiking, rock climbing, and protecting nesting raptors.

The Moses Spring Trail continues on the other side of the road, and it climbs on a gentle grade. Passing marker **1**, indicating California buckeye, and marker **2**, for the plant community known as foothill woodland, you walk parallel to Bear Creek, which is downhill and right in a boulder-filled ravine. Rock climbers practice their sport on the cliffs across the creek, and you can watch them ascending via ledges and cracks, safely protected by colorful strands of rope anchored to the rock. Marker **3**, right, indicates toyon, a shrub also called Christmas berry because of its bright red berries. At a fork marked by a trail post, the High Peaks Trail departs right, but you angle left, still on the Moses Spring Trail.

As you continue your climb beside the creek, the trail here is lined with shrubs such as manzanita, buckbrush, lupine, redberry, and bush monkeyflower. Marker **4**, right, is for the spires and crags that give Pinnacles National Monument its name. Now you are amid impressive rock faces and towers, many of which have climbing routes. Gray pines, whose long roots seek water to sustain them during our hot, dry summers, are indicated by marker **5**, left. Soon the route crosses a watercourse which may

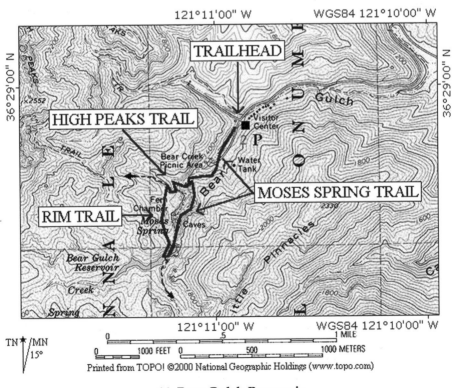

46. Bear Gulch Reservoir

While in Pinnacles National Monument, enjoy this popular picnic spot at Bear Gulch Reservoir.

be dry, swings right, and then passes marker **6**, left, for mosses, which are also capable of surviving long dry spells. The trail reaches the foot of a soaring rock face pierced by a 100-foot-long tunnel, which you can walk through without crouching if you are 6 feet tall or less. On the other side of the tunnel is marker **7**, left, indicating various species of lichens, which are composed of an alga and a fungus living together as one organism.

At a junction marked by a trail post, the trail through Bear Gulch Cave, currently closed to protect roosting Townsend's big-eared bats, goes straight, but you veer right and climb on a gentle grade. On the left is marker **8**, for coast live oak, a species that always grows near a permanent source of water. Now the trail makes a couple of tight switchbacks, taking you past an access point for climbers. Marker **9** is for the riparian community, found in canyon bottoms beside flowing water. Beside the trail here are poison oak, hollyleaf cherry, and blue witch. On your right is marker **10**, indicating poison oak.

Now the trail is pressed against the bottom of a cliff face that has fractured into horizontal bands of eroded rock. Working your way through a possibly wet area, you come to marker **11**, right, for Moses Spring, a year-round water source. This beautiful, shaded area has a large rock platform you can use as a vantage point to study the narrow canyon that holds Bear Creek and the Bear Gulch Cave. This is a "talus cave," so called because it was formed when rock debris—in this case huge boulders—fell from the cliffs above and wedged themselves in narrow spaces between the canyon walls.

Passing marker **12**, left, for manzanita, a chaparral shrub adapted to dought and fire, you inch along a sandy ledge beneath an overhanging cliff, and then climb a set of rock steps. Marker **13**, left, indicates hollyleaf cherry. Here the trail is hewn from the rocks and runs between the boulders that form the roof of the cave below. In places there are gaps between the rocks, and you can see down into the cave's dimly lit recesses. You follow the trail as it switchbacks past several access points for climbers, giving you more opportunities to watch these graceful athletes scamper up vertical rock walls. Ahead is a cluster of markers—**14**, for chaparral; **15**, for buckbrush, a *Ceanothus* shrub also called wild lilac; and **16**, for chamise, the dominant chaparral shrub.

Now descending on rock steps that may be wet or covered with loose gravel, you are confronted with a large boulder partially blocking your way. Ducking under it and then staying left, you find more steps to help you downhill. The cliff walls beside the route may be dripping with water, and the air feels delightfully cool and moist. After passing marker **17**, indicating Bear Gulch Reservoir, which was built by the Civilian Conservation Corps (CCC) in 1936, you cross Bear Creek on a rock bridge and then reach a junction. Here the trail to the closed cave goes right, but you turn left and walk upstream beside the creek.

Ahead and above is a rock dam forming Bear Gulch Reservoir. Water spills over the dam and cascades down into Bear Creek. Using a handrail for support, you climb a narrow and possibly wet set of steps carved beside the edge of a cliff that rises steeply to your right. At the top of the steps, just past the 1-mile point, you find Bear Gulch Reservoir, a beautiful body of water set amid rolling hills and colorful rock outcrops. Two trails depart from this scenic spot. Across the dam, left, is the Chalone Peak Trail, described in Trip 48. Straight ahead is your route, the Rim Trail, which loops back toward the visitor center.

The reservoir is a lovely spot to have a picnic or to spend the day relaxing. You can also explore the trail to North Chalone Peak by following the route description that begins on p. 219 (Trip 48). When you are ready to leave the reservoir area, follow the Rim Trail uphill on large rock steps, making a right-hand switchback after about 100 feet. The trail follows a gravelly ledge that has been gouged out of the cliffs. A vantage point above a steep drop, right, gives you a chance to look down into the canyon that holds Bear Creek.

Soon the trail widens and runs through an area of chaparral, mostly chamise, with some manzanita, buckbrush, and hollyleaf cherry. Now descending over rough ground, you step across a seasonal stream, and then follow the trail on a winding course. At a junction marked by a trail post, you join the High Peaks Trail by turning sharply right, and follow it downhill via a series of switchbacks. At a junction with a climbers-access trail to Discovery Wall, you turn sharply left, still on the High Peaks Trail, and continue descending until you reach Bear Creek. Now a short and easy climb quickly brings you to the junction where you began this loop. Here the High Peaks Trail ends, and you retrace your steps by continuing straight on the Moses Spring Trail to the parking area.

47

Pinnacles National Monument
HIGH PEAKS LOOP

Length:	5.3 miles
Time:	3 to 4 hours
Rating:	Difficult
Regulations:	NPS; entrance fee; no bikes, no dogs.
Phone:	(831) 389-4485
Web site:	*www.nps.gov/pinn*

Highlights: This loop, one of the premier routes in the Pinnacles, uses the Condor Gulch, High Peaks, and Moses Spring trails to traverse the High Peaks, a fantastic area of cliffs, spires, and outcrops that crown this national monument. In addition to sweeping views, this route provides an up-close look at a wide variety of native plants, especially chaparral shrubs. Lucky hikers may see raptors, such as golden eagles and prairie falcons, which nest in the cliffs. **Caution: The route through the High Peaks area involves climbing and descending steep rock faces**. Steps have been cut in the rock to make the going easier, and metal railings are provided in places for added safety. Do not attempt this route without proper footwear, or if you suffer from vertigo. A large pack would be a hindrance where you must negotiate narrow passages.

Directions: Same as for "Balconies Caves" on pages 204–06, but when you reach the junction with the paved road signed for the CHALONE CREEK PICNIC AREA, curve left over a bridge and go another 1.2 miles to the Bear Gulch Visitor Center and a parking area on the left. Weekends, especially in spring, are very crowded here. Plan to arrive early in the day or visit during mid-week.

Facilities: Picnic tables, fire grates, rest rooms, water, phone, and visitor center with displays, maps, books, brochures, and helpful staff.

Trailhead: At a wood bridge opposite the visitor center, on the north side of the road.

Once across the wood bridge, which spans a tributary of Bear Creek, you turn sharply left onto the Condor Gulch Trail and begin a climb through a savanna of blue oak and gray pine. Beside the trail are chamise, toyon,

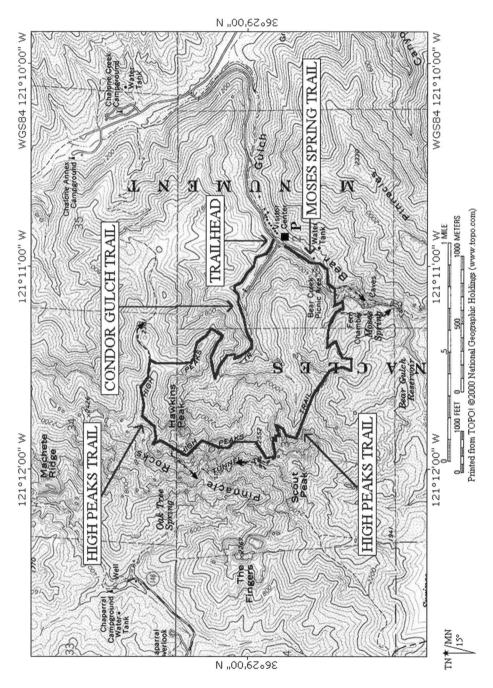

47. High Peaks Loop

California sagebrush, mountain mahogany, and California buckwheat, all common in the Pinnacles. The countryside around you is rugged, featuring steep hills capped by rocky outcrops. Looking up a draw to your left, you catch glimpses of your goal, the High Peaks, a jagged line of cliffs reaching for the sky.

In spring, the hills beside the trail may be dotted blue, red, and orange with bush lupine, paintbrush, and wallflower. The botanical variety here is amazing—look for shrubs such as blue elderberry, hollyleaf cherry, redberry, bush monkeyflower, and poison oak. Turkey vultures may be circling overhead, and western scrub-jays may complain about territorial violations. Other birds to look for here are acorn woodpeckers, white-breasted nuthatches, California towhees, and western bluebirds.

As you approach a wall of rock ahead, the trail curves right and wanders amid stands of tree-sized manzanita and coast live oak. At about the

Hikers follow the Condor Gulch Trail at Pinnacles National Monument.

1-mile point, the trail makes a switchback right and climbs through a corridor of chaparral. Several more switchbacks help you gain elevation and bring the High Peaks into clearer view. Soon you reach the Condor Gulch Overlook, left, where a short trail, lined by a metal rail, runs along the edge of a precipitous cliff. From here you can trace the route, which has already climbed about 600 feet, back toward the visitor center.

Back on the Condor Gulch Trail, now rocky and eroded in places, you make a long, rising traverse across a south-facing hillside cloaked with black sage, bush poppy, and wooly yerba santa. The expansive views let you appreciate the uniqueness of the Pinnacles: although many of the neighboring hills are steep and rugged, and some are pierced by rock outcrops, no other nearby location has as much exposed rock in such dramatic formations. To the east, a line of ridges—the Diablo Range—eventually disappears in the distant haze above the Central Valley. Curving left around the shoulder of a ridge and still climbing, you head north for a saddle on the skyline.

Approaching the saddle, you have the High Peaks looming on your left—this is the realm of ravens, golden eagles, and prairie falcons. In places the dirt trail disappears, and you walk on rock slabs, following a course defined by thoughtfully placed stones. At a **T**-junction just west of and slightly higher than the saddle, the Condor Gulch Trail ends, and you turn left onto the High Peaks Trail, which brings hikers up from Chalone Creek to the High Peaks. With a very steep drop on your right, you follow a mostly level rock-and-gravel path carved from a hillside that rises and then crests immediately left. Across a deep canyon, right, is an impressive rock formation that vies with the High Peaks for your attention.

Now descending for the first time since you left the trailhead, the route curves left and soon brings you to the heart of the High Peaks, a collection of fantastic cliffs, outcrops, and spires, with names like Chaos Crags, Dragonfly Dome, Long's Folly, and (my favorite) Photographer's Delight. After making a switchback left, you have a dramatic view west toward Juniper Canyon and the area around the Chaparral Ranger Station. A right-hand switchback leads to a junction with the Tunnel Trail, which hikers from the monument's west access point can use in conjunction with the Juniper Canyon Trail to reach the High Peaks.

Here you continue straight, with the highest pinnacles now on your left. Passing through a slot between two cliffs, you descend past a huge spire that rises right. Now climbing gently, you soon reach a spot where the dirt trail gives way to rock steps. After climbing these, you arrive on a ledge where you turn sharply right and confront a steeply angled rock wall, at about the 3-mile point. A route up the wall is provided by notches gouged in the rock, and a metal railing alongside gives you extra support. Be careful of loose rock on the steps, and beware of ill-mannered hikers who may try to push past you.

An athletic climb puts you atop another ledge, where you have dramatic views to the east, taking in all the ground you covered since leaving the trailhead. The next pitch angles up beside a cliff face overhanging from the right, and then you work your way across a narrow ledge guarded by a metal rail. Where the ledge temporarily disappears, a short, wooden walkway suspended over a dizzying gap takes its place. At last, you reach level and open ground, where you can enjoy a well-deserved break. Past this point, the trail winds through rock boulders and then reaches a steep cliff that you descend via rock steps, aided by a railing.

Once down on level ground, you turn sharply left, but not before gazing west and downhill to a meadow that may be filled with wildflowers. More steps and railings help you downhill over rough ground, but soon you enjoy easy walking, lovely wildflowers, and 360° views that take in the High Peaks, most of which are now due north, and the rich agricultural lands of the Salinas Valley, which is west. Descending gently just below a ridgecrest, you reach a trail post and a junction, right, with the Juniper Canyon Trail. About 100 feet ahead, you have a rest bench, right, and then another trail post, left. Here a short trail continues straight to a rest room, but your route, the High Peaks Trail, makes a switchback, the first in a series, to the left.

A beautiful sea of chaparral clinging to the side of a deep canyon, left, is the stage for your gradual descent out of the High Peaks area. Passing a rock formation called the Anvil at about the 5-mile point, the trail swings left around it and then wanders downhill to a junction, right, with the Rim Trail, which goes to Bear Gulch Reservoir. Here you bear left and begin another series of switchbacks, descending past several access points for climbers, until you reach Bear Creek, which flows underneath the trail amid a jumble of huge boulders.

Now climbing gently, you soon reach a junction; here the High Peaks Trail ends, and the Moses Spring Trail, which also leads to the reservoir, goes both right and straight. You continue straight, enjoying views, left, across the creek of towering rock walls, where climbers attached to colorful ropes for safety may be splayed like spiders. Arriving at a paved road that serves a parking area, you cross it and find the continuation of your trail, which goes through a picnic area on its way back to Bear Gulch Visitor Center. Staying right at a fork, you walk about 30 feet to a paved road. Now you bear left and go several hundred feet to the parking area for the visitor center.

Pinnacles National Monument
NORTH CHALONE PEAK

Length: 9 miles

Time: 4 to 5 hours

Rating: Difficult

Regulations: NPS; entrance fee; no bikes, no dogs.

Phone: (831) 389-4485

Web site: *www.nps.gov/pinn*

Highlights: Using the Moses Spring and Chalone Peak trails, this strenuous out-and-back route gains more than 2,000 feet from the trailhead to the summit of North Chalone Peak in about 4.5 miles. None of the climbing is steep, and you are rewarded at almost every step by wonderful views of the chaparral-clad hills, deep wooded canyons, and towering rock pinnacles that make this such a special place.

Directions: Same as for "Balconies Caves" on pages 204–06, but when you reach the junction with the paved road signed for the CHALONE CREEK PICNIC AREA, curve left over a bridge and go another 1.2 miles to the Bear Gulch Visitor Center and a parking area on the left. Weekends, especially in spring, are very crowded here. Plan to arrive early or visit during mid-week.

Facilities: Picnic tables, fire grates, rest rooms, water, phone, and visitor center with displays, maps, books, brochures, and helpful staff.

Trailhead: Southwest end of parking area.

Follow the route description for "Bear Gulch Reservoir" on pages 210–13. When you reach the reservoir and the junction with the Rim and Chalone Peak trails, you turn left and walk across the rock dam. Now on the other side, you turn right and follow the Chalone Peak Trail as it skirts the reservoir's shoreline. Soon the trail, lined with chamise, manzanita, buckbrush, bush poppy, and hollyleaf cherry, veers away from the water and starts to rise on a gentle grade. The Sisters, a popular climbing wall, is uphill and left.

In spring, paintbrush, bluedicks, California poppies, and shooting stars provide colorful accents to the scene of green grass, orange rock, and blue sky. Passing a trail post, right, and then stepping across a little stream, you continue ascending past stands of gray pine, live oak, and

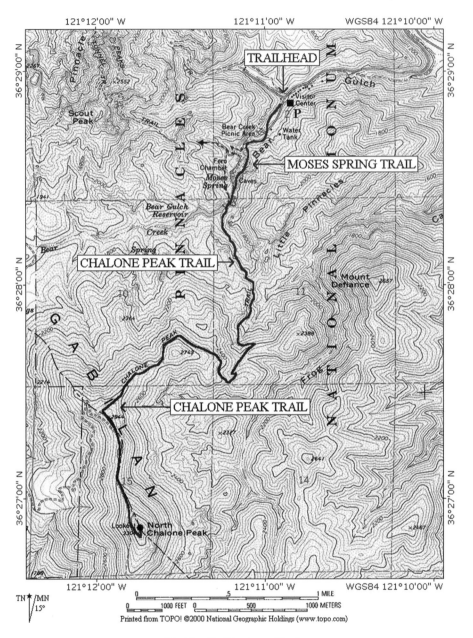

48. North Chalone Peak

mountain mahogany. The view behind you is arresting—the reservoir, which is encircled by fantastic rock formations, forms a perfect foreground for the High Peaks, a toothed range biting into the sky. Your route heads generally south on a steadily rising grade, then curves left near the head of a canyon holding a tributary of Chalone Creek.

Now about 1,000 feet higher than at the trailhead, you make a switchback to the right and begin to spy your goal, North Chalone Peak, crowned by a lookout tower, southwest. The route levels briefly as you cross a saddle, but there is plenty of high ground ahead. Several more switchbacks put you atop the next saddle, which is oriented east-west. Here you follow the trail, which is indistinct, to the right as it curves around a shoulder of North Chalone Peak. Your efforts are rewarded by fine views of the High Peaks, which rise slightly west of north.

Where the trail angles left, at about the 3-mile point, stands of blue oak frame a lovely view of the Salinas Valley, which contains the Salinas River, a bright ribbon of water, and some of California's richest agricultural land. Up here, however, the terrain is rocky, windswept, and fire-scarred, with burnt remnants of chamise poking up from the ground. Yet fire is a boon to some plants, and there may be colorful displays beside the trail of bush poppy, star lily, and fiddleneck. Soon you reach a gate and a sign giving distances ahead to the peak, 0.8 mile, and back to the visitor center, 3.5 miles.

Passing through the gate, you now have a barbed-wire fence on your left, and a very rough dirt road merging from the right. After a short, level walk, you reach the base of North Chalone Peak's summit pyramid. Here the road curves around the southwest side of the peak, climbing on a moderate grade. Near the summit, you make a switchback left, and then, on a gentler grade, make a switchback to the right. Now you are atop North Chalone Peak (3304'), having come up more than 2,000 feet from the trailhead. The only thing higher for miles around is the lookout tower rising several stories above you. This is perhaps the best vantage point in the Pinnacles for getting a complete overview of the national monument.

Bush poppy, a shrub often found in chaparral.

The 360° views extend southwest across the Salinas Valley to the Santa Lucia Range, east to the hazy hills of the Diablo Range, and, on a clear day, northwest to Monterey Bay. South Chalone Peak, slightly lower in elevation than its cousin, is southeast. Photographs on an interpretive panel located just east of the lookout tower show the effect of air quality on visibility: haze and pollution can cut visibility from about 200 miles to 40 miles or less. Monitoring equipment here on the peak keeps track of air quality year-round. (A toilet is located just downhill from the display panels.)

No doubt you will want to linger on the summit for a while, reaping the scenic rewards of your arduous hike. When it is time to leave, simply retrace your steps to the reservoir. There you have a choice of trails: either return to the parking area via the Moses Spring Trail, or follow the route description in "Bear Gulch Reservoir" on p. 213 to return via the Rim and High Peaks trails.

The lookout tower crowns North Chalone Peak, where you have a great view of Pinnacles National Monument.

Appendix A: Selected Reading Material

MONTEREY BAY AREA & CALIFORNIA

California Coastal Commission. *California Coastal Access Guide*. 5th ed.
Berkeley: University of California Press, 1997.

California Coastal Commission. *California Coastal Resource Guide*. 5th ed.
Berkeley: University of California Press, 1987.

Emory, Jerry. *The Monterey Bay Shoreline Guide*. Berkeley: University of
California Press, 1999.

Gudde, Erwin G. *California Place Names*. 4th ed. Berkeley: University of
California Press, 1998.

Lavender, David. *California*. Lincoln: University of Nebraska Press, 1972.

Marinacci, Barbara, and Rudy Marinacci. *California's Spanish Place-
Names*. 2nd ed. Houston: Gulf Publishing Company, 1997.

Monterey Bay Aquarium Foundation. *Natural History of the Monterey Bay
National Marine Sanctuary*. Monterey: Monterey Bay Aquarium
Foundation, 1997.

NATURAL HISTORY

Burt, William H., and Richard P. Grossenheider. *A Field Guide to the
Mammals: North America North of Mexico*. 3rd ed. Boston: Houghton
Mifflin Co., 1980.

Clark, Jeanne L. *California Wildlife Viewing Guide*. Helena, MT: Falcon
Press, 1992.

Coffeen, Mary. *Central Coast Wildflowers*. San Luis Obispo: EZ Nature
Books, 1996.

Faber, Phyllis M. *Common Wetland Plants of Coastal California*. 2nd ed.
Mill Valley: Pickleweed Press, 1996.

Faber, Phyllis M., and Robert F. Holland. *Common Riparian Plants of
California*. Mill Valley: Pickleweed Press, 1988.

Kozloff, Eugene N., and Linda H. Beidleman. *Plants of the San Francisco
Bay Region*. Pacific Grove: Sagen Press, 1994.

Lanner, Ronald M. *Conifers of California*. Los Olivos: Cachuma Press,
1999.

Little, Elbert L. *National Audubon Society Field Guide to North American
Trees, Western Region*. New York: Alfred A. Knopf, 1994.

Lyons, Kathleen, and Mary Beth Cooney-Lazaneo. *Plants of the Coast
Redwood Region*. Boulder Creek: Looking Press, 1988.

Matthews, Mary Ann. *An Illustrated Field Key to the Flowering Plants of
Monterey County*. Sacramento: California Native Plant Society, 1997.

National Geographic Society. *Field Guide to the Birds of North America*.
3rd ed. Washington: National Geographic Society, 1999.

Niehaus, Theodore F., and Charles L. Ripper. *A Field Guide to Pacific States Wildflowers*. Boston: Houghton Mifflin Co., 1976.

Pavlik, Bruce M., et al. *Oaks of California*. Los Olivos: Cachuma Press, 1991.

Peterson, Roger T. *A Field Guide to Western Birds*. 3rd ed. Boston: Houghton Mifflin Co., 1990.

Schoenherr, Allan A. *A Natural History of California*. Berkeley: University of California Press, 1992.

Sibley, David Allen. *The Sibley Guide to Birds*. New York: Alfred A. Knopf, 2000.

Stebbins, Robert C. *A Field Guide to Western Reptiles and Amphibians*. 2nd ed. Boston: Houghton Mifflin Co., 1985.

OTHER

Darvill, Fred T., Jr. *Mountaineering Medicine*. 14th ed. Berkeley: Wilderness Press, 1998.

Letham, Lawrence. *GPS Made Easy*. 2nd ed. Seattle: The Mountaineers, 1998.

Wilkerson, James A. *Medicine for Mountaineering & Other Wilderness Activities*. 4th ed. Seattle: The Mountaineers, 1992.

Bush lupine, a flowering shrub.

Appendix B: Information Souces

GOVERNMENT AGENCIES

Bureau of Land Management (BLM)
Fort Ord Public Lands (831) 394-8314

California Department of Fish and Game
Elkhorn Slough National Estuarine Research Reserve (831) 728-2822

California State Parks (CSP)
Monterey District (831) 649-2836
Santa Cruz District (831) 429-2851

Carmel Department of Forestry (831) 624-3543

**Monterey County Department of
Parks and Recreation** (888) 588-2267

Monterey (City of) Parks Division (831) 646-3866

**Monterey Peninsula
Regional Park District (MPRPD)** (831) 372-3196

National Park Service (NPS)
Pinnacles National Monument (831) 389-4485

**Santa Cruz (City of) Department of
Parks and Recreation** (831) 420-5270
Pogonip (831) 420-6207

U.S. Fish and Wildlife Service (USFWS)
Salinas River National Wildlife Refuge (510) 792-0222

OTHER ORGANIZATIONS

California Native Plant Society (916) 447-2677

Carmel Business Association (831) 624-2522

Friends of Santa Cruz State Parks (831) 423-1840

Monterey Bay Aquarium (831) 648-4888

Monterey Bay National Marine Sanctuary (831) 647-4255

**Monterey Peninsula Visitors and
Convention Bureau** (831) 649-1770

Mountain Parks Foundation (831) 335-3174

National Geographic Maps/TOPO!	(415) 558-8700
National Steinbeck Center	(831) 775-4720
Pacific Grove Chamber of Commerce	(831) 373-3304
Pacific Grove Museum of Natural History	(831) 648-5176
Pebble Beach Company	(800) 654-9300
Santa Cruz County Conference and Visitors Council	(831) 425-1234 (800) 833-3494
Santa Cruz Museum of Natural History	(831) 429-3773
Sempervirens Fund	(650) 968-4509
Wilderness Press	(510) 558-1666

About the Author

David Weintraub is a professional photographer and writer based in San Francisco and Cape Cod. His photographs and articles have appeared in many newspapers, books, and magazines, including *Audubon*, *Backpacker*, *Sierra*, *Smithsonian*, and *Sunset*. His other Wilderness Press titles are *East Bay Trails*, *North Bay Trails*, and *Adventure Kayaking: Cape Cod and Martha's Vineyard*. You can visit David on the Web at *www.weintraubphoto.com*.

Photo by Steve Gregory

Index